"In this timely meditation, Alan Noble reminds us that brokenness, loneliness, and purposelessness will not be conquered by living our best life, finding our true self, or even belonging to the right family, club, or church. To the contrary, our greatest fears and anxieties are not problems to be solved but mysteries to be embraced through the knowledge of self that comes only from knowing that the self belongs to Christ."

John Inazu, Sally D. Danforth Distinguished Professor of Law and Religion at Washington University in St. Louis

"Alan Noble's book is exactly what we need. It shows the severe weaknesses of the supposedly liberated modern approach to identity and lifts up the biblical and Christian confessional resources (the sixteenth-century Heidelberg Catechism) that can heal us. As you can see from Alan's copious notes, he has read deeply in the many great critiques of the modern self written over the past two generations. But while powerful and penetrating, these volumes are inaccessible to the average person and therefore they have not gotten the traction in our culture that they should. Alan is, I hope, the beginning of a new generation of scholar-writers who can bring the insights of these thinkers down to earth and apply them in the most practical, compelling, and helpful form. May Alan's tribe increase!"

Tim Keller, Redeemer City to City

"Alan Noble has dedicated his life to the real things of the kingdom of God, and with *You Are Not Your Own* he helps us sift through the clutter of modern life to focus on what is most real. Alan understands that the very calling of discipleship is to follow Jesus in our time and circumstances—we cannot follow Jesus any other way. I expect this book will become a touchstone for many, and it confirms Alan as one of the most astute Christian writers of his generation. *You Are Not Your Own* will shape how you think about your life with Jesus."

Michael Wear, founder of Public Square Strategies and author of *Reclaiming Hope: Lessons Learned in the Obama White House About the Future of Faith in America*

"*You Are Not Your Own* is astonishing in its breadth and its depth, but even more remarkable for its compassionate and practical wisdom. This is an exceptional book by an exceptional voice for our times."

Karen Swallow Prior, author of *On Reading Well: Finding the Good Life through Great Books*

"In *You Are Not Your Own*, Alan Noble offers a deep diagnosis of the dysfunction and disease in our contemporary culture. And he shows that the challenging hope offered in the first question of the Heidelberg Catechism—that I belong not to myself but to Jesus Christ—is the only cure to this sickness. This is a rich book, eloquently and perceptively exploring the damage inflicted by the myth of autonomy and offering the healing resources of the Christian faith. Anyone hoping for a deeper understanding of our contemporary malaise or wanting to explore what it might mean to belong to Christ should read this timely, well-written, and wise book."

Tish Harrison Warren, Anglican priest, author of *Liturgy of the Ordinary* and *Prayer in the Night*

"Alan Noble has given us a gift. Using one of the most beautifully articulated truths in creedal history as its guide, *You Are Not Your Own* examines one of the great sicknesses of our age—the soul-crushing malady of self-belonging. With the learnedness of a professor, the meticulousness of a tutor, and the empathy of a friend, Noble guides the reader through crucial questions around personhood, identity, and meaning. And he does so in a manner that is at once exposing and healing for those exhausted (and seduced) by modern life. Importantly, this book offers more than cultural insight and a Christian anthropology; it offers much needed hope, not by commending religious techniques that only add to the burdens of self-optimization, but by commending Christ—the one to whom alone we must belong. Here is a book that is penetrating, accessible, convicting, and in the end, hopeful."

Duke Kwon, lead pastor of Grace Meridian Hill and coauthor of *Reparations: A Christian Call for Repentance and Repair*

YOU ARE NOT YOUR OWN

BELONGING TO GOD IN AN INHUMAN WORLD

ALAN NOBLE

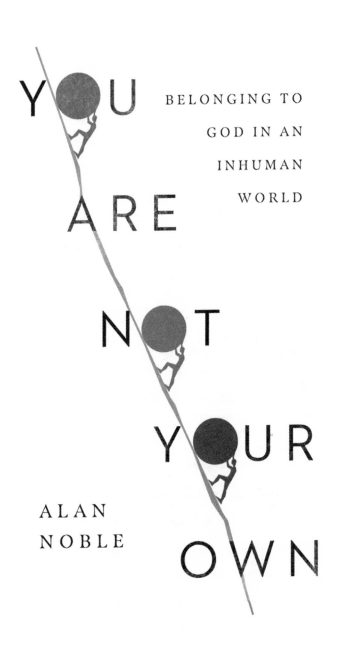

An imprint of InterVarsity Press
Downers Grove, Illinois

InterVarsity Press
P.O. Box 1400, Downers Grove, IL 60515-1426
ivpress.com
email@ivpress.com

InterVarsity Press® is the book-publishing division of InterVarsity Christian Fellowship/USA®, a
movement of students and faculty active on campus at hundreds of universities, colleges, and schools of
nursing in the United States of America, and a member movement of the International Fellowship of
Evangelical Students. For information about local and regional activities, visit intervarsity.org.

Scripture quotations, unless otherwise noted, are from The Holy Bible, English Standard Version,
copyright © 2001 by Crossway Bibles, a division of Good News Publishers. Used by permission.
All rights reserved.

While any stories in this book are true, some names and identifying information may have been
changed to protect the privacy of individuals.

Published in association with the literary agent Don Gates of The Gates Group,
http://www.the-gates-group.com

The publisher cannot verify the accuracy or functionality of website URLs used in this book beyond the
date of publication.

Cover design and image composite: David Fassett
Interior design: Jeanna Wiggins
Image: man pushing boulder: © ATZ / iStock / Getty Images Plus

ISBN 978-0-8308-4782-2 (print)
ISBN 978-0-8308-4783-9 (digital)

Printed in the United States of America ♾

InterVarsity Press is committed to ecological stewardship and to the conservation of natural resources
in all our operations. This book was printed using sustainably sourced paper.

Library of Congress Cataloging-in-Publication Data

Names: Noble, Alan, 1981- author.
Title: You are not your own : belonging to God in an inhuman world / Alan
    Noble.
Description: Downers Grove, IL : InterVarsity Press, [2021] | Includes
    bibliographical references.
Identifiers: LCCN 2021021126 (print) | LCCN 2021021127 (ebook) | ISBN
    9780830847822 (print) | ISBN 9780830847839 (digital)
Subjects: LCSH: Identity (Psychology)—Religious aspects—Christianity. |
    Theological anthropology—Christianity.
Classification: LCC BV4509.5 .N63 2021 (print) | LCC BV4509.5 (ebook) |
    DDC 248.4—dc23
LC record available at https://lccn.loc.gov/2021021126
LC ebook record available at https://lccn.loc.gov/2021021127

P 24 23 22 21 20 19 18 17 16 15 14 13 12 11 10 9 8 7 6 5 4 3 2 1

Y 41 40 39 38 37 36 35 34 33 32 31 30 29 28 27 26 25 24 23 22 21

IN HONOR OF LARRY PRATER,

a man who lived his life imperfectly but

earnestly—not as his own, but as a gift

to his family and friends.

CONTENTS

Introduction

AN INHUMAN CULTURE

A DEFINING FEATURE OF LIFE in the modern West is our awareness of society's inhumanity and our inability to imagine a way out of it. This inhumanity includes everything from abortions, mass shootings, and widespread coverups of sexual abuse to meaningless jobs, broken communities, and TV shows that are only good for numbing our anxiety for thirty minutes.

We weren't made to live like this, and most of us know it. But either we don't care, or we don't think we can do anything about it. So, the mode that best describes our day-to-day experience is "survival." Ask an honest parent, student, or employee and they'll tell you that their goal for the day is to survive—to "get through the day," or "make it through." Existence is a thing to be tolerated; time is a burden to be carried. And while there are moments of joy, nobody seems to be actually flourishing—except on Instagram, which only makes us feel worse.

Strikingly, even as our standard of living in the West continues to rise, our quality of life doesn't. It is possible to make the case that our world is getting better. The dramatic decrease in extreme poverty is one clear example of our world becoming a bit more humane. But "life is more than food, and the body more than clothing" (Luke 12:23). Often, the very techniques that improve our material lives are the ones that alienate us from each other or from creation. The advances in agriculture that afford us a tremendous variety of food at our table for very little cost also disconnect us from the seasons, the earth, and our neighbors. And so, while our material well-being has improved in some important ways, judged by many of the qualities that truly make life worth living (meaning, relationships, love, purpose, beauty), the modern world is sick. Perhaps we are less physically sick than in the past, but spiritual and mental sickness is still sickness.

If this sounds morose or hyperbolic, bear with me. This isn't going to be a whiny pessimist's rant about how terribly unfair the world is, or how we all need to move to farms or return to medieval feudalism to escape the ills of modern life. But we do need some clear-eyed hope.

And if the idea that modern life is basically inhuman sounds ridiculous to you, I'd just ask you to suspend your disbelief for a while as we consider some examples of our culture's disorder in the subsequent chapters.

Of course, plenty of people still live lives filled with pleasure and fun and even occasionally real joy. But I'd like to suggest that more often than not, our contentment with or optimism about modern life is only sustainable by denying our nature as persons, ignoring the suffering around us, dismissing the consequences of our lifestyles, distracting ourselves from our anxiety, or entertaining misplaced hope that experts will someday soon solve our problems. As Kierkegaard understood, the deepest despair occurs when we are unconscious of being in despair. When we accept how deeply dysfunctional our world is, contentment isn't really an option for us. We can still be grateful to God for His love and grace, but we can't be content with the disorder of our human society.

For Christians, particularly those of us from a tradition with a strong doctrine of depravity, nothing I've said so far is surprising. Yes, the world is fallen. Sin reigns. People are awful. None of this is new. Ever since the fall, life has been corrupted by sin. But while this is all true, is it possible we've made that an excuse for not rooting out the *particular* problems of our times? There are specific, deeply embedded ways that sin manifests in our society today, as we shall soon see. Identifying the specific sins of a society has long been the way the church has prophetically challenged culture, from Paul's critique of worshiping an "unknown god" to Augustine's criticisms of luxury in Rome to the Reformation. And confronting these evils will require more (but not less) than "opting out" of sin individually. Christians have an obligation to promote a human culture, one that reflects the goodness of creation, the uniqueness of human persons as image bearers, and Christ's love.

But this book is not a renewed call to the front lines of the culture war. I won't be arguing that we need God in America again, or that everything is going to hell because we took prayer out of schools. In fact, if everyone in America started attending church, I doubt that any of the major issues facing our society would be resolved. We'd probably find ourselves just as unwell and just as burned out. The only real difference is that we'd have an evangelical spin to our counseling and our programs of self-improvement. For you see, Christians in America are carriers of contemporary disease too.

Like the rest of western society, the church in the West tends to be good at helping people cope with modern life, but not at undoing the disorder of modern life. Too often the church's response to deep societal ills has been, "Go in peace, be warmed and filled." We offer spiritual self-improvement, prayer, counseling, medication, exercise, discipline, wealth, government aid, charity, education—all of it a Band-Aid, but we leave the disease untouched, or perhaps muted, anesthetized. To the young man struggling with addiction to porn, we offer a thin image of the gospel, self-discipline, and grace (hopefully), but the systemic objectification of bodies, the cultural glorification of sex and romance as a means of existential justification, and the anxieties and inadequacies that often drive porn use go largely unaddressed and even unacknowledged. We just accept as a fact of life that our world is inhuman, and that the human body will be objectified to sell products. We try to teach our young people to cope, and then we lament when they fail.

I AM MY OWN AND I BELONG TO MYSELF

These ills are grounded in a particular understanding of what it means to be human: we are each our own, we belong to ourselves. From the early political liberalism of the seventeenth century, with its language of individual liberties and rights, over time westerners began to think of themselves as naturally sovereign: "The modern political idea, that we are owners of ourselves . . . has widened to encompass all of aspects of existence. The sovereign man who is only like himself, who Nietzsche had imagined, has now become the norm."[1] From this idea flows the belief in the virtue of freedom as limitlessness.[2] To be your own and belong to yourself means that the most fundamental truth about existence is that you are responsible for your existence and everything it entails. I am responsible for living a life of purpose, of defining my identity, of interpreting meaningful events, of choosing my values, and electing where I belong. If I belong to myself, then I am the only one who can set limits on who I am or what I can do. No one else has the right to define me, to choose my journey in life, or to assure me that I am okay. I belong to myself.

But the freedom of sovereign individualism comes at a great price. Once I am liberated from all social, moral, natural, and religious values, I become responsible for the meaning of my own life. With no God to judge or justify me, I have to be my own judge and redeemer. This burden manifests as a desperate need to justify our lives through identity crafting and expression. But because everyone else is also working frantically to craft and express their own identity, society becomes a space of vicious competition between individuals vying for attention, meaning, and significance, not unlike the contrived drama of reality TV.

Some of us respond to this competition by rising to the challenge and submitting to the tyranny of self-improvement, which demands constant optimizing, always making healthier choices, always discovering ways to be and do and work better. In chapter three, I will refer to this group as the Affirming because their basic posture toward society is one of affirmation. Others, a group I'll call the Resigned, accept that they will never be able to successfully compete and turn to the allure of despair, killing time with immersive entertainment until death comes or circumstances change.

For both the Affirming and the Resigned, life is marked by unrestrained desire and consumption. Either we desire ever greater heights of self-mastery and excellence, or ever more entertainment and pleasure (or both). The market is happy to aid us in these quests. But unlimited desire and consumption always leave us exhausted and empty. There is always more to buy, always some way to improve, always something else to watch, always something else to try. To cope with our exhaustion and emptiness, we self-medicate.

Some drink, some take prescription anti-depressants or stimulants or anti-anxiety meds,[3] some eat, some binge watch *Friends*, some work more, some work out more, some cut themselves, some immerse themselves in the news, some immerse themselves in porn, some play video games, some shop, some sleep, some become K-Pop stans, some scroll endlessly through Instagram, some post endlessly on Twitter, some argue online, some obsess about their health, some obsess about the environment, some protest online, some protest to be famous online, some travel, some attempt suicide, some attempt self-improvement, some abuse people, some join extremist movements, some join multi-level marketing programs, some take up yoga, some take up gambling, some participate in extreme sports, some participate in illicit romance, some daydream about being diagnosed with a disease that will justify their mediocrity, some invest in self-care, some invest in Bitcoins, some discover a new identity, some modify their bodies, some modify their diets, some embrace victimhood, some embrace mocking victimhood.

Self-medicating is the norm in our society. Because if we don't medicate, we're not sure we can get through the day.

● ● ●

This is the fundamental lie of modernity: that we are our own. Until we see this lie for what it is, until we work to uproot it from our culture and replant a conception of human persons as belonging to God and not ourselves, most of our efforts at improving the world will be glorified Band-Aids.

The first question and answer in the Heidelberg Catechism reads:

Q. What is your only comfort in life and death?
A. That I am not my own,
but belong with body and soul,
both in life and in death,
to my faithful Savior, Jesus Christ.[4]

A proper understanding of our personhood requires we recognize that we are not our own. At our core, we belong to Christ. This doesn't just mean that we give mental allegiance to Christ or discover our true identity in Him. The truth is deeper and more beautiful than these phrases convey. For one thing, our understanding of *identity* tends to be distorted by modern conceptions of image and representation. To belong to Christ is to find our existence in His grace, to live transparently before God.[5] And this belonging to Christ necessarily entails belonging to His body, the church, and to our families and neighbors. An anthropology defined by our belonging to God is diametrically opposed to the contemporary belief that we are autonomous, free, atomistic individuals who find our greatest fulfillment in breaking free from all external norms. Our selves belong to God, and we are joyfully limited and restrained by the obligations, virtues, and love that naturally come from this belonging. This living before God is not easy. It requires sacrifice and humility, perpetual repentance and dependence upon Christ. In a secular age such as our own, it requires an intentional effort to remember that we belong to Christ, and that belonging is not merely a doctrine, but a reality that touches every aspect of our lives.

Maybe the cure sounds worse than the disease. If our lives are not our own, are we not enslaved? Isn't that the definition of a loss of freedom? Perhaps nothing seems worth that price. In the coming chapters we'll explore that possibility. For now, allow me to show how the belief that we are our own fundamentally forms our inhuman society. Then we can consider the alternative: accepting and embracing our belonging to Christ, which unites us with Him and gives us the ground to delight in this world even as we work to make it more human.

No significant idea in this book is original. Some I learned from wiser people than myself, some I came to on my own and later discovered in others' writing. But nothing here is really original. And that's not false modesty—it's a comment on the nature of the problem.

The basic idea that the modern world makes us ill, and that part of that illness comes from individualism, technocracy, and consumerism, has been explored in detail since at least the Second World War. Theologians, sociologists, poets, musicians, politicians, historians, and philosophers have all made these points. And yet, here we are. Here we remain.

I offer the following book in the spirit of these lines from T. S. Eliot's *Four Quartets*:

And what there is to conquer
By strength and submission, has already been discovered
Once or twice, or several times, by men whom one cannot hope
To emulate—but there is no competition—

There is only the fight to recover what has been lost
And found and lost again and again: and now, under conditions
That seem unpropitious. But perhaps neither gain nor loss.
For us, there is only the trying. The rest is not our business.[6]

Indeed, all of this has already been discovered by better men and women I "cannot hope to emulate." For further exploration of this book's themes, I recommend to you Walker Percy's *Lost in the Cosmos* and *The Moviegoer*, C. S. Lewis's *That Hideous Strength*, T. S. Eliot's *Four Quartets* and *Choruses from "The Rock,"* *Capitalism and Progress: A Diagnosis of Western Society* by Bob Goudzwaard, *OK Computer* by Radiohead, *The Weariness of the Self* by Alain Ehrenberg, Zygmunt Bauman's *Liquid Modernity*, Patrick J. Deneen's *Why Liberalism Failed*, Josef Pieper's *Leisure: The Basis of Culture*, Wendell Berry, Jacques Ellul's *The Technological Society*, and so on.

But there remains the fight to recover what has been lost, for we have lost it. Or at the very least, we have not taken advantage of the wisdom of those great minds who came before us. What I hope this work contributes is to recontextualize the argument in the twenty-first century and to think specifically in terms of self-ownership and self-belonging, from which I believe a number of our problems stem.

Despite the fact that this cultural critique is old and fairly uncontroversial, very little has changed. And it feels less likely to change now than fifty or one hundred years ago; the conditions "seem unpropitious." But, as Eliot says, I am not responsible for changing the world or even for creating something "original." My responsibility is to address what I believe to be one of the most pressing issues for my community. And so, I'll try. How successful I am is not my business, although I suppose it is yours. Please like and subscribe.

A final note: I did not write this book as a critic positioned safely outside of society. It is very much the product of someone living within society, affected by the same problems, tempted by the same desires, and burdened by the same anxieties as those I describe. There is a popular genre of nonfiction in which the author recounts their personal journey from a bad life to a good one, a disorganized life to an organized one, depressed to happy, poor to wealthy, out of shape to fit, and so on.

This is not that book, and I am no guru. Follow Christ. Follow in the footsteps of wise, righteous elders in your life. And have grace for everyone. Lord knows we all need it.

I AM MY OWN AND
I BELONG TO MYSELF

The milieu in which [man] lives is no longer his. He must adapt himself, as though the world were new, to a universe for which he was not created. He was made to go six kilometers an hour, and he goes a thousand. He was made to eat when he was hungry and sleep when he was sleepy; instead, he obeys a clock. He was made to have contact with living things, and he lives in a world of stone. He was created with a certain essential unity, and he is fragmented by all the forces of the modern world.

JACQUES ELLUL, *THE TECHNOLOGICAL SOCIETY*

Z OOCHOSIS is the common term for that thing that lions do at the zoo when they obsessively pace back and forth in their cages. The technical term is *stereotypies*: "repetitive, invariant behaviour patterns with no obvious goal or function," which occur in "captive animals."[1] But *zoochosis*, a portmanteau of zoo and psychosis, is much less euphemistic and sterile than *stereotypies*.[2] These are animals driven to *psychosis* from being in captivity.

Despite the best efforts of zookeepers to recreate the animal's natural environment, a zoo is still a zoo. The lion is still caged. People still point, stare at it, and take photographs all day long. The lion still smells churros and hotdogs cooking. He still hears the cries of animals that belong on entirely different continents. He still sleeps in what smells like an artificial cave. His meals, while scientifically engineered to meet all his dietary needs, never satisfy his desire to hunt. And with the noise of people and the sight of concrete, fences, and bars, he feels both exposed and alone. His anxiety is, really, quite natural.

The zoo exhibit was not built for the lion. Well, okay, technically it *was* made for him. In fact, some of the top African lion experts designed his habitat and diet. These scientists know more facts about lions than he knows about himself. He knows only the urgings of his own instincts, but the scientists know the history of his entire species, the intricate workings of his internal organs, and the latest research on the behavior of African lions.

And yet still he paces, back and forth. Day after day. Still the habitat does not feel quite right. Yes, this space was made for "a lion," but not *this* lion, or even an African lion. It was made for a "lion" that probably doesn't exist, one who is naturally at home in a cage. And no matter how the zookeepers modify and optimize the habitat, they will always assume that he is the kind of creature who can live a good life confined in the middle of a zoo in the middle of a city on a foreign continent—a tool to bring people entertainment and education.[3]

The lion's best hope is to adapt to his new environment. This may not be possible in his lifetime, but if he is not too anxious or bored to have sex, he may start a line of lions bred in captivity who manage to feel more at home in an artificial habitat. Of course, even then two thoughts trouble us. The grandchild of our original lion has a note on his plaque that acknowledges that he was "bred in captivity," and once you've read the plaque you can't help but think that it is somehow less of a *real* lion. It's a zoo lion. And then we feel sorry for him, sorry that our drive to capture and contain and understand and display all the wonders of the earth has perverted one of those wonders. Something has been lost. But that's best-case scenario. It's more likely that the zoochosis continues.

Strangely enough, almost everyone who visits the zoo recognizes that something is not right about the lion. His zoochosis is plain for anyone to see. You have almost certainly witnessed animals in the zoo with this behavior, even if you didn't know the term for it. And perhaps you, like me, have found yourself caught up short before the pacing animal, thinking, *This poor beast is mentally ill. He doesn't belong here. It's driving him mad, but there's nothing we can do for the poor fellow. Zoos will be zoos, and even if I boycott this place, I'm only one person. I hope they at least can give him something to settle his nerves.* The lion does not belong in the cage, but so long as people are fascinated by animals, zoos will exist. So the best thing we can hope for is progress in habitat design and maybe some animal pharmaceuticals. For most visitors to the zoo, determinism overcomes our discomfort at the sight of anxious, compulsive animals.

●　　●　　●

Although we are not caged in the same way as lions at the zoo, contemporary people in the West often suffer from our own kind of zoochosis. Just like the lion, our anxiety stems from living in an environment that was not actually made for us—for humans as we truly are. The designers (who happen to be us, by the way: only humans are capable of creating inhuman environments for themselves) had a particular idea of the human person in mind when they created the modern world. Before you can build a habitat for humans, you must have an idea of what humans *are*. What do they do? How do they live? Why do they live? What do they need? Where do they belong? When you can answer these questions, you can begin to design institutions, economies, practices, values, and laws accordingly—the building blocks of a society.

In some ways, history is the story of civilizations misunderstanding anthropology in one way or another, leading to terrible results. So my argument is not that the modern world has done something new by misinterpreting human nature. Instead, I'm asking *how* modern society has misinterpreted humans, and what are the implications of that false anthropology.

Let's consider a few examples of the way in which our human environment creates inhuman conditions.

INCELS

In 2014, a twenty-two-year-old man in Isla Vista, California, killed six people, wounded fourteen others, and then killed himself out of frustration over his "involuntary celibacy." Elliot Rodger targeted sorority women near the campus of the University of California, Santa Barbara, who he blamed for not finding him sexually desirable. Rodger uploaded a "manifesto" to YouTube before launching his attack, in which he explained the great injustice of the world: that beautiful women chose stupid jerks over "supreme gentlemen" like himself. Since 2014, Rodgers has been cited as an inspiration in at least five more mass killings (with a total of forty people killed and forty-three injured), including the infamous Parkland High School shooting. These men either identified as "incels" (involuntarily celibate) or sympathized with the incel subculture. While there have always been some men who resent women for spurning their advances, the internet has created a space for these men to support one another, form a community, and develop their own vocabulary and philosophy.

Just outside of the incel subculture we find men's rights activists and pickup artist subcultures, which share the incel culture's obsession with sex and misogyny. Each of these internet communities is horrifying in its own way, but they are also following a vision of the good life fed to them by our culture through advertising, entertainment, and celebrities. How many commercials did these killers watch over the course of their lives that glorified the attainment of beautiful women? I suspect that many young men today—and to a lesser extent, women—walk around with a view of sex not far removed from Elliot Rodger's thinking: "If someone beautiful, popular, desirable, and cool enough would give themselves to me sexually, I could know that I matter in the world."

The way we understand sex, love, and meaning is sick.

STAY-AT-HOME MOMS

Imagine that you are a mother of two small children who wants to stay home and can afford not to work (an increasingly difficult choice in many cities). First, you have to get over a lifetime of cultural programing that has equated a meaningful life with a successful career. It's not just that you've been taught that you have the freedom to work outside the home; from your earliest school memories every model of a successful person has been someone working outside the home, and every teacher has stressed the importance of a college education to prepare you for the workforce. Maybe you were raised in a more conservative religious environment where there was social pressure to marry young and stay at home, but even then, that communal pressure works against the rest of culture, which continues to treat the good life as the career life. But maybe you are able to beat back this cultural programing and convince yourself that caring for young children is one of the most fulfilling and natural forms of human work. You don't judge your friends for having careers, but you feel that forgoing one for a time is the right decision for your family. In your better moments, you even realize that the entire idea that your income determines your worth as a person is utter nonsense that can't stand up to three minutes of scrutiny. But most of the time you feel both the pressure to stay home and the pressure to work outside it.

Second, you have to deal with the loss of close community. It is normal for young people to leave their hometown after graduating high school or college, separating themselves from family and friends in order to pursue a good job for themselves or a spouse. But doing so means you stay home with two small children and no family within three hundred miles. You have a few friends in the area, but because of urban and suburban sprawl, "getting together" is always an ordeal. In the day-to-day struggle of motherhood, you find yourself alone with the kids almost all the time. It begins to get depressing.

Third, when you do hang out with other adults, the topic of conversation almost always centers around their jobs, leaving you with little to contribute. You dread meeting new people because you know one of their first questions will be, "So, what do you *do*?" And you'll have to say, "I stay at home with my kids." Maybe they'll be nice and say, "I think that's great of you to sacrifice like that for them!" but it'll be hard to shake the feeling that they view you as living a purposeless life. Just like you, they were raised to think that accumulating wealth through a successful career is what makes a person valuable and interesting. And all you do is care for the minds, bodies, and souls of vulnerable human beings.

Fourth, even if you'd like to work part time to exercise some of your gifts outside the home, our economy makes it incredibly difficult to find meaningful, satisfying work. Companies either want to employ you full time as a skilled worker, or part time in a largely mindless position (cleaning, taking orders, etc.)—the kind of repetitive labor you already do at home.

The way we treat mothers, careers, and work is sick.

THE MENTALLY ILL

Among young Americans, there has been a dramatic increase in mental illness diagnoses.[4] College campuses have been ground zero for these issues, but most schools have failed to keep up. In my own experience as a professor, students suffering from mental illness are not "snowflakes." On the contrary, many times I've had to urge students to take advantage of our school's mental health services because they prefer to keep their problems to themselves and muscle through, even as their lives are falling apart.

Young people are torn up over broken families, childhood abuse, anxiety, depression, loneliness, dread that they will never amount to anything, impostor syndrome, choice paralysis, porn addiction, suicidal ideation, the death of parents—profound and extensive brokenness. One survey found that nearly 43 percent of undergraduates "felt so depressed that it was difficult to function" in the past year, and 64 percent said they "felt overwhelming anxiety."[5] Between scholarly research on the mental health crisis on college campuses and my own experiences, I've come to assume that in any given class, several students will be suffering from a diagnosed mental illness, others will be the survivors of sexual abuse, and many will struggle with depression, anxiety, and aimlessness. While the rise in mental illness diagnoses can be partially explained by heightened awareness and decreased taboos, that isn't the whole story. Something has changed. Our kids are not all right—and the rest of us aren't doing much better.

According to the CDC, "During 2011–2014, 12.7% of persons aged 12 and over . . . took antidepressant medication in the past month."[6] The widespread use of psychiatric medications led one historian of psychiatry to remark, "We've come to a place, at least in the West, where it seems every other person is depressed and on medication. You do have to wonder what that says about our culture."[7] More alarming is the trend of declining life expectancy in America. In November of 2018, the CDC director released a statement that said, "Tragically, this troubling trend is largely driven by deaths from drug overdose and suicide."[8]

A significant segment of the American population finds life unbearable. Some cope with medication, but others turn to opioids or suicide. In their carefully researched study of declining life expectancy, economists Anne Case and Angus Deaton repeatedly point to the loss of *meaning* experienced by less educated Americans who have experienced the loss of fulfilling work, marriages, churches, and communities.[9]

One partial explanation for this despair is that many people are "burned out." Author Anne Helen Petersen has explored the phenomenon, particularly as it affects millennials, which she calls the "Burnout Generation." For many modern people, every moment of the day must be spent on work—self-improvement, personal branding, making connections, optimizing, and side-hustles. Financial crises, student loan debt, and economic uncertainty drive much of this obsession with working and self-improvement, but the effect is burnout, exhaustion, and an inability to handle simple life tasks.

Comparing historical examples of exhaustion with the experience of millennials, Petersen concludes, "Burnout differs in its intensity and its prevalence: It isn't an affliction experienced by relatively few that evidences the darker qualities of change but, increasingly, and particularly among millennials, *the* contemporary condition."[10] Although she focuses on millennials, my guess is that both younger and older people share many of these experiences: the pressure to work longer hours, develop a social media brand, and constantly improve their lifestyle, all while being inundated with warnings about debts, injustices, crime, and health. A life of unending and unrewarded competition and self-improvement through increased efficiency and optimization is overwhelming, depressing, and unsatisfying. This is not what we were made for, and we know it, but rather than confront the problem, we blame ourselves and work harder.

The way we live together is sick.

UNSUSTAINABLE CONSUMPTION

One of the more convenient features of contemporary western life is that we don't often have to acknowledge the way our actions affect the world.[11] A perfect example of this is our consumption of products—especially plastics.

Modern consumption has an almost supernatural quality to it. The products we find on the shelf in the market have almost no sense of being *made* by someone. They appear like manna, miraculously created, sealed, and delivered for our satisfaction. When we finish using the product, we merely throw the plastic container in a bin and it disappears, like magic.

If my daughter asks me where a toy came from, I can explain to her how it was designed by someone and manufactured and sent from overseas. And if she asks where the toy goes once it breaks and is thrown away, I can explain landfills or recycling plants. But my actual experience of the product's manufacture and disposal is entirely theoretical, even mythical. I don't know who made the toy or who bottled the water. I don't know exactly where they go after they are thrown out. I understand these things in principle but not in practice, which is why it can be so unsettling to visit a landfill and face the endless sprawl of waste I helped create.

Contributing to the magical feel of consumption is my supernatural faith in the capacity of landfills and recycling plants to absorb everything I dispose of. I never question whether my consumption might have a physical limit. I trust that as long as I pay my disposal fees, my trash and recycling will be taken from me. Like Mary Poppins's carpetbag, landfills are imagined to be infinite in capacity.

One way we justify believing that our consumption has no meaningful negative effect on the world is the massive systems of recycling to mitigate the use of landfills. But as it turns out, this, too, involves magical thinking.

Recently released documents from oil and plastics companies have shown that from the beginning of the push to recycle plastic in the 1990s, these companies have known that it was economically unsustainable. Recycling is complicated and costly. Plastics have to be cleaned and sorted, and every time plastic is recycled it degrades. It is cheaper to make new plastic. But because it helped us feel that we could consume plastic goods without consequences, corporations spent millions to promote recycling, and we believed the myth.[12] To make the myth work, we sent most of our recycling to China, until they stopped accepting it in 2018. With nowhere else to send their valueless plastic, some cities with mandatory recycling started dumping plastic bottles back into landfills. Others shipped their recycling to South Asian countries that still accepted it, creating environmental problems in impoverished port cities.[13] And while most consumers continue to believe that their consumption is safe because their water bottles are recycled, our landfills continue to grow.

The way we consume is sick.

●   ●   ●

While personal responsibility plays a role in each of these problems, none can be reduced to personal choice alone. The frustrated and bitter young man who cannot attain the sexual validation society has taught him to pursue can choose to love and respect women rather than hate them, but he can't change society's view of sex. The mother who struggles to live a fulfilled life at home can choose how she responds to societal pressure that denigrates her work and valorizes careerism, but she cannot change society's view of families and the workplace. Those suffering from mental health issues can (sometimes) choose treatments that lead to healing, but they can't fix the sources of anxiety in the modern world. Consumers can individually elect to use metal water bottles, but the majority of the products they buy will still contain or be packaged in plastic that has nowhere to go except the landfill. In each case, society—the human environment—is inhuman because it is opposed to the way humans ought to live.

And these are merely the tip of the iceberg. There's also endemic porn use, the rise of white nationalism and the alt-right, meaningless jobs, clergy sex abuse scandals, Hollywood sex abuse scandals, our disconnection from the natural world, declining birth rates, the intransigence of abortion, and escapism through addiction to technology. No single cause can explain the presence of these social ills, but they share important characteristics: they are systemic in nature, they are inhuman, and they all rely on a particular set of assumptions about what it *means* to be a human. The way we understand ourselves, the way we relate to and live with one another, the way we labor, and the way we rest all show signs of disorder.

●   ●   ●

Most people understand that society is inhuman in basic ways—that we live in a habitat ill-suited for us. But like the fate of the lion in the zoo, the progression of society feels determined. Even if we object to the way the lion is treated, what can we do to stop it?

- Self-checkout is a little less human than interacting with a cashier, but stores have to cut costs to remain competitive.

- Objectifying the human body is degrading, but you can't stop people from viewing pornography.

- Consuming poorly made products is depressing, but if they weren't poorly made we couldn't afford them.

- Filling our days with tedious labor soothed by streams of entertainment is boring, but what's the alternative?

- It's ridiculous to feel validated because an attractive person gives you attention, even more so when the "attention" is a like on Instagram, but it *does* feel affirming.

- The healthcare industry should want people to live healthy lives and get the care they need, but nobody blames them for primarily caring about profitability. That's the free market.

- The mechanization and standardization of education ignores the uniqueness of every student, but education is expensive enough as it is.

- It isn't natural to spend fifteen hours a day staring at a screen, but here we are.

And so we resign ourselves to the progress that we ourselves are designing.

We've created a society based on the assumption that we are our own and belong to ourselves. But if this anthropology is fundamentally wrong, then we should expect people to suffer from their malformed habitat. And that is precisely what we discover. The difference between us and the lion is that we are more successful at treating our zoochosis and adapting to our environment. We don't mind pacing back and forth, especially if we can listen to a podcast while we do.

THE BURDEN OF SELF-JUSTIFICATION

If I am my own and belong to myself, the first and most significant impli-cation is that I am wholly responsible for my life. This is both an exhilarating and terrifying thought. And it's not just that I am responsible for my personal survival, for food and shelter and so on. I also need a reason to live. I need purpose and direction. I need some way to know when I am failing at life and when I am succeeding, when I am living ethically and when I am not. I must have some way of determining on my deathbed that I lived a good, full life.

Human life is simply too hard and too miraculous to lack a purpose.[14] We need something to make sense of the fact that we are alive and to justify that life. Unlike animals, who can survive by instinct, humans have the capacity to question our own existence, to ask why we should live, and why we should put up with suffering. Mere survival isn't enough. Living for the sake of living and having children doesn't cut it for most people, so we adopt visions of the good life to work toward—reasons to live and ways to make sense of our life stories.

That's another thing humans are uniquely capable of. We can choose our reasons to live. Some live to see their children grow up. Others live to conquer their fears or find happiness. And as we age, we often change our vision of a fulfilled life. When we were young, we might have believed that finding the "right one" would give our lives meaning and purpose and sig-nificance, but after fifteen years of being married to the "right one," we may find our purpose in a career or trying to find a new "right one."

We're all confronted with the challenge of justifying our lives at one point or another. Some are hit with this question following years of living on autopilot. After high school, college, marriage, kids, and the start of a good career, we wake up one morning unsure why we are doing anything at all. Yesterday was just like today, and tomorrow will be the same. You aren't going anywhere. And there doesn't seem to be much of a point to any of it. Life is stressful and exhausting, and despite moments of pleasure and a few notable successes, you can't shake the feeling that you've been just "going through the motions" your entire life. We sometimes call this a midlife crisis, but increasingly I encounter young college students who wrestle with these same debilitating questions. My suspicion is that such moments come to almost everyone living in western society at one point or another.

For other people, the obligation to justify their life is an exciting challenge, like climbing Mount Everest, but for existence. They might describe their goal as to "feel alive," which is a very odd phrase when you consider it. Only someone who's alive can try to "feel alive," and if they are alive, then whatever they feel is already what it feels like to be alive.

So what is behind this odd phrase? What do we mean when we say we want to feel alive? I believe there are two desires at work here. Sometimes it is a desire to tangibly feel our aliveness in a world that constantly mediates experience through technology and screens and busyness. Intellectually, we know we are not robots, but every once in a while, it's good to jump out of an airplane because no robot would do something so absurd. We are more than cogs in a machine because we are capable of acting irrationally.

Alternatively, to "feel alive" is the desire to live our lives to the fullest. We are all going to die, and if we don't do something meaningful and significant then we will have wasted the only thing that truly matters. We may write a bucket list of experiences we want to have before we die.[15] We must climb this mountain, visit all fifty states, plant a thousand trees, or raise successful children before we die. Whatever our goals, we want to feel like we've done enough to make our lives worthwhile, to feel like *we* mattered. To feel alive.

We have many other ways we speak of justifying our lives. We want to know that our lives "made a difference," "told a good story," "meant something," or that they were "full" or "rich" or had a "lasting impact." However we frame the challenge, according to our contemporary anthropology, we each have to *find* some explanation for our life.

● ● ●

Justification also involves an explicitly moral dimension. We desire to know that we are righteous. In a few pages we will look at the question of values more broadly, but here I want to consider how morality and justification overlap. We have a sense of this connection when we ask ourselves, "Am I okay?" or "Am I a good person?" Some may experience this as feelings of shame or guilt, a pervading sense that they are morally inadequate or corrupt. When these impressions become overwhelming, they rise to the level of justification: my life lacks value or purpose because I am not a good person.

The great difficulty is that if we are our own, then our moral horizons cannot be given, only chosen. And that means that the only assurance we can ever have that we are living morally must come from within ourselves.

No one can absolve you or pardon you. As we'll see in the next chapter, the best other people can do is offer their opinion. Similarly, no one has the right or ability to tell you what your life means, why it matters, or what your purpose is. Of course, a lot of people have suggestions. They may even be quite forceful in persuading you to devote your life to the environment or to healthy living or to some god, but these are always mere suggestions. If your life is your own, nobody can decide why your life matters except you. You have to live your truth.

Again, this is both exciting and frightening. It means we don't have to follow in our parents' footsteps. We don't have to adopt our community's values or its vision of the good life. We are free to discover the meaning of our own life—but we're also burdened to discover it. We can only ignore the question for so long before we break down. At one point or another life will become so difficult and painful that the only way we'll be able to keep going is by telling ourselves that we have a purpose. We are going somewhere with our life, and that matters.

THE WEARINESS OF BEING YOURSELF

If I am my own and belong to myself, then I must define who "I" am. My parents can name me, and the government can issue me a Social Security number, but only I can decide my identity. And much like the responsibility to justify ourselves, the responsibility to define ourselves is not something we can opt out of. To be human is to have an identity. And the contemporary understanding of humanity decrees that each of us has the freedom and responsibility to define that identity.

Think about this: the basic story we tell ourselves in the modern world is of self-discovery. Our films, novels, and TV shows repeatedly follow the story of a protagonist who longs to know who they truly are, to uncover their authentic self, to throw off the expectations of fathers, teachers, and the rest of society in order to follow their own path. Pick virtually any Disney animated film of the last three decades, or any number of recent dramas about defying gender or sexual norms. In literature, many of the great novels of the mid-twentieth century are explicitly about self-discovery: *Invisible Man* by Ralph Ellison, *The Bell Jar* by Sylvia Plath, or *Ceremony* by Leslie Marmon Silko. We might even say that self-discovery is our contemporary hero's journey.

Who are you? What is your personality? What motivates you? What are you passionate about? How do you perceive yourself? How do you want the world to see you? These questions are not easily answered, and our answers often change during different seasons of our lives. But what doesn't change is the obligation to answer them, to define who we are—publicly. When that obligation feels overwhelming, we call it an "identity crisis." Many people suffer from a chronic identity crisis, shifting from one identity to another throughout their life.

We take it as a matter of course that to be a teenager is to suffer through an identity crisis. Young adulthood is a period in which you find yourself, define yourself against your parents and your past, and explore different possible identities. And this crisis is distinct from the natural discomfort many teenagers feel as they go through puberty. Just as young people are learning to feel normal in a rapidly changing body, they are also under cultural pressure to discover who they are. Whatever identity they choose (which is almost always defined by the market) will be contested by those with other, different identities, so that they never quite feel secure.

Not that adults are any more secure in their identities. Although we are likely to frame it in language of growth rather than exploration (which is mostly for the young), the anxiety remains the same. When it manifests as a midlife crisis (which is still fundamentally about redefining *who* you are), the anxiety can lead people to make sudden and drastic life choices with profound consequences.

One of the more demoralizing experiences of growing older has been witnessing so many couples end their marriage over a midlife crisis. One spouse feels their identity is inadequate compared to other people (*I don't matter, or feel full or significant*), or perhaps they get lost in considering all the possible identities they could adopt (*What if I weren't married to a woman who leaves me sexually unfulfilled? What if my career wasn't held back by my children? What if I could live in a better city?*). In any case, one or both parties come to believe that their real, satisfying, authentic life can only be achieved by severing the marriage. Sometimes it involves an affair. Sometimes it involves abandoning their religious faith or political beliefs or sexual or gender identity. I have seen this take place with people close to me.[16] We've all seen it occur publicly among Christian celebrities.

My point here is that married adults in the West have the relatively common experience of waking up one day and concluding the roles, relationships, obligations, and lifestyles that once defined their identity are no longer fulfilling. And in that moment, a modern person can come to feel that it would be immoral *not* to follow this new, truer identity—even if it hurts many people around them. Of course, if we really are responsible for discovering and expressing our identity, the moral pressure to be true to yourself regardless of how it affects others makes perfect sense.

People haven't always experienced identity crises as normal. In fact, where modern people suffer from identity crises, earlier societies suffered *spiritual* crises. The best example of this is Dante's *The Divine Comedy*, which famously begins: "Midway on our life's journey, I found myself / In dark woods, the right road lost."[17] One reason these lines have resonated with readers for centuries is that the poet is describing a common human experience: waking up halfway into life only to discover you are lost. Perhaps you wake up one morning questioning whether your life is worth living. Or you might wake up wondering who you are. Regardless, the image of suddenly discovering that you are off the "right road" and lost in the "dark woods" is a resonate one. But the "right road" meant something different to Dante than it does to us today. Dante has not lost his identity; he is not confused about who he is. He has lost his spiritual vision.

Soon after he finds himself in the dark woods, Dante sees the sun rise over a mountain. He desperately tries to climb the mountain and get closer to the sun (which represents the Son of God and divine illumination), but he is stopped by three animals representing his sins. At this point the poet Virgil appears and leads Dante through Hell and Purgatory and up to Paradise. For Dante in the fourteenth century, the question was not "Who am I?" but "Who is God?" and "How can I grow in Christlikeness?" *The Divine Comedy* describes one man's efforts to know God, but it is also the poet's way of describing the spiritual journey that everyone must take. In the process of knowing God, Dante learns more and more about himself, about his sins, and the ways God has blessed him. But self-knowledge is a byproduct of knowing God; it is not the goal. The goal is to know God and become like him.

If *The Divine Comedy* were written today, I think it would be the story of one man's efforts to know and express himself—that's the life journey that every modern person must take. The "right road" would not represent the way of Christ, but a process of self-revelation and actualization. The "dark woods" would represent an identity crisis, and the beasts blocking the way to self-actualization would be cultural expectations and self-doubt instead of sins. A modern *Divine Comedy* might still include religion or God, but only insofar as they help the protagonist discover their real, true self—a complete reversal of the Italian poet's original vision. From Dante's spiritual crisis to our modern identity crisis, the search moves from external to internal sources. One way to understand that shift is to recognize that unlike the fourteenth-century poet, contemporary people tend to believe that they are their own and belong to themselves, and as a result, their identities are in question. We can lose our "self" in ways that wouldn't have made much sense to Dante.

●   ●   ●

Even when we discover our true self or create our own identity, we still need some kind of external validation, and so we must express ourselves—a process called "expressive individualism." We are our own and belong to ourselves, but identity always requires the acknowledgment of other people. There's a tension here, and you can find it all over our culture.

On one hand there is the pull of autonomy: "I am my own; only I can define myself; it doesn't matter how other people see me, only how I see myself." But on the other hand, there is the pull for recognition that is inherently a part of identity: "People must acknowledge me for who I am and see me how I desire to be seen." A teenager listens to music that reflects and expresses her personality to other people, even though the lyrics are explicitly about rejecting the judgments and opinions of other people. A middle-aged man wears a shirt that reads, "Only God can judge me," but clearly wants you to judge him based on his shirt. We strive to independently define our identity, but we are always dependent upon others for the recognition of that identity.

The resolution of this tension is simple but idealistic: we want everyone to recognize and affirm our identity precisely as we define that identity at this moment in time. No one has the right to define me, but in order to have an identity, I need them to see and affirm me. And in order to get people to see me, I need to express myself—a lot. The more people who witness and affirm my identity, the more secure I feel. I believe this partially explains the glorification of fame (and infamy!) in our times. We are shaped by the logic of the attention economy, where attention to ads, apps, articles, images, videos, trending topics, and so on is a measure of value.

When your identity requires public recognition and affirmation, you can never really stop expressing yourself. No person is significant enough to permanently ground your identity with their gaze of approval, although we sometimes allow ourselves to think so. Particularly when we are young, insecure, and infatuated, we can easily imagine that if he or she would only look at us approvingly, then we'd feel secure as a person. Later in life, we might imagine a career or artistic achievement as the definitive grounding of our identity. But it is never enough.

And the terrifying thing is that everyone else in society is doing the exact same thing. Everyone is on their own private journey of self-discovery and self-expression, so that at times, modern life feels like billions of people in the same room shouting their own name so that everyone else knows they exist and who they are—which is a fairly accurate description of social media. To be recognized is to draw the gaze and the attention of others. To be affirmed is to draw their positive gaze. But if we are all responsible for creating and expressing our own identities, then everyone is in competition with everyone else for our limited attention, and no one is secure enough in their own identity to ground us with their approval. How can we cope with such fierce competition?

THE UNCERTAINTY OF MEANING

If I am my own and belong to myself, then I am responsible for creating meaning in my life. No one else can decide what love means, what my experiences means, what the sunlight bursting through leaves on a tree means. Humans cannot live without meaning. We must interpret our world to navigate it. The only question is where that meaning comes from.

There is no shortage of interpretations to choose from. All art, religion, and culture are attempts at interpreting meaning in the human experience. The greatest minds in human history have helped us make sense of life. They have given songs that try to articulate our experience of loneliness and paintings that attempt to capture the beauty of nature. They have offered rituals solemnizing the sacred moments in our lives like marriage, childbirth, and death.

But if we are our own, then all these great minds like Plato, Jesus, Michelangelo, and Shakespeare can do is *recommend* certain interpretations. They are only ever options. We have to decide for ourselves what each moment of life means. And that, like every other part of our contemporary anthropology, is both a great freedom and a terrible burden.

No one really questions whether we can find meaning in life, or that finding meaning is one of the keys to a fulfilling life. In her book, *The Power of Meaning*, Emily Esfahani Smith studies some of the most respected sources of wisdom in the world to determine what they all agree on as ways to have a meaningful life. The subtitle of her book is *Crafting a Life That Matters*, which perfectly reflects the assumption that we are individually responsible for our life and whatever meaning we find in it. What she discovers is that the modern world is experiencing a "crisis of meaning," and that belonging, purpose, storytelling, transcendence, and growth are the universal keys to experiencing a meaningful life.[18]

Johann Hari's *Lost Connections* describes a slightly different kind of crisis, but offers a strikingly similar solution. For Hari the question is, why are modern people so depressed? Rejecting the "chemical imbalance" explanation that has driven the sales of antidepressants and therapy, Hari argues that what we really need are deeper, more meaningful connections with other humans, with work that matters, and with values that motivate us.[19]

In both of these books the authors understand the nature of meaning in the same way. Both of them conclude that modern people in the West are experiencing a loss of meaning, and that meaning is essential to a good life, but how do we *get* meaning? For Smith, Hari, and Steven Pinker (who has written a book-length defense of the modern enlightened world) meaning is primarily something we *feel*, not something we discover or recognize.[20] It is a subjective, internal experience, not an external reality (or, more properly, an internal-external reality) that we acknowledge.

But if we are our own, meaning can only ever be internal because no one has the right or ability to impose meaning upon us. Artists, philosophers, and religious leaders can make recommendations about what things mean, but nothing more. And if I don't like their recommendation, I can shop elsewhere. If I like the meaning of sex conveyed in a particular romantic film, then I can choose to adopt it as my own. But if I find it too restrictive or emotionally intimate, I can find a different story, perhaps a pornographic one, that interprets sex purely as an act of personal pleasure or power. These are not just two different depictions of sex; they are claims about what sex *means*, its purpose, value, and significance.

Another way of understanding our predicament is that in the modern world, meaning cannot be imposed upon us from an outside source. Instead, our experience of life is something we impose meaning upon. The closest our society comes to imposing meaning on people is requiring us to act in certain ways. Politicians and other leaders can require us to act *as if* certain things have definite meaning. For example, national holidays are an effort to force citizens to act as if a date were sacred. Flag codes try to establish definite meaning to a flag by fining people for not treating the flag correctly. An employer may ask you to smile at each customer as if you were happy to see them. But to you, the Fourth of July means a backyard party with your family and friends, and the American flag means right-wing politics or freedom, and persuading yet another customer into buying something they don't really need is depressing. We have the freedom and obligation to interpret our lives for ourselves, and "meaning" is the name we give to the subjective result of our interpretations of life.

● ● ●

The problem is that meaning doesn't *feel* subjective. In fact, what gives meaning its ability to carry us and make sense of the world is its weightiness outside of your head. When a loved one dies, your sorrow doesn't feel like a personal interpretation. Certainly, your relationship with them colors the meaning of their death for you, but the meaning of loss goes beyond your head. Or, at least, it *feels* like it goes beyond your head. The death of this person, the love of this man or woman, the beauty of this poem, the injustice of this event—all of these meanings seem to touch upon a reality that is independent of you. Whether you were to acknowledge it or not, the love a small child feels for his mother when he is held in her arms has a definite meaning. The very thing that makes such a hug so powerful and reassuring is that it seems to communicate something objectively true about existence; in this case, something like "You are safe and loved."

How can a modern person who is responsible for creating meaning for themselves deal with the sense that meaning really isn't something they create? For the existentialist philosophers of the mid-twentieth century, life is absurd and tragic precisely because meaning only *seems* to have some objective reality. We experience life as if it were meaningful, when in actuality, there is no meaning except what we impose. Life requires a great deal of courage to face, not just because it is hard and painful, but because it doesn't objectively mean anything, and to go on living requires us to choose to see meaning where there is none. According to this line of thinking, the task of each individual person is to reject the meanings imposed by tradition, authorities, and custom—which are all false—to acknowledge that life is meaningless, and to choose to create meaning anyway. Not everyone has the courage to live authentically, but for authors like Jean-Paul Sartre and Albert Camus, living with the knowledge that life is meaningless and one day you will die is the only way to truly live. Everything else is self-delusion. Life may be absurd but knowing that it is absurd is better than living a lie.[21]

The existentialist answer to the problem of meaning might sound depressing to you, but it doesn't have to be. If you are your own, you can choose to see the inherent meaninglessness of existence as a kind of blank canvas. All you have to do is erase the drawings put there by tradition, tune out all the critics who want to tell you how to draw, box out the other artists who keep trying to draw on your canvas, and create your own masterpiece. Alternatively, you can choose to deny your freedom to draw. You can follow a highly detailed drawing tutorial on YouTube that produces something lovely and utterly inauthentic, but that would require you to deny that you are your own and are wholly responsible for creating a life of meaning.

THE QUANTIFICATION OF VALUES

If I am my own and belong to myself, then I'm also responsible for determining right and wrong for myself. No other person or institution has the authority to impose their morality on me. I may choose to abide by social norms and laws in order to make my life easier and more pleasant, but that's a choice I make for my own interests, not because there's anything inherently right about the social norms and laws. "Morality" turns out to be the assertion of someone's will upon someone else—an exercise of power, not truth.

In such a society, the basis for our moral positions is ultimately personal preference or deep feeling, something internal and private. We may use terms like "equality" or "justice" as we argue for a law or criticize the behavior of others, but if we are our own, then the only thing underneath those values is our preference for certain ideas of equality or justice. In *After Virtue*, the philosopher Alasdair MacIntyre has described this perspective on values as "emotivism":

> The specifically modern self, the self that I have called emotivist, finds no limits set to that on which it may pass judgment, for such limits could only derive from rational criteria for evaluation and . . . the emotivist self lacks any such criteria. Everything may be criticized from whatever standpoint the self has adopted, including the self's choice of standpoint to adopt.[22]

You have probably heard someone make a moral claim based explicitly on the way it makes them feel, and perhaps you thought they were being overly sensitive or emotional. But MacIntyre argues that most of us are operating as emotivists; even when we appeal to "impersonal criteria," it is a mask to cover our personal preferences. And if we belong to ourselves, all we ever have is our own perspective, whether expressed explicitly or behind a mask of objective standards.

I am my own, therefore, I owe no obedience or submission to anyone. It sounds like a perfect recipe for anarchy. As Mitya says in *The Brothers Karamazov,* "Without God . . . everything is permitted."[23] A few pages later, Mitya notes, "If he does not exist, man is chief of the earth, of the universe."[24] We find a similar thought in Nietzsche's concept of the Übermensch: the man who accepts the death of God and chooses to establish a new morality by his own will.[25] Or we can look at Joseph Conrad's *The Heart of Darkness.* When Mr. Kurtz journeys into the heart of the Congo looking for ivory, he discovers that without the constraints of society and the church, all he has left to guide his morality is his personal conscience, which turns out to be a paltry substitute. He is radically free to be a cruel oppressor. Religious critics and even some pragmatic agnostics have argued that we need to believe in God in order to live morally because we will only have a reason to deny our selfish and destructive impulses if we believe in a moral source outside of ourselves. And yet, over a hundred and thirty years after Nietzsche declared the death of God, Western civilization has not actually fallen into chaos and anarchy. Why is that?

From a historical perspective, modern liberal democracies are actually quite orderly. Western democracies are incredibly safe compared with other periods of history. We almost never worry about bandits when we travel. Political corruption and the abuse of power are relatively restrained. And we enjoy more basic human rights than at any other time in history. This raises an important question: If we all choose our morality for ourselves, why hasn't the West fallen into utter chaos?

I think there are two primary reasons why our contemporary anthropology doesn't lead directly to anarchy. The first is that with the loss of a moral order established through religion, modern people are left with "human concerns" and gravitate toward universal benevolence, as the philosopher Charles Taylor has described.[26] With a vision of human solidarity, we feel an obligation to improve all human welfare. Society then becomes a space for "mutual benefit," where we help each other by helping ourselves.

Not everyone feels this sense of human solidarity. Like all other modern moralities, it is optional. And as Taylor points out, there is nothing that requires me "to take universal human welfare as my goal; nor does it tell me that freedom is important, or fulfillment, or equality. Just being confined to human goods could just as well find expression in my concerning myself exclusively with my own material welfare."[27] Indeed, some people do deny that universal human welfare is their problem. They remain focused on their own, individual happiness. And if they are their own, why shouldn't they? But for the most part, modern people have a vaguely defined sense that they ought to leave the world better than they found it, that they should relieve suffering and fight injustice wherever it is found. When we participate in such activism, it is easier to convince ourselves that our lives matter. We are valuable and significant because we make the world a better place.

The second reason we don't live in a post-apocalyptic wasteland is that even when you give people freedom to determine morality for themselves, they generally choose to live peaceful, orderly lives. The loss of objective morality does not lead to violence, but it does lead to consequentialism. Following the Golden Rule makes life easier and more pleasant for everyone. Being faithful to your wife improves your quality of life. Paying for a music streaming service is simpler than pirating music. On the whole, being evil is a terrible way to live, and pragmatic humanism is beneficial.

But while we can trace a reduction in certain crimes in the past few centuries, that does not mean that contemporary people are more moral than those in the past. Perhaps it's true, but I'm not sure how anyone could prove it. The prominent humanist Steven Pinker has used statistics on falling crime to argue for the success of the Enlightenment project (which includes the belief that we are our own and belong to ourselves).[28] This contemporary anthropology doesn't only affect whether or not people act morally. It also changes the way we understand moral laws and our motives for acting morally.

Once we accept that morality has no objective existence, we tend to privilege moral judgments that can be supported by data because data (and specifically "efficiency") are the closest things we have to universal values or a common good. For us, a moral law is an evidence-based law that has been proven to reduce suffering or increase human flourishing. For example, some argue that regardless of questions of human dignity, prostitution should be legalized, because legalization will reduce violence and venereal diseases. As Steven Pinker has argued, "human dignity" is a squishy phrase used to smuggle in all kinds of baseless taboos and prohibitions.[29] We can count the number of victims of sexual violence, but we can't measure the loss in human dignity that occurs when a person sells their body. We can't even agree that human dignity is a thing, or that prostitution is an affront to that dignity. If we are each responsible for our own moral laws, then we have no right to impose a value like "human dignity" on another person, even if we believe it's for their own good. But measurable harm is a different matter altogether. Once you can quantitatively demonstrate the harmfulness of a behavior, then you can regulate it.

I suspect that it is precisely the measurability of "universal benevolence" that modern people find so reassuring. We want to know how many malnourished children we can feed for twenty-five dollars a month, how many lives were saved through international medical aid, how effectively education can improve social mobility, and so on. Reducing measurable harm is the overarching goal, and measurability is the key. We might not agree on what counts as "human welfare," but we can agree that decreasing harm is good.

All across the political spectrum you will find experts making primarily data-driven moral arguments for policies or social norms. Even Christians, who ought to believe in an objective moral law revealed by God, tend to rely heavily on data and evidence-based arguments. It just feels natural in our society. And I think it feels natural because Christians, like everyone else, tend to think of themselves as autonomous. And among autonomous individuals, the language of numbers is the surest foundation for morality.

Which brings us to another implication of our contemporary anthropology on morality: everything is in flux. Once you begin grounding morality on data, you must be ready to change moral norms and laws when the data calls for it. For some thinkers (and I suspect Steven Pinker would fit here) this is a great advantage of utilitarianism.[30] It is a moral system that operates more like science than religion. We update and modify our morality based on new information.

While quantified morality is the closest thing we can have to a shared morality, even it remains optional. Even when we know the evidence-based reasons to behave in a certain way, there's nothing objectively requiring you to accept the conclusions of data. You are free to litter or hold bigoted views. It's just that it's much easier and less costly to follow the data. One reason you may choose to adopt a moral position that contradicts our best data is that it is useful in expressing your identity. When morality becomes a matter of personal perspective, individuals can make moral arguments in order to show the world the kind of person they are. You don't have to oppose war or global warming because they are objectively wrong, or because we can quantify the harm they cause. You can oppose them because it feels right and reflects your brand or personality. Later, when your values change, the causes that define you can change as well.

THE INSECURITY OF SELF-BELONGING

If I am my own and belong to myself, then any and all associations, ties, and relationships I have are voluntary. I might lend myself out for forty, fifty, or eighty hours a week in exchange for pay. And I might figuratively "belong" to my spouse or kids or my community. But in the end, these are choices I've made about how I want to live my own life, which belongs only and ever to me.

I might just as well not lend myself out to a particular employer, or I could choose to not work at all, keeping all of my time for myself. Ideally, I'd find a job that allows me to *feel* as if I were free, even though I have promised myself for eight hours of labor per day, five days a week. If I have choices, I am still, basically, essentially, my own, and I don't belong to anyone—not even, really, to my family.

I "belong" to my wife only to the extent that I choose to belong to her. I owe her some fidelity, but it's a negotiated, contractual fidelity. I promise not to sleep with other women so long as she promises not to sleep with other men, but fantasies can't really be policed, and if for some reason one of us decides that our belonging together is not as fulfilling as we hoped, we are legally free to separate. I may even feel a kind of moral obligation to leave my wife to be with someone more fulfilling, perhaps a more authentic relationship. After all, if I am completely responsible for my life, then the greatest moral failure would be for me to fail to pursue what I desire most. I owe it to myself to be happy, and I cannot rely on anyone else to provide that happiness. So I can only belong to my wife tentatively.

Likewise, I belong to my kids in a narrowly defined legal and biological way, but both law and biology are fluid. I'm legally responsible for feeding and caring for my children, but they don't have any hold on my *identity* unless I want them to. I can love them and provide for them, but I can also allow them to grow up to be free individuals, just like myself. If they choose to visit me in my old age, that will be nice, but I'll understand if they're too busy. I wouldn't want to be a burden to them as my parents were to me.

My biological connection to my children is stronger than the legal obligation, but properly understood, biology merely explains why things are. It can't tell us how things ought to be. And in fact, most of the greatest achievements in human history have involved humanity's refusal to accept the physical world as it is: vaccines, genetically modified food, wind turbines, the airplane. I may not be able to undo the fact that my children share my DNA, but I don't have to accept that our shared genes *mean* anything. They are an accident of biology. The coincidence of genetic similarity.

I may also choose to associate myself with a specific community, but even if I was born and raised in one city, that place has no formal hold on me, neither the people who live there or the natural environment. Sometimes it can be hard to shake the emotional baggage of the place you grew up. It feels like it is a part of you, even if you don't want it to be. But that can't be objectively true if I am my own. It is only a feeling. With enough determination, I can leave my hometown behind. Leaving home to follow our vision of the good life is an essential part of our modern hero's journey. In a traditional hero's journey, the hero returns home after a period of testing and growth so that he can liberate or cure his home. But I don't think we need to come home anymore. And if we do come home—if we do allow our community or hometown to have some pull on us—it's only because we choose to let it.

• • •

The modern person belongs everywhere and nowhere at once. In her bestselling book *Braving the Wilderness*, popular author Brené Brown advocates for just this idea of belonging: "True belonging is the spiritual practice of believing in and belonging to yourself so deeply that you can share your most authentic self with the world and find sacredness in both being a part of something and standing alone in the wilderness."[31] For the mature person who accepts that they belong to themselves, Brown declares that they will be free to be completely alone or completely committed to wherever they are, because true belonging is inside them. And according to Brown, the freedom to belong wherever you choose to be (because you belong to yourself) requires serious courage. As we saw before, the defining dynamic of our modern anthropology is the tension between the excitement and terror of radical freedom.

We are free to join and leave our communities, to live in one place and adopt a digital community completely divorced from that place, to dwell in a city but never inhabit it. But we also have no place to ground us, no relationships that can make demands on us. Neither our bodies nor the Earth can contain us, because our bodies can be transformed, and the Earth is not our responsibility.

When they are asked to define freedom, contemporary people usually imagine the absence of constraints. In many ways, liberal democracy is premised on this conception of freedom. Humans cannot be truly human without freedom, and freedom means that no one can control me, coerce me, obligate me, or limit me. As we shall see in the following chapters, this understanding of freedom as limitlessness has shaped the way our society structures itself.

• • •

What these implications have in common is that they all come with a responsibility: the responsibility to justify our existence, to create an identity, to discover meaning, to choose values, and to belong. We might collectively refer to these as the *Responsibilities of Self-Belonging*. Of course, not everyone feels each of these responsibilities in the same way to the same extent or at the same time. You may feel tremendously burdened to live a significant life, while your neighbor may be quite obsessed with his identity. And over the course of a lifetime, we prioritize different responsibilities. I am not describing a monolithic experience of the modern world that is necessarily caused by a particular anthropology. Humans are rarely that simple, and whole societies never are. But this much I believe to be true: to the degree that our society has largely adopted the belief that we are our own and belong to ourselves, we all feel the Responsibilities of Self-Belonging. This is also true: there is another to whom we belong, and living before Him frees us from the unbearable burden of self-belonging.

2

HOW SOCIETY HELPS YOU BE YOUR OWN

I T TURNS OUT THAT WE NEED a lot of help to be our own. As we saw in the last chapter, the contemporary understanding of anthropology involves many burdensome responsibilities, even if they are responsibilities to ourselves. And our society equips us to fulfill these responsibilities.

A central purpose of a well-functioning society is to promote "human flourishing" or to help people achieve the "good life." But it is difficult to promote human flourishing when flourishing looks different for literally every single person. The best we can do is help each other live "authentically." By an "authentic life" I mean a life of accepting and embracing the Responsibilities of Self-Belonging discussed in the previous chapter. To live authentically means to justify your own existence, to express your identity, to interpret meaning for yourself, to judge according to your own moral compass, and to belong where and only where you choose.

I'm borrowing the term *authentic* from the French Existentialists, but they're dead, so I don't think they'll mind. While I do not believe that existentialism has had a significant direct influence upon our society, it seems clear that a kind of latent, unacknowledged existentialism is the defining philosophy for our time: we come to feel that our existence is the only thing we can truly know, and to live authentically to that existence means to choose our identity. It's not that people are reading Sartre and becoming convinced of his arguments. Instead, we naturally adopt our society's understanding of the human person as we grow up in society, and that understanding leads to a kind of existentialist outlook.

Our understandings of the world are not primarily cognitive or rational; they're habitual. We pick them up from cultural practices that stress our individual, radical freedoms, from depictions of freedom as limitlessness, from the people and actions that our society valorizes. Societies define, reinforce, and pass on certain values, but perhaps more importantly, they provide the scaffolding for people to flourish according to those values. If human life requires the pursuit of authenticity, then we need a society that allows us to explore, redefine, and express ourselves. Society's role here is not only reactive, however; it also forms us. By equipping us to pursue this vision of the good life, society also reinforces this vision of the good life. As a result of this mutual reinforcement, it is exceedingly difficult for us to envision an alternative to bearing the Responsibilities of Self-Belonging.

But, if we are not in fact our own, then living "authentically" will not produce human flourishing, and a society that compels us to live "authentically" will only make us increasingly distressed, exhausted, and alienated.[1]

HOW SOCIETY PROVIDES JUSTIFICATIONS

The burden of justifying your own life is too much to bear. How can you be sure that your life matters? There are billions of people in the world today, and billions more have come before you. Long after you are gone the world will keep turning and people will go on eating and drinking and making love. You will be forgotten just as you have forgotten your great-grandfather's name, or at least your great-great grandfather's. No matter how remarkable you are, historically, statistically, you are unremarkable.

And yet, to be a person is to be remarkable. The human person has the capacity for history-altering actions, for literary masterpieces, and civilization-defining innovations, as well as imaginative violence and creative evil. Your mind can contemplate the ability to contemplate your existence on a small rock flying through space. It can discover the nature of that small rock and the physical laws that describe it hurling through space. But your mind can also fix its attention upon clichéd sitcoms and memorize vapid songs.

Justifying your life would not be so difficult if humans had less potential for greatness, pettiness, and wretchedness. But we do, as history attests. So we need models of what it looks like to live a significant and moral life—

examples of how to live a life worthy of the miracle of being. When we try to make sense of the purpose of our life, we look to models of people who appear to be fulfilled, who have achieved a kind of flourishing or meaningfulness. However, they must only be models, not standards, because a standard implies an obligation to follow while models are optional. You can safely try on one style of validation without fear of failure. Another way to justify your life is always available.

The primary way society helps us to justify our lives is through stories. People can only pursue ideals they can envision, and stories embody visions of the good life. They help us imagine how we might live a full life. When a film movingly portrays a young couple finding happiness in romance, viewers can begin to imagine their own lives validated through a romantic relationship. When an athlete tells her story of overcoming adversity to win a gold medal, we can imagine our lives justified through some great achievement. When we see happy, attractive, wealthy young people on YouTube living their best life and sharing it all online, we can believe that fame or attractiveness or wealth can make our lives meaningful. When a well-produced TV commercial promises you that buying a Mazda will make you "feel alive," you start to think that maybe, just maybe it will. Even though every other purchase you've made in life has failed to give you that sense of purpose and fullness, on some level, you still think, *Maybe this time it will happen.* Then again, you may be disgusted by the advertisement of another fossil-fuel guzzling machine, and instead think about the example of brave young climate change activists: *If a thirteen-year-old girl can give her life to save the planet, maybe I can, too. And that would be something real, something lasting, something unambiguously important.* There are models of fullness for every lifestyle or value you can imagine.

Since we each are responsible for our own existential justification, it is not enough for society to offer one or two or even a hundred visions of the good life. We need an endless stream of them, enough for every day of the year, for every person in the world. We need options. And this turns out to be a wonderful thing for storytellers. Viewers don't just enjoy a good film; they *need* stories to make sense out of their existence. And since no one story can definitively model the good life, viewers will always need more stories. It's no coincidence that we live in such a story-saturated culture. When you account for ads, songs, books, social media, the news, film, and TV, nearly our entire day is made up of consuming stories. I don't suppose we could make sense of life otherwise. Society provides.

•   •   •

To feel existentially justified, we also need assurance that we are living a righteous life. Are my choices moral? Am I an ethical shopper? Am I doing enough for important social causes? Whether or not you think of yourself as trying to live morally, you are. The only question is what your moral vision is. Everyone is oriented toward some moral horizon of what it means to be good. When we are our own, that vision must be drawn from within. Even if we choose to adopt an ethical system, like utilitarianism or Christian ethics or humanism, our choice is made from our inner resources.

For most of us, the desire to be a "good person" expresses itself in terms of universal benevolence, like working to end suffering and injustice in the world. In particular, we want other people to be able to fulfill their Responsibilities of Self-Belonging. Whenever a person or group is prevented from finding their own purpose in life, to define themselves as they wish, to interpret meaning as they will, and to belong wherever they choose, we feel responsible to advocate for them. Two immediate problems confront us, however. First, even if we advocate for some oppressed groups, how can we be "good people" when we still ignore the vast majority of evil and injustice in the world? Second, how do we decide who deserves our compassion or aid? Who precisely is the victim?

The first challenge is made considerably more difficult in a global, information-rich society. The modern person is aware of more suffering and injustice than a person living at any other time in history. That doesn't mean that there is more suffering. In fact, according to some measures like violence and poverty, there is less suffering and injustice in the world than ever before. But we are exposed to all of it. Every horrific murder, rape, or kidnapping is national news, along with natural disasters, political corruption, famines, civil wars, bigotry, pandemics, and so on. I am aware of far more than I can ever do anything about. On the other hand, I do have the option to address most problems in the world. I may not be able to effectively address them all, but I can always give to another charitable organization, I can always advocate for the oppressed, I can always be more conscientious about the environment, I can always be a better ally. There is always more for me to do. A problem with universal benevolence is that we are not universal; we are painfully finite. And yet it is not uncommon for people (especially on social media) to insist that you *must* care about everything. Society provides us with opportunities to feel like we are improving the world and therefore living lives of purpose and value. Unfortunately, those opportunities present endless obligations.

Society does provide us with a way to determine who deserves our compassion, however. We ought to show compassion and offer aid to anyone who suffers or is inhibited because of factors beyond their control. The philosopher Michael Sandel associates this view with "luck egalitarian" philosophy.[2] This conception of justice "bases our obligation to help those in need not on compassion or solidarity but on how they came to be needy in the first place." While luck egalitarianism emphasizes personal responsibility with an expansive enough view of history, biology, and the environment, it's possible to view almost anyone, or no one, as a deserving victim. There are factors beyond our control at work in every action we take. Perhaps your neediness is the result of your bad childhood, genetics, systemic racism, a medical condition, or any other part of our inhuman society.

The important thing is that we establish that someone deserves our compassion. And this is exactly what we witness in our public discourse about justice and equality. We argue over all the ways someone has been disadvantaged in order to decide whether they are worthy of our compassion, to decide whether they are the oppressor or the oppressed. In this debate, disadvantages take on social capital. As Sandel notes, "Liberals who defend the welfare state on the basis of luck egalitarianism are led, almost unavoidably, to a rhetoric of victimhood that views welfare recipients as lacking agency, as incapable of acting responsibly." Quite rightly, Sandel finds this philosophy to be immoral. It assumes that we are capable of establishing with certainty who "merits" our compassion and who doesn't. But the real world is more complicated than that. It also leads to a "rhetoric of victimhood" and creates perverse incentives to commodify our disadvantages, to leverage them for social gain. Rather than lead to a more just and compassionate society, we turn suffering into another arena for competition.

One alternative to luck egalitarianism and the inevitable competition over merited compassion can be found in David Foster Wallace's commencement speech for Kenyon College, titled "This Is Water." Wallace warns the graduating seniors against allowing their default thinking to control them, because our default is to be self-absorbed. He encourages them to actively choose what to think about. So instead of focusing on how the person in front of you in line at the grocery store is in your way, you could consider that maybe they are having a much worse day than you. Maybe she stayed up all night nursing a husband dying of cancer. Maybe the man driving the disgustingly large SUV was traumatized by a car accident. We can call this ethic "as-if egalitarianism." Wallace takes a step beyond the luck egalitarianism that Sandel finds so prominent in contemporary society. Instead of *establishing* when someone merits our compassion or aid, Wallace encourages us to treat them *as if* they merit it, because it's technically possible that they do.[3]

Here are the two primary frameworks society offers us for trying to meet the demands of universal benevolence. Either we believe that we are good people because we identify and aid those who are most disadvantaged, or we are good people because we act as if people are disadvantaged and deserve our aid. At the heart of both frameworks is the assumption that compassion, desiring the good of others, is something that is merited. And each of us is responsible for judging that merit.

Stories are also a common source of moral options. The stories we tell and participate in make arguments for various moral positions: tolerance, respect, inclusivity, equality, self-reliance, honesty, fidelity, creativity, authenticity, and so on. There is no shortage of stories offering moral ideals. But our exposure to the cacophony of often contrasting moral values does little to aid us in feeling that we are okay or "good people." For that, society provides therapy: specifically, therapeutic techniques of self-assurance.

We develop the ability to look at ourselves in the mirror and grant self-assurance. You need to be able to look at yourself and your choices without regret, we are told. As we shall see in a later chapter, humans long to have someone look into their face with loving acceptance. The "well done" spoken by a parent to their child does not lose its importance with age. It only grows exponentially as we become more aware of the profound moral complexities of the adult world, when the stakes change from sharing a toy with your sibling to risking your job by speaking out against an injustice. Then the word spoken from the parent, who we now realize is just as morally beleaguered as us, is no longer commensurate with the problem. We can try to reassure one another that we are good people, but it's merely an analogical reassurance. The real thing can only come from a source of moral judgment, from someone who defines the horizon of moral action. And if we are our own, we ourselves are that source of moral judgment.

Others can try to comfort us, but we are responsible for ourselves. And so we find the multiplication of techniques that help us accept who we are, live authentically, and teach us to assure ourselves: visualization techniques, self-confidence building exercises, self-care, surrounding ourselves with positive friends, therapy, and so on. Society provides.

HOW SOCIETY PROVIDES IDENTITIES

Humans are the only creatures that can worry about "being someone." Everyone else is too busy staying alive to bother with doing so. But it matters to us a great deal that we know who we are and that the people around us can witness and affirm that identity. To live authentically, you must live true to yourself, and that means that you must know just who your "self" is and be able to express it in a loud, competitive, and hostile world.

Society aids us by offering an endless number of possible identities to choose from and by developing more and more means of expressing those identities. So great is this role in society that large portions of our economy are entirely devoted to facilitating our personal quest for identity and self-expression. Hardly any product or service exists that does not intentionally express something about the consumer.

I have described two parts to the responsibility of identity: knowing and expressing. But it is a little deceptive to speak of them as separate, as if you could do one and not the other—as if you could discover your true self and keep it to yourself. Expressing your identity is the same step as discovering or creating it. Every time we tell the world something about ourselves, it's like putting a piece of a puzzle together. We feel a little more confident in our identity. When I announce my love of the band Fugazi on Twitter, I am both expressing something about myself and making that self more solid and definite. I give shape to my life by expressing it. The band Fugazi helps me express myself by giving me a style to identify with, and Twitter helps me know myself by providing a platform to announce my preferences. When you start to think about all the ways our society facilitates self-expression, it's quite staggering.

Consider how we use a Facebook profile. I "like" my favorite TV shows, movies, celebrities, political pundits, world religions, sports teams, bands, and online communities. With every like I express who I am. I can also post pictures of myself that communicate tiny things about me through my pose, clothing, expression, setting, framing, editing, and caption to whoever has access to the photos. You might learn something about what I find pleasurable, or how I view my body, or how seriously I take myself.

None of this is entirely new. Photography is nearly two hundred years old. But what *is* new is how cheap, easy, and fast it is to capture an image of myself and project it to the entire world via a "profile" that explicitly represents *me*. There was only so much self-expression you could convey when a photograph required you to hold perfectly still for fifteen minutes. But today the possibilities are endless, and nearly effortless. The average preteen in America has the same basic tools for publicity that only the biggest Hollywood stars had sixty years ago. Where the paparazzi or celebrity gossip magazines used to publish every major life event in a star's life, Facebook allows every user to make the same announcements. Instead of being asked by a pesky reporter to share our opinion about a recent political story, we share articles on Facebook with our personal commentary. These tools for professional self-expression are only multiplying, providing new ways of sharing our thoughts, feelings, voice, body, interests, and values with the world. And with every piece of information we share, we define and validate our identity.

Our society not only provides limitless options for defining our identities and expressing them, but it also facilitates the acknowledgment and affirmation that we all seek. As we discussed in the last chapter, identity is only meaningful when there are other people who can witness your identity. We have a need to be seen and affirmed; it is an inherent part of what it means to have an identity. Facebook and many other social media platforms give us more and more spaces and ways to be seen. In fact, being *seen* is such a basic desire for modern people that you'd have to work very hard *not* to be seen. Privacy is hard to maintain, not only because corporations want to use your information to sell you more stuff, but also because society *assumes you want to express your identity.* Self-expression is the default. Privacy is the anomaly. If you don't believe me, Google your name.

Everyone wants to be affirmed. We desire to be looked directly in the eyes by some authority figure (a father, mother, teacher, God) and told that we are accepted and loved. The beauty (efficiency) of social media is that we can quantify affirmation. When you post a selfie on Instagram, you can receive direct and specific feedback through likes and comments. You can track the number of people who have viewed a Facebook or Instagram story, or the number of people who clicked on your Twitter profile through a specific tweet. You have endless combinations of preferences and brands and values with which to craft an interesting and popular identity, endless opportunities to share that identity, and concrete ways to measure your affirmation. And here is the critical point: our society is designed for humans who *must* define and express themselves.

As our lives have moved increasingly online, so has our focus for self-definition and expression. But it would be a mistake to think of expressive individualism as primarily a digital phenomenon. Social media platforms have adapted to meet *our demand* for radical personalization, but so too has every other industry in our society. Take the medical industry, for example. The modern human body is plastic through and through. Our bodies can be modified to ever greater extremes: plastic surgery, gender reassignment surgery, sterilization, tattoos, and piercings. Eye color, hair color, and skin color can be modified. Limbs can be removed. Even our minds are malleable: neuroplasticity describes our brain's ability to change. Through practices like cognitive behavioral therapy, you can intentionally modify the way you see and inhabit the world.

We can disagree on which of these procedures is ethical and which is not, but we cannot disagree that the number of ways you can modify your body to fit your identity has increased and will only continue to increase with new technological and medical innovations. The only limit to your identity is what society and your credit card will tolerate. And society will continue to provide options—so make sure to take care of your credit score.

HOW SOCIETY GIVES US MEANINGS

At the turn of the twentieth century, poets and authors and artists faced an acute challenge: fewer and fewer people shared a common collection of symbols, myths, beliefs, and images in the West. Without common references, it's hard for artists to communicate. Secularization, globalization, and industrialization shattered the old cosmos with its relatively stable and common set of symbols and ideas, leaving us with an exponentially growing index of private symbols and meanings.

Consider, for example, how mass advertising and mass media changed the number and variety of images a person sees per day.[4] Artists could no longer assume that their audience would resonate with Christian imagery or allusions to Greek literature or even certain basic experiences of nature that prior generations would have shared: harvests, the changing of seasons, or nightfall, as electricity changed the way we experience night. Meaning had to be made anew, which was essentially the motto of literary modernism: "Make it new!" urged Ezra Pound. Make it new, not for novelty's sake, but because the modern world with its speed and innovation and mechanization and loss of faith required a new language. And the process of making it new has not slackened for a moment since the early 1900s.

Self-ownership requires us to discover meaning for ourselves, not to trust traditional or communal interpretations (unless we choose to). We need ways of understanding the meaningfulness of life that are as varied as our lives. But the power of meaning is that it *feels* as if it transcends our personal experience. It feels as if it is grounded in some reality beyond us. I do not experience joy at a beautiful sunset as a primarily or exclusively subjective experience. It feels as if I am taking part of something greater than me. Here is the challenge for modern people: we need experiences of meaning that feel like they resonate beyond us, beyond our heads, but we need them to remain optional. They can't actually demand us to interpret the experience in a specific way. I need to feel like my love for my wife is objectively good and real and yet still something that I choose and can unchoose if I wish. And society has happily obliged.

In the previous chapter we briefly considered the role of philosophy, theology, and the arts in the meaning-making experience. I mentioned how great artists and thinkers can recommend ways of interpreting life, of experiencing love or suffering or beauty or loneliness. And while it is certainly true that Shakespeare has much to teach us about love and tragedy, contemporary people are not limited to canonical authors and artists.

For every person in America there is an artist or genre or medium that elucidates and dramatizes their experience of the world. The power of these cultural works is that they give us a sense that our interpretation isn't purely subjective. Our experience has a grandness to it when it is interpreted through a moving song or story.

Think about the near-universal experience of being rejected or dumped by someone you love. Why do so many people immediately turn on sad music? Because we want our experience of loss to mean something beyond our head. We want that feeling of rejection or loneliness or alienation to resonate, to be as big and objective as it feels inside of us. Powerful creative works give a sense of reality to the way we interpret the world. Of course, you don't have to listen to music that validates emotions of rejection or loneliness. You can find a cultural work to interpret your experience any way you choose. Where one person may choose to listen to breakup music, someone else who believes they were treated unfairly listens to angry music, and someone else interprets the breakup as God's will. For this person, a religious romance novel helps them feel the tragedy of the loss while inspiring them with a higher purpose.

Music may be the most common example of cultural work that helps us interpret life, but society provides entire lifestyles and subcultures to elucidate and dramatize meaning for us. Imagine you're a lonely, angry, young White male living in a small midwestern town who is convinced that the Jews or some other minority group are working to ostracize and emasculate you. If you search SoundCloud long enough, you'll discover a band that embodies your identity, and their music will help you interpret important moments of your life. What does it "mean" that you can't get a job or a date? Their music can provide answers, or at least models of interpretation that you can choose. But through this music you discover a larger community of bitter young men. They have their own philosophy, style of dress, slang, political affiliation, and so on. And all of these things work together to make sense of your life experiences.

Or imagine you're a middle-aged woman who wants to relive her youth by partying and clubbing. You can find music, clothing, and community that will affirm your feelings, give you an identity, and interpret your life. And the same is true for any of us. Whatever your background, whatever identity you choose, there are songs, bumper stickers, YouTube channels, and clothing styles that reflect the particular way you make sense of the world. So that even though you are responsible for finding meaning in life, you can always find someone else to validate that meaning and give it grandeur.

● ● ●

We are individually responsible for creating meaning, but choosing to identify within a larger community can be an effective way to share the burden of interpretation and validation. Why bother starting from scratch when you can just join a community that provides a framework of meaning for you? Plus, it can help you express your identity and give you a greater sense of purpose. For a non-trivial number of self-identified evangelicals, I suspect church pragmatically fills this function. Membership at a church can provide you with a place to belong in a community, a way of interpreting everything from the daily rhythms of life to politics and global events. It can also help you define yourself. At their best, local churches remind us that we are not our own but belong to God, and in so doing, they disrupt contemporary understandings of meaning and identity. It must be said, however, that far too many churches have adopted the contemporary anthropology. They assume that we are our own and provide us with options for meaning and identity like any other community.

The great danger in allowing a community to aid you in discovering meaning is that at some point the community is going to overstep its bounds and try to enforce meaning. Perhaps you attend a church because it "feels like home." You appreciate that the church community shares many of your own political attitudes. But then one Sunday morning the pastor denounces as sin some behavior that you hold quite dear. You are likely to feel betrayed by the community and leave to find one that actually "feels like home."

Belonging in a community is contingent on fitting with the way you interpret the world. A church (or any other institution or community) can help you with the Responsibilities of Self-Belonging so long as it does not infringe on your self-belonging. But when it does, there is always another community ready to welcome you.

●   ●   ●

Rituals are another significant way society aids us in the Responsibilities of Self-Belonging. The most significant moments in our lives tend to be solemnized by some kind of ritual or ceremony. Historically in the West, weddings, funerals, and baptisms have been celebrated with specific Christian rituals that mark these events and define their meaning in our community. Christians still practice these rituals, but today there are millions of other rituals to choose from.

We mark time and significance with parties, graduations, award ceremonies, trips, tattoos, songs, and purchases. And even the three traditionally Christian ceremonies have grown more personalized to reflect the meaning attached to them by individuals, many of whom are not religious. There is no one standard for a wedding ceremony in the twenty-first century. The structure, length, tone, elements, and location of weddings are all individually determined. In fact, the intense personalization of wedding ceremonies is part of their charm (and profitability). They allow couples to define what love and marriage means for them.

Humans need rituals, or "liturgies" as James K. A. Smith calls them, in order to make sense of our lives, to give them shape and substance.[5] But without a shared sense of meaning, we need increasingly diverse options for rituals. We need the ability to create entirely personalized rituals.

One dramatic example of personalized rituals is Ritual Design Labs, a Silicon Valley company that helps people develop rituals that fit their specific needs. In 2018 they led a class at Stanford University on designing rituals to make humans more comfortable riding in autonomous cars.[6] While I don't think we're going to see a wave of companies specifically devoted to designing rituals, we will continue to see individual markets, fields, and social spaces design their own rituals to help give meaning to their work.

It's common for companies to have their own ceremonies to solemnize events or achievements. Even when we know that a ritual has been created whole cloth to promote team bonding or celebrate life milestones—to give an experience a particular meaning—the physicality and drama of the ritual can have a deep pull on us. Think of "The Dundies" episode of *The Office*, where Michael Scott tries to force his employees to care about his made-up awards. It's a bit pathetic, but it also feels very human. It's natural for us to interpret our experience through communal rituals, even when they have no roots in tradition, culture, ethnicity, religion, or anything else.

Society doesn't just give us recommendations for how to interpret meaning in our lives. It also enables us by limiting the power of depression, primarily through antidepressants. If you've suffered with depression for any extended period, you'll know that the sense of the meaninglessness of life can be overwhelming. What used to give you joy and purpose suddenly feels utterly empty. You know you ought to feel something, but you can't escape the fog of hopelessness or numbness. You no longer desire sex, your favorite foods taste bland, and none of the sitcoms are funny anymore. When you're in a depression like this, the only meaning you can discover in life is its apparent meaninglessness. Sometimes you feel disembodied, like the world is out there experiencing things, and you're floating thirty yards above everyone, untethered from anything real or meaningful. The material world continues to exist, but it appears naked before you, denuded of any significance or importance. Raw material moving according to physics, biology, and custom.

I hope you've never suffered this way, but many of us have. In the following chapters we'll consider the rise of mental illness in America and how it relates to all we've been discussing, but for now we just need to see how society works to help us create meaning by reducing the effects of mental illness. While there are certainly good and proper uses for them, it is remarkable that psychiatric medications seem to be a necessity for millions of people to even get to the place where they can feel meaning at all, let alone choose meaning for themselves. And society is happy to provide any aid necessary.

HOW SOCIETY GIVES US VALUES

In the absence of a shared system of values, humans gravitate toward values that are quantifiable. Certainly, many other values are promoted in society from differing voices: PETA wants me to value all living creatures equally, a car commercial wants me to value freedom, a politician wants me to value nationalism. But we perceive these values as highly negotiable options, what the philosopher Zygmunt Bauman called "the until-further-noticeness of human bonds and networks."[7] As in, "I believe in the sanctity of marriage until a more attractive person comes along, at which time I'll give notice of my new values."

The fluidity of ethics in the modern world could lead to a condition called "anomie," a lack of social norms to guide our behavior and life. And this is where I believe the power of numbers rescues a great many people from a moral aimlessness. Specifically, the modern value of "technique" gives people a way to function in society without getting lost in our own personal preferences.

●   ●   ●

When most people hear the word "technique," they think of technology or a method for doing a task well. In his book *The Technological Society*, the philosopher Jacques Ellul gives us a definition of technique that is extremely valuable to interpreting our society: "Technique is the totality of methods rationally arrived at and having absolute efficiency . . . in every field of human activity."[8] Whenever we use reason to create methods to achieve efficiency, we are practicing technique. For Ellul, one defining characteristic of technique is that in the modern world it subsumes all values under efficiency. Efficiency becomes the greatest good and a way of re-assuring our conscience: "Technique provides justification to everybody and gives all men the conviction that their actions are just, good, and in the spirit of truth."[9]

When Ellul says "every field of human activity," he means it, as I have discovered. While drafting this chapter, I began to experience considerable pain in my shoulders from sleeping on my side. Like a normal person, I turned to Google for answers. One of the top results was an article titled "Best Practices for Side Sleeping." I had no clue there was an entire science devoted to studying the optimal way to sleep on your side, but I *should* have known, because the drive for maximizing efficiency in every activity is a considerable aspect of modern life.

An interesting example of this can be found in the field of "leadership," a broad category that has come to include everyone from CEOs to pastors. Why are leaders encouraged to care for the well-being of their employees? Why do experts recommend allowing workers to have regular breaks, and encourage office parties or other social activities? We've heard the answer a million times: treating workers well increases productivity. A happy worker is a productive worker. Note that this method of leadership *appears* to be motivated by a value higher than efficiency: the welfare of fellow humans. If workers are taking coffee breaks, they'll have less time to work, so isn't management really putting "people before profit"? And yet the rationale for giving them breaks is not that it is good for them as human persons, or that it would be immoral to overwork people made in the image of God. Far from it. Kindness, respect, and love are utilitarian means to maximize efficiency.

Remarkably, all of this occurs out in the open. Leaders rarely hide the fact that efficiency, not charity, motivates their policies. On the contrary, it's common to hear management publicize their motive: "At Work Corp, we value our employees and their families. Employees who are satisfied with their home life are four times as productive as those who are dissatisfied. That's why we are thrilled to begin offering paid family leave for pregnancies, medical emergencies, and other family life crises." It should seem odd to us that managers can openly admit to treating their employees humanely primarily to increase profits (especially because it raises the question of what they'll do when humane policies decrease profits), but we've become so deeply committed to technique that none of this phases us. Actually, knowing that family leave will increase our productivity and, therefore, benefit the company may ease our conscience about using the benefit. We don't need to feel guilty about using paid family leave if we know it will benefit our employer in the long run!

The moral superiority of efficiency is so deeply ingrained in us that one author who recently wrote a book about "a world obsessed with work" advocated for increased "recovery time" to avoid worker burnout and to increase creativity. The tag of a *Bloomberg* interview with the author reads, "Recovery time is key to innovation and output, says digital anthropologist Rahaf Harfoush."[10] Why should we give recovery time to exhausted employees? So they can increase their output. To combat burnout, Harfoush appeals to efficiency.

We use this same logic to justify our leisure outside of work. It's okay for me to nap because it'll help me be more alert so I can finish this task. It's okay for me to watch this game because I need to give my brain a rest. It's okay for me to spend time with my kids because data shows that reading to children is the most effective way to improve their vocabulary and lifetime earnings. It's okay for me to go for a run because it will improve my health. And so on.

Examples of technique can be found everywhere in our society, and while we might not have consciously conceived of them as a phenomenon, I suspect that we often have a similar response to technique when it appears in our lives. We experience a sense of weariness, urgency, and a moral burden. You might say to yourself, "I just need to . . ." after learning of another technique for living. Perhaps you read a headline describing the latest research on how to lose weight and keep it off. Or perhaps it's an article outlining strategies for raising well-adjusted or successful children. Or it's a journaling method that promises to bring order to your chaotic life. Or instructions for how to properly wash a blouse or tie. Or a new Bible reading plan. Or a self-care regimen. Or an app that designs a workout based on your interests, weight, height, age, sex, and available time. Or a method for organizing your house. And you say, "I just need to follow this advice, then I'll won't have all these problems."

Efficiency has many healthy applications when it is not treated as an *ultimate* good. But according to Ellul, technique does not easily abide other values. Efficiency tends to push out other considerations, or at least subjugate them. For example, it's a wonderful thing to develop a more efficient way to farm so that you can provide more food for your neighbors, but when your concern for efficiency leads you to ignore the way a farming technique *harms* your neighbors or the environment, you are under the spell of technique.

What's remarkable is the way technique has effortlessly crept into every single corner of modern life. And in virtually every instance, we treat the more efficient method as a moral obligation. While we may hesitate to make moral judgments about people's sex lives (because that's a private matter), almost everyone wants to reduce the rate of teen pregnancies.

In the previous chapter, I used the example of prostitution to explain our near-universal embrace of efficiency as the greatest good. Some advocates for the legalization of prostitution point to the quantifiable harm of prohibition. If legalization reduces sexual and state violence, incarceration rates, and venereal diseases, and enables impoverished women to provide for themselves and their families, then clearly it is more efficient to legalize it. After all, every social harm is a drain on society and, therefore, an inefficiency.[11] There are considerable problems with our justice system, but left out of this logic is the question of whether there may be some nonquantifiable moral reason for opposing prostitution. This question is not worth answering, however, because if it cannot be measured, we cannot publicly debate it. You define human "dignity" one way and I define it another, but we can both follow the data that points to a measurable reduction in harm.

While this tendency to appeal to efficiency and data is widely used on the political left, the political right, and even the religious right, are just as enamored by it. There is an ongoing debate among conservatives (particularly religious conservatives) about outlawing or strongly regulating pornography.[12] The libertarian wing of the Right opposes such restrictions on liberty, but some social conservatives argue that since there is data that demonstrates psychological and physical harm caused by addiction to pornography, it's a public health crisis.[13] Again, social harm is a drain on society and therefore inefficient. Similarly, some pro-life activists have stressed the physical and psychological harm associated with abortions. None of these appeals to data and efficiency feel odd to us because as Ellul has argued, efficiency has established itself as the greatest good.

There is no space in contemporary life that has not become subject to the dominion of rational methods for achieving maximum efficiency, from the marriage bed to art and warfare. That's not to say that we never prioritize other values—we certainly do—but our one agreed-upon value in nearly every sphere of life tends to be efficiency. And the methods for improving our lives that fill self-help books, podcasts, and conferences are exactly the way society aids us in our responsibility to determine what moral living looks like. Society can do very little to help us decide whether promiscuity or fidelity is more ethical since we are our own, but it *can* provide us with the contraceptive methods, the married-sex-life strategies, and the erotic material to make our choice efficient. This tremendous emphasis on personal optimization reflects a society made for humans for whom efficiency is the greatest good.

● ● ●

In the absence of universal values, we turn to efficiency, and in the absence of a vision of the common good, we turn to identity politics, the organizing of political coalitions based on religion, race, ethnicity, gender, sexuality, or cultural preferences. While the phrase has some negative connotations among conservatives, identity politics is the dominate shape of contemporary politics across the political spectrum. Middle-class White evangelicals without a college education are just as much a political identity group as Black college graduates and transgendered people of color. That doesn't mean that all identity groups have equal justification for acting as political movements; it's merely an observation about the state of current American politics.

Like the rest of our society, identity politics is inherently antagonistic. Groups are generally formed through shared experiences of oppression or shared acts of aggression, and they offer a political vision alongside a set of social values.

If we are hopelessly our own and belong to ourselves, then there can be no substantial common good for us to work toward, politically or socially. The best we can do is try to stay out of each other's way. We see this in the influential political philosophy of John Rawls, who believed "freedom consists in pursuing our own conception of the good life while respecting the right of others to do the same."[14] Charles Taylor calls this the "proceduralist liberalism of neutrality" and points to it as one of the reasons western countries are so politically fragmented.[15] So long as the state remains committed to neutrality in regard to the good life, the "common good" can only ever be toleration.

Instead of a common good, we have billions of private goods. The best we can do is join forces with other people with intersecting identities. Identity politics is one way that society offers us a vision for political action in the absence of a common good. If we are radically our own, we can't hope to build a political vision that encompasses the entire nation, or even a local community. But we can form collective action groups to defend our private interests.

Identity politics cannot be entirely explained by the anthropology I'm laying out in this book, but it is a factor. History is clear that discrimination and oppression force people into collective political action for their survival. In fact, ignoring the oppression of particular identity groups is not a retreat from identity politics, but the defense of a dominant identity group. But it is possible to name and oppose discrimination against groups of people while placing that fight for justice within a larger vision of the common good. When we see ourselves as our own, however, it is difficult to even conceive of a common good that looks like anything other than John Lennon's "Imagine": vapid, incoherent, and unimaginative wishful thinking. So society provides identity groups for us.

HOW SOCIETY LETS US BELONG

I have been speaking of our collective Responsibilities of Self-Belonging, which refers to all the ways in which modern people feel responsible for their existence. In this section we will focus on a different kind of belonging: our human need to be rightly placed in the universe. Of all the Responsibilities of Self-Belonging, the burden to belong somewhere may be the most dependent on the support of society. It's one thing to be responsible for choosing where and to whom you belong in this life, but it's another thing altogether to have the freedom to act on that choice.

Belonging requires a society that facilitates fluidity. Our tendency is to place obligations on one another. We are naturally social beings and when we live in a community, that community will organically draw us into its life, making us a member, placing burdens and responsibilities on us as well as conferring rights and privileges.

Even the land does this. Living in a particular place for an extended period of time organically etches something of the natural environment upon you. Perhaps you find yourself belonging to a place because the changing of the seasons becomes a part of your rhythms of life. People who have lived in the Northeast often speak of the way the leaves change colors in the fall, a phenomenon that holds no sway over me because I've never experienced it. Growing up, the smell of onion fields reminded me that the California high desert was my home. It conjured up years and years of memories.

We find the same principle at work in human relationships: when you commit to being with someone, it always feels like an aberration when the relationship fails. Think back to a valued friendship that has ended. Even if it ended on bad terms—even if you discovered that your friend had betrayed you—you experience the breaking of that friendship as a loss of belonging.

What is true of friendships is even truer of romantic relationships. Most people experience break-ups as a severing of self. When you have intimately united yourself with someone, any cleavage of that union will involve a displacement. This is precisely why we need a society with robust means to help us overcome our natural tendency to belong. Society must liberate us or we will grow roots. Society must help us "brave the wilderness," in Brené Brown's language.

And society provides. Consider how easy and normal it is to move away from your hometown. It's practically a rite of passage to graduate from high school and move off to college. In this phase of life, we view the world, or at least the country, as a wide-open space to choose from. You can live anywhere. This kind of freedom only works if we have infrastructure that makes cross-country moves affordable and easy. The replacement of the natural world with human construction weakens our ties to particular places. Good roads, moving companies, cheap and disposable furniture, and plenty of housing options make this possible.

But more than our physical displacement, the expansion of our legal, commercial, and personal identities onto the internet makes all the hassle of moving simple. If I move to a new state, almost all the critical parts of my public person remain the same. My credit cards, my banking, many of my bills, my social media presence, and even my cell phone number can all remain the same. They never really belonged where I lived anyway. In that respect, my public persona resides just as much if not more online than off.

Not only does technology allow us to move more easily, it also allows us to stay unattached wherever we are. I am not obligated to get to know my neighbors. Everyone politely minds their own business unless some catastrophe happens. Even my commerce keeps me free from entanglements. For one thing, most stores are major chains and it's difficult to feel a sense of solidarity with a chain supermarket. When I enter a chain store, I perceive the employees differently than if I enter a locally owned business. With the former, a corporate mask covers the employees so that even if they are technically my neighbors, I feel like I'm primarily interacting with an agent of or avatar for Walmart, not a person. This alienation from my neighbors could lead to awkward interactions, but for the most part it doesn't because technology has adapted so that I don't have to interact with people while shopping. Digital boxes attached to poles can price items for me. Self-checkout shields me from even the most basic pleasantries with a checker. In exchange for this freedom from belonging to people in a community, I only have to accept constant surveillance by security cameras. At my local Walmart, multiple flatscreen displays hang from the ceiling right above the self-checkout section to forcefully remind shoppers that even if an employee is not around, you are still being watched.

The good news is that other technological innovations allow me to avoid the Walmart experience entirely. Even in my small city of thirty thousand people, I can have my groceries delivered. With an app, I can select all the items I want, choose a time window for delivery, and pay with a credit card. The items I can't have delivered from the local grocery store, I can order with two-day free shipping from Amazon Prime. Virtually all of my consumer needs can be met with little human contact and, therefore, very few obligations to belong. I don't have to witness my neighbor's suffering or joy. I don't have to feel like we have something in common. I don't have to feel responsible for their well-being.

It has never been easier to be socially "connected" to people without the necessity of actually connecting with people. In my life, I have made two major moves. First from the desert of Southern California to Waco, Texas, and then from Waco to Shawnee, Oklahoma. After each move, my wife and I have made a concerted effort to belong to a community: to join a church and a small group and to make friends. And then we'd have to move again. Across these transitions and the loss (or diminishment) of close friendships that naturally happens with any move, two of my closest friends have been Richard Clark and Derek Rishmawy. We talk almost daily through private messages, sharing personal burdens, prayer requests, praises, questions, anger, confusion, and exhortation.

While it is certainly true that online friendships aren't the same as in-person ones, the number of differences is decreasing. I can write my friends wherever I am and get an instant response as if they were in the room with me. I can play video games with my friends, so that we are "doing" something together. We can record podcasts together. And if I wanted to, I could extend this to include more and more online communities and fewer and fewer in-person ones. A well-produced multiplayer video game can provide common goals, bonding, friendships, and even romance. Or if I feel too "mature" for games, I can get deeply involved in an internet microcommunity: groups devoted to modifying drones, to maximizing (efficiency!) a certain workout program, or to conspiracy theories. Microcommunities form around podcasts, websites, YouTube channels, Instagrammers, religions, cars, decades, diets, and so on. Technology has effectively freed me from any need to belong to where my body is. I may have to sleep here, but I don't have to *be* here.

Marriages and families are harder to treat so fluidly, but society offers what it can here too. No-fault divorce makes the ending of marriage about as easy as it can be. Social safety nets, which are generally good things, absolve us from the responsibility to care for injured, disabled, ill, poor, or elderly family members. The elderly are a particularly instructive case of how society enables us to choose our belonging. Historically, caring for your parents and grandparents was a basic part of life. Just as they belonged to you, caring and providing for you when you were a child, you belonged to them and were expected to care and provide for them in their old age. But we have gone so far from that norm that many elderly people feel guilt and shame at the prospect of having to rely on their children. More than once I have heard someone express the desire to live in an assisted living home rather than being a "burden" to their children who would have to wipe their butts. Sadly, their children usually agree. So most cities in America have enough assisted living facilities that adult children don't have to personally care for their parents, unless they choose to. Society provides.

A final example: Pornography provides a way for couples to "belong" to each other legally and yet be emotionally and physically autonomous. Sex, it turns out—or at least sex in a healthy marriage—requires a great deal of time, effort, vulnerability, and self-denial. If you're not married, trust me. If you are married and have not had this experience, be patient. Good sex doesn't abide autonomy. The act itself is the most intimate, affirming, vulnerable, self-giving expression you can share with a person. Once the common storms of life—stress, work, children, money problems, boredom, age—kick in, cultivating a rich love life with your spouse is difficult. For periods it may feel impossible. And the thing about porn is you can experience almost any sexual fantasy whenever you want, without any emotional labor or self-giving, and usually for free. This means that in a marriage where the couple does not want to separate but are no longer are "in love," society has provided an efficient way for each spouse to experience some form of sexual stimulation without the destabilizing effects of an affair.

The choice to belong to your spouse or not has been highly aided in modern times by the ready availability of pornography. It's not uncommon for couples, particularly couples with children, to stop having intercourse over time and to supplement that loss with porn. For other people, pornography makes the choice to belong to yourself and forgo marriage altogether easier to bear. Again, society provides.

• • •

The Responsibilities of Self-Belonging are considerable, and the pressure to fulfill them is too much for most people to bear. But society responds to our needs by equipping us to be our own and belong to ourselves.

In a sense, the tools needed are the tools of "self authoring." Bestselling author and psychologist Jordan Peterson actually sells an online course for anyone who wants to improve themselves through self authoring. If you pay for the full package, you're asked to write responses to a series of prompts about your past, your present, and your future goals. I have no doubt that much of this reflection is helpful: we tend to avoid honest introspection. But I find two things remarkable about the program. First, it is called "Self Authoring." Peterson frames the process of self-improvement in terms of writing a better life for oneself—which makes perfect sense if we are our own. What could be worse than to abdicate the storyline of our life to some ghostwriter, whether it's your parents' ideals or societal norms? Clearly, we ought to take up the pen and author our own life story. Second, as Peterson describes in a YouTube video advertising the program, the origin of the "Self Authoring" suite was, at least in part, corporate consulting.[16] Peterson was brought into corporations to help make employees more productive, and he discovered that through this method of "self authoring," employees were able to define their goals and more effectively work toward them. So from the beginning, Peterson's self authoring method is rooted not in the human person but in efficiency in the business world. This is not a coincidence. Just as corporations must optimize by increasing efficiency in order to stay competitive, so individuals need to optimize in order to fulfill our Responsibilities of Self-Belonging.

The systems and techniques and norms society has developed to help us cope with the Responsibilities of Self-Belonging come with their own problems. Society makes us a kind of promise: it will do its part to help us live authentically if we'll accept the Responsibilities of Self-Belonging.

But does society enable us to live the good life? Are the methods and tools we have covered in this chapter effective? What if this whole time society has been constructing systems, techniques, and norms based on a false understanding of what a human person is? If that's the case, we'd expect to find an inhuman society. And so we do. But we'd also expect that a proper understanding of the human person would give us a more human society. And so it does. Before we can consider an alternate anthropology, one which assumes that we belong to Christ, as well as the hope it can offer us in life and death, we need to understand how contemporary society utterly fails to keep its promises of a fulfilled life through the Responsibilities of Self-Belonging.

3

HOW SOCIETY FAILS US

*So obvious are the impotence and distress of all men in face of the
social machine, which has become a machine for breaking hearts
and crushing spirits, a machine for manufacturing irresponsibility,
stupidity, corruption, slackness, and, above all, dizziness. The reason
for this painful state of affairs is perfectly clear. We are living in a
world in which nothing is made to man's measure; there exists a
monstrous discrepancy between man's body, man's mind and the
things which at the present time constitute the elements of human
existence; everything is disequilibrium.*

SIMONE WEIL, *OPPRESSION AND LIBERTY*

THE LOGIC, SPIRIT, AND ECONOMY of contemporary pornography
is a near-perfect reflection of society's failure to provide us with the
tools necessary to meet the Responsibilities of Self-Belonging. Pornography
assumes that we are each our own and belong to ourselves. It's a tool that
promises to give us a kind of personal validation, a sense of identity, a taste
of meaningfulness, and a glimpse of intimate belonging. But by its own
logic, pornography, like modernity, is an empty promise. Rather than helping
us meet our responsibilities and cope with an inhuman world, it exacerbates
our condition. Rather than bringing us closer to our humanity, it dehumanizes
at every turn, turning our intimacy into instrumentality and leaving us

addicted, depressed, exhausted, lonely, and bored—which also happens to be an accurate description of our society in general.

Contemporary pornography is merely a continuation of a long tradition of human efforts to depict sex and the sexualized body. Some might argue that there's really no difference between erotic murals in the homes of ancient Pompeii and what the average, healthy, imaginative, sex-positive young man or woman accesses on their smart phone today. Humans have always creatively depicted sex and sexualized bodies. What does it really matter whether they're drawn by hand or filmed and uploaded to the internet? Is there a meaningful difference between kids today hiding porn on their smartphones in 2021 and kids hiding copies of *Playboy* under their mattresses in the 1981?[1]

It is not the same; the internet has changed pornography. And those changes reflect our contemporary anthropology. Consider the power of choice. Today you can find a pornographic depiction of virtually any fantasy. If you can dream it, you can find it. And you can probably find it for free within three minutes. When you inevitably get bored of that fantasy, just dispose of it and find something new—indefinitely. Humans have always been able to imagine all kinds of sexual scenarios, but we haven't been able to make them exist, unless you happened to be a tremendously powerful despotic ruler. We all have the power of Caligula now.

With just an internet connection and a smart device you can entertain yourself with real humans performing any sexual fantasy you desire, no matter how debased, abusive, or bizarre. And on the off chance that you can't find what you want, with a little money you can contact a pornographic performer and ask for a private video, customized and personalized to your tastes. Contemporary pornography is the most affirmative experience we can have.

But you say, "I can't have *anything*. What I'd really like is a video of a particular coworker and me having intercourse, and since she won't even go out for coffee with me, there's no chance of that happening." Don't worry, technology will find a way. And it almost has. With the rise of "deep fakes," it's now possible to create realistic videos where one person's head is replaced by another's. Currently this technology is used to create bootleg porn of famous actresses. The user takes footage of the actress, uses a program with advanced AI, and splices it with an existing pornographic video. The result is a realistic pornographic video of your favorite celebrity, whether or not she has actually done the sex scenes. And given enough time and images, it's possible to use this same technology with your coworker, without her permission. Because your coworker, like most of us, has posted many images of herself online, you have all the raw material needed.

If this discussion has turned your stomach, that's a good sign. It *ought* to turn your stomach. But what I'd like you to see is that contemporary pornography puts the individual user at the center of the universe. We have a godlike freedom to pursue any fantasy we wish. We can consume the most intimate human experience, taking in image after image after image, amassing a collection of human intimacy so vast and diverse that you come to feel that by rights you should have access to anyone's body for your own pleasure. That's one reason why young people—particularly young women—are so often pressured into sending nude photos and videos of themselves to their boyfriend or girlfriend. When so many bodies are so widely available for (primarily) the male gaze, exposing yourself can feel like the ante everyone pays to play the game.

Another result is that the economic value of exposing your body for the sexual gaze of others has dramatically fallen. During the Covid-19 pandemic of 2020–2021, the *New York Times* reported that a website allowing people to sell pornographic images of themselves had grown from one hundred twenty thousand "content creators" in 2019 to over one million. Unemployed and desperate, these content creators sold images and videos of themselves to pay their bills.[2] But with over one million people selling content on top of an already vast market of pornography, one body simply isn't worth that much. Nobody's body is worth very much—which makes it even easier to imagine that you deserve to see whatever fantasy you desire.

In following your erotic preferences, you feel a sense of self-expression. The kinds of people you look for, the kinds of acts, the settings, the music, the tone and mood—all of it reflects your identity. By consuming moments of intimacy, you feel yourself become a little more real and more powerful. Your existence feels justified as you consume the intimacy of others. Perhaps you feel more "alive" with the thrill of accumulating images. Or perhaps you feel a sense of belonging, since belonging *to* someone is central to the act of sex, even its most mediated forms. But as with all consumption, you can never linger long; it never satisfies, which is why it's good that search engines and internet speeds can accommodate your appetite. As quickly as you can imagine a fantasy, you grow dissatisfied with it. The thrill of the hunt, of discovery, is always inevitably followed by the letdown. Possession loses its edge.

For a moment, you felt a sense of intimacy, of passion, of sexual conquest, of power, but you know it's a game. It isn't real. Even when the videos are created by amateurs and lack all the benefits of professional editing, it never feels genuinely intimate. This is the unspoken logic of pornography: this beautiful, unique human is giving themself to me, exposing themself intimately *for me*, and so I must matter.[3] In the act of sex, two people give themselves as vulnerably as possible. They may put up psychological or physical barriers to protect themselves from intimacy and union, but the act itself is inseparable from a profound sense of giving, unity, openness, and therefore belonging. Any abuse of sexual intimacy is a uniquely evil affront against someone's personhood precisely because it treats that personhood as a means to an end.

Even in highly mediated and artificial forms of sexual intimacy, like edited pornographic videos, there remains the feeling that the viewer is receiving special access to someone's person by virtue of their worthiness. I believe the best description of this this feeling is "tiny and meaningless and—sad-making," a phrase used by one of J. D. Salinger's characters to express a pathetic effort to feel existentially justified through a grotesque game of make-believe.[4] What we will discover is that, as with pornography, many of our attempts to meet the Responsibilities of Self-Belonging are "tiny and meaningless and—sad-making."

It is an "unspoken" logic of pornography because if we name it, if we admit that in pornography we momentarily allow ourselves to believe that a mass-reproduced image represents intimate and personal affirmation, then it would lose much of its power. It is also unspoken because, for men at least, it's easier to admit to being biologically driven by lust than emotionally driven by loneliness or inadequacy. And as the sociologist Alain Ehrenberg argues in his history of depression, inadequacy is the pathology of contemporary depression.[5] Sex, even masturbation, cannot help but involve the heart. When the moment passes, however, and you are faced with how tiny and meaningless and sad-making your fantasy really was, you may feel more alone and inadequate than ever. And to alleviate the renewed feelings of inadequacy, you return to pornography.

So a tool created to help give you justification, identity, meaning, value, and belonging cannot fulfill its promise. It only leaves you worse off than before: depressed and inadequate, anxious and addicted.

●   ●   ●

To cope with the inhumanity of our society, we develop newer and better techniques, which, being based on a false anthropology, only extend that inhumanity in new ways, requiring further coping techniques.

Consider the case of a married man who suffers from depression and anxiety. These conditions primarily surface as a general apathy toward life, a feeling of inadequacy, and fatigue. Maybe the meaninglessness of his work is the source of his despair, or a midlife crisis in which he doubts his contribution to the world, or burnout after decades of desperately trying to get in shape or get a promotion. Take your pick. The more depressed and anxious he is, the more alienated he becomes from his wife. He feels too depressed to initiate sex and she feels too emotionally distant to initiate. The longer they stay apart, the more depressed and anxious he becomes. Soon, his feelings of inadequacy seem to be affirmed by their lack of intimacy: "Maybe I am not desirable?" He feels an acute lack of belonging. To cope with his mental condition, he begins taking an antidepressant. Using the technique of modern psychiatric medication, he is able to lower the symptoms of his depression and anxiety to a manageable level. In a few weeks, he mostly feels like his old self. He is more productive at work and finds that he can enjoy most of life's simple pleasures.

Unfortunately for our hypothetical husband, the most common side effect of antidepressants is loss of sexual desire.[6] Now that he is no longer too depressed to have sex, he has lost the desire and maybe even the ability to have sex. Except there is still pornography. And the drama and endless novelty of porn renews the desire deadened by antidepressants and age. More importantly, porn gives him freedom from emotional and physical vulnerability with his wife and mitigates his fear of sexual failure. He experiences a mediated simulation of belonging rather than risk the failure of actual belonging with his wife.

Thus, technique (porn as a tool for sexual validation and belonging) is used to cope with a problem (lack of intimacy and belonging) created by a technique (antidepressants) to cope with a problem (depression and anxiety), which grew from the inhuman conditions of modern life.

The darkest part of the unspoken logic of pornography is the idea that the porn actors are free, consensual, aware, liberated individuals, using their freedom to express themselves, make money, and please others. Because they are their own and belong to themselves, they are free to treat their body, their intimate personhood, as a tool, a commodity, to objectify it and use it instrumentally for personal gain.

And if I am my own, I have no moral responsibility to a performer. If an adult elects to offer a good or service, or to take a job creating a good or performing a service, then I am free to participate in it. I am free to treat others as means to my ends, as tools, as instruments for my personal fulfillment—so long as they are compensated. And if an adult chooses to upload their own amateur pornography, then I am free to enjoy that too. If I cannot tell whether the adult really *chose* to make that video or image public, or whether that adult is indeed an adult, I should not be held responsible. I was an ignorant, free consumer.

The dynamic of choice, consumption, power, and identity in pornography mirrors our broader cultural practices. The same spirit of endless choice that gives contemporary pornography so much of its power can be experienced walking down the cereal aisle of a grocery store. In other words, porn doesn't ask users to adopt new or different ideas of choice, consumption, and identity. It's the very same dynamic of choice we have practiced our entire lives. Consumption is one way we cope with depression, anxiety, insecurity, and identity crises. We choose, consume, and dispose of objects in order to affirm our existence, define our identity, give meaningfulness to our dull lives, and belong to or possess someone beyond ourselves. In other words, contemporary pornography rests on a particular conception of the human person, a conception that is widely shared in society, even by many who find pornography distasteful or offensive.

Pornography can only offer a shadow of fulfillment, and even then it is fleeting. As is the case with many of the coping mechanisms of modernity, addiction follows, ending in burnout.

THE UNFULFILLED PROMISE OF A GOOD LIFE

Our society is a constructed environment built for humans who are their own and belong to themselves. This environment includes the tools (the internet, antidepressants), spaces (cities, the suburbs), laws (no-fault divorce, free speech defenses of pornography), values (efficiency, individualism), and practices (self-expression, consumption) that reflect and reinforce that anthropology. Each of these elements, like the pagan gods of ancient Rome, promises to aid us in living a good life so long as we pay them proper devotion and tribute.

Implicit in our society is the promise that you can become a fully realized human if you:

1. Accept that you are your own and belong completely to yourself.

2. Work every day to discover and express yourself.

3. Use all of the techniques and methods perfected by society to improve your life and conquer your obstacles.

If you adjust to living in this habitat, you will be happy. And if you aren't a fully realized human, it's either because there's some injustice in the environment (an inefficiency), a flaw in your will to improve (another inefficiency), or some natural/biological hinderance (also an inefficiency!). But society is self-correcting: collectively, we are purging the injustices, improving ourselves, and overcoming the burdens of the natural world—a process we call "Progress." Our hope in Progress lets us overlook the brokenness of society.

But by its own standards, our society cannot fulfill its promise. The gods are mute. And those who make them become like them.

•   •   •

One reason society fails to fulfill its promise is that a society premised
on the sovereign self has no discernable ends, only an ever expanding and
ever demanding number of means. The goal of our striving cannot be
reached because it is self-defined. The image of our fulfilled life is forever
shifting. One day we may believe that the good life looks like climbing the
corporate ladder, but the next it may look like pursuing social justice. The
ends of our lives are uncertain, but there are plenty of means to pursue
them. We know what our obligations are, but there is no model of what the
fulfillment of those obligations looks like because there cannot be. All we
have are our intuitions.

What does a fully realized Alan Noble even look like? The optimistic
answer (what I will call "Affirmation" in a few pages) is whatever I sincerely
believe to be most true about myself and my identity. Robert Bellah and
Charles Taylor have both rightly described this idea as "expressive individualism."[7] This sounds wonderful, but it's not really a proper *end*. To be
"true to myself" is to be "true" in an unconventional way. To be true to yourself
is categorically different from being true in an empirical or logical sense
because there is no external or objective way to judge or reassure ourselves.
How can you ever be sure that you are being true to yourself? How can you
ever know if you are being authentic? You are utterly alone in your judgment—
sovereign, but alone. And to make matters worse, you cannot trust yourself.
The human mind is capable of tremendous self-deception. Maybe you are
least true to yourself when you are trying to be like yourself!

When you cannot envision the purpose of your life, you must instead
focus on the means of getting there. Society's promise of fulfillment turns
out to be commitment to find more and more ways (means) of feeling authentically myself, knowing that there can be no arrival.

To make matters worse, the Responsibilities of Self-Belonging require
godlike powers to sustain, leaving us exhausted, tired, burned out, and
finally bored. We are always *becoming* a fully realized human and never
arriving. Nobody ever arrives because there is no destination outside ourselves to arrive at. If we are our own and belong to ourselves, then we are

always only who we are. No more. No less. All we have are options and shifting opinions and an overwhelming feeling that whatever the standard might be, we aren't measuring up. Our work is inadequate, our house is inadequate, our tastes are inadequate, our spouse is inadequate, our body is inadequate, our education is inadequate, our cooking is inadequate, and so on. Society cannot fulfill its promise because it never really offered a clear goal. In this sense, the promise of society is more like a warning: You will keep searching, keep expressing, keep redefining, keep striving for your autonomous personhood until you die.

Sometimes you will hear people try to make this obsession with means into a virtue: "It's not about where you're going, it's how you get there." But if you dwell on these claims long enough, the best you can do is say with Albert Camus, "The struggle itself toward the heights is enough to fill a man's heart. One must imagine Sisyphus happy."[8] In his famous essay, *The Myth of Sisyphus*, Camus suggests that human life is much like the fate of Sisyphus from Greek mythology, who was damned to spend eternity pushing a boulder up a mountain, only to watch it roll down again. Life, then, is an endless, arduous, meaningless existence. Also, to be clear, Sisyphus is in Hades. If all society can promise us is a life in Hades pushing the boulder of the Responsibilities of Self-Belonging, then it's not much of a promise. It may be an absurd fate that we can choose to face with dignity, which is essentially what Camus means by the "struggle" filling "a man's heart" and imagining Sisyphus "happy," but it's not the promise of a fulfilled and self-actualized life that society made to us.

●　　●　　●

Another way society fails to fulfill its promise is by introducing new problems to solve old ones as society progresses. New tools create new anxieties and new competitions. New spaces confine us in new ways.

Fast food and other prepackaged processed foods give us extra time to be more competitive. Energy drinks give us the alertness to work extra hours. But both deteriorate our health. Smartphones allow us to feel connected even as society isolates us, but it does so at the cost of addiction and privacy. Online dating opens up a world of possibilities for single people while also dramatically increasing competition and decreasing the effort needed to deceive someone you are dating. The information explosion makes it easier for us to fact check our politicians and more susceptible to conspiracy theories. Globalism has given us endless products to express our identity, which has made identity more contested than ever.

Society responds to its failures by creating new tools, spaces, laws, values, and practices that assume we are our own and belong to ourselves. And these new elements help us cope even as they introduce new problems. The problem may be in you (a lack of will), them (an unjust society), or it (nature). But what goes unquestioned is our understanding of the human person itself. We can debate the use of a particular technology, or how to stop police brutality, or whether to modify our bodies—but not our sovereignty.

Society also fails to fulfill its promise because the Responsibilities of Self-Belonging end up being profoundly dependent on other persons. As we saw in chapter two, justification pulls us out of ourselves to seek validation through stories or some other external source. Identity always assumes an *other* to whom we are presenting ourselves and from whom we seek affirmation. Meaning inherently feels external or it isn't worth the name. Our desire for justice implies values that transcend individual biases. And by definition, belonging is relational. To be our own and belong to ourselves we must do the impossible work of holding ourselves up while relying on others to hold us up, which is exhausting.

In the end, many find themselves in a state of burnout. As I discussed earlier, Anne Helen Petersen wrote a widely read and discussed article on millennial burnout[9] in 2019. The popularity of her article stemmed from the way readers resonated so deeply with the condition she describes:

> Why can't I get this mundane stuff done? Because I'm burned out. Why am I burned out? Because I've internalized the idea that I should be working all the time. Why have I internalized that idea? Because everything and everyone in my life has reinforced it—explicitly and implicitly—since I was young. Life has always been hard, but many millennials are unequipped to deal with the particular ways in which it's become hard for us.

Petersen argues that "burnout" goes beyond "exhaustion" and becomes a habit: "Exhaustion means going to the point where you can't go any further; burnout means reaching that point and pushing yourself to keep going, whether for days or weeks or years." Millennials often suffer from workaholism, happily working more than forty hours a week and feeling guilty when we aren't working. But even when we aren't "working," we are optimizing ourselves (applying technique to our personhood) so that we can have a fuller and satisfying life. While Petersen rightly points to changing economic conditions as a cause of burnout, in another article Derek Thompson identifies the deeper significance of workaholism: it functions as a religion. He writes, "What is workism? It is the belief that work is not only necessary to economic production, but also the centerpiece of one's identity and life's purpose; and the belief that any policy to promote human welfare must always encourage more work."[10] In other words, the burnout that many people feel is not merely the product of being overworked. There's an existential restlessness beneath our drive to "self-optimize."

COMPETITION IS THE HEART OF SUCCESS

Perhaps the most significant way society fails to fulfill its promise is that in a world where we all take the Responsibilities of Self-Belonging seriously, we experience escalating and spreading competition, not peace or self-actualization. Everyone must strive to make their personhood visible and affirmed. Everyone must define their identity against everyone else. Everyone must pursue constant self-improvement. Despite all the public handwringing over participation trophies, my sense is that most people feel themselves to be constantly competing, whether they want to be or not. In J. D. Salinger's *Franny and Zooey*, Franny quits her college theater department not because she's afraid of the competition, as her boyfriend suggests, but because she's afraid she *will* compete.[11] And so too, many of us feel that we have two choices: drop out or devote ourselves to endless competition.

When my son was in second grade, the local elementary school posted the top AR reading scores in the hallway, updated weekly and sorted by grade and for the entire school, grades 1–5. Every student that walked down

the hallway was greeted with a reminder of who the smart kids were and
where their intelligence fit relative to other students in their grade level and
in the school. There are several remarkable assumptions in this school's
practice. The first assumption, broadly shared across the nation and probably
mandated by the state, is that reading ability can be meaningfully quantified
and measured. The second is that reading is *the kind of thing* that one com-
petes in: part of the experience of learning to read is beating your friends
at it. Both assumptions are the products of technique's influence over the
school system, particularly the emphasis upon standardization and metrics.
The quest for constant improvement of efficiency through better practices
is tied up with our obsession with data and competition.

In the big scheme of things, a school posting reading scores in the hall
is insignificant. But it is an example of a much larger and more troubling
phenomenon. Michael Sandel and Malcolm Harris have noted that K–12
and college students are under increased pressure to compete and achieve.
Because we have taught our children that we live in a meritocracy where
the winners are responsible for their success and the losers are responsible
for their failure, all of life becomes part of the game. At every stage, our
children are either improving and developing, working toward an impressive
college application and resumé, or they are falling behind. In his book *Kids
These Days*, Harris documents the way "a lot more kids are working a lot
harder." Elementary schools have increased homework and high school AP
classes have exploded in popularity.[12] Parents come to view their child as

> a capital project. Realization—the tendency for firms to reduce every
> interaction to a number so that they'll be easier to optimize—has
> come to apply more and more to people themselves as productive
> tools. Risk management used to be a business practice; now it's our
> dominant child-rearing strategy.[13]

Harris's description of modern parenting is overwhelmingly cynical, but
he gets at an important truth. If we live in a strict meritocracy, parents ought
to do whatever they can to prepare their children for competition. That
means reducing risk and increasing activities that provide some discrete
benefit. And so Little League is valuable since it can teach teamwork and

improve the health of a child, not because baseball is a beautiful sport. Children's shows use the best research in emotional learning and child development to improve the viewers' emotional intelligence, rather than just telling a good story. To be a modern parent is to live with the anxiety that you are not doing everything you possibly can to raise children who can compete in a global marketplace.

Sandel has witnessed the crushing weight of meritocracy in his college students. In his book *The Tyranny of Merit*, Sandel claims that the dramatically rising emotional distress among college students is directly a result of our meritocratic system: "Years of anxious striving leave young people with a fragile sense of self-worth, contingent on achievement and vulnerable to the exacting judgments of parents, teachers, admissions committees, and ultimately, themselves."[14] This certainly fits my own experience teaching college. But as Sandel argues, the problem is much broader than anxious college students. Our meritocratic system—which turns competition over efficiency into a judgment of human value—morally malforms both the winners and the losers: "Among the winners, it generates hubris; among the losers, humiliation and resentment."[15] In Sandel's view, the heart of meritocracy is what I have been calling the contemporary anthropology: "The more we view ourselves as self-made and self-sufficient, the less likely we are to care for the fate of those less fortunate than ourselves. If my success is my doing, their failure must be their fault. This logic makes meritocracy corrosive of commonality."[16] Our faith in merit is spiritually and morally harmful for parents and children, teachers and students, winners and losers, individuals and communities. And it is based on the belief that we are our own.

If Jacques Ellul is correct that we live in a society governed by technique, then we should expect our interactions to be marked by competition because the essence of efficiency is competition: contrasting one method against another to discover the best practice. And meritocracy is a powerful way to reward those who master techniques.

We cannot overlook the influence of capitalism either. For example, we tend to conceive of competition as a kind of purifying fire that brings out the best in all of us. Competition drives us to greatness, inspires innovation,

and motivates us to improve. But competition has also contributed to the
condition Josef Pieper calls "Total Work," where every facet of our lives is
marked by productivity of one kind or another.[17] Work obligations follow
us home. They interrupt our sleep and family time. Social events become
opportunities to network. And, as Pieper points out, the only real exceptions
to work are activities that increase productivity. You can have vacation days
because allowing a certain number per year has been proven to increase
productivity by making employees happier. Total Work is the logic of technique applied to all labor—those who will not accept this logic will fall
behind, but that's okay because it's their own fault. That is meritocracy.

With few exceptions, competition is treated as the answer to our problems.
There are many good things to be said for the power of market competition
to improve our quality of life, but it is important to see how it also affects
our perception of the world.

Whether or not capitalism *necessarily* makes us hypercompetitive is not
my question. But when workers compete for limited jobs, coworkers compete
for promotions, and companies compete for shoppers, we should not be
surprised when we also quite naturally compete for social media platforms,
for attention, or even love. Let me encourage you to spend a day looking for
examples of competition in society. Once you start looking, you quickly
find that almost all our interactions are framed in some way as a competition,
often aided by technology (like the fitness apps that automatically post your
workout results on social media).

The presence of metrics introduces the specter of competition into any
activity. And as we discover ways to measure more things with greater accuracy, metrics have expanded into every area of life.

A few months after my wife bought a hybrid car for her daily commute,
I took it on a short road trip to Arkansas. The entire drive there and back to
Oklahoma I was fixated on improving my gas mileage. The car's dashboard
displays real-time data on your fuel efficiency and even gives a report card
when you stop the car, complete with percentage grade and areas for improvement. The next time my wife drove her car I mentioned my scores and
asked if she was able to match or beat my fuel efficiency. At the time, a gallon
of gas in Oklahoma was less than two dollars, and even if you tried to burn

fuel as inefficiently as possible the car wouldn't get worse than forty miles per gallon. There was no reason for me to be competitive with my wife, yet there I was, driving the car like a video game, striving to beat my previous high score and bragging about it. Why? The very presence of metrics invited me to measure myself against my past efforts and those of others.

In addition to fuel efficiency, I have access to metrics on the time I spend on specific apps, how many hours of Netflix I've watched, how many steps I've taken, how many floors I've climbed, how many hours I slept last night, how many tweets I've posted, how many likes I've received, how my income compares to others, the current value of my home, my credit score, my bank balance, my weight, my unread messages, and so on. Each metric nudges me to compare myself with others and improve. Taken individually, many of these data points are healthy and helpful, but collectively they overwhelm us with the sense that all of life is essentially a competition.

Technology also makes us more aware of the various lifestyle options available. We have more examples of success and more intimate insights into the lives of others. Few modern people allow themselves to consciously admit that they use social media as a platform for competition and comparison, but we know it. Just as we dare not admit that in porn we imagine real intimacy with a desirable person who affirms us, so we dare not admit that through social media we pursue affirmation through comparisons and engagement:

> We all know what we see on Facebook or Instagram isn't "real," but that doesn't mean we don't judge ourselves against it. I find that millennials are far less jealous of objects or belongings on social media than the holistic experiences represented there, the sort of thing that prompts people to comment, *I want your life.* That enviable mix of leisure and travel, the accumulation of pets and children, the landscapes inhabited and the food consumed seems not just desirable, but balanced, satisfied, and unafflicted by burnout.[18]

It's all very tiny and meaningless and sad-making, but here we are.

●   ●   ●

We certainly don't need to live in a consumer capitalist society governed by technique to live fundamentally antagonistic, competitive lives. The first murder in the Bible resulted from a competition between two brothers, one of whom didn't acknowledge they were competing, while the other saw only competition. We are selfish, vain creatures who naturally compare ourselves to one another and strive to dominate. Even so, doesn't the way our current society is ordered encourage our innate desire to compete? This is not a difference of kind but of quality. Yes, we have always been selfish, but when you are constantly reminded and pressured to improve, do better, overcome, and beat your neighbor or classmate (or your spouse's fuel efficiency score), it will shape your desires. And it has. We are taught from an early age that there are winners and losers, and only those who can compete will survive and flourish, whether on the field of AR reading scores or romance.

A society committed to the belief that we are our own and belong to ourselves will develop into a hypercompetitive society, one in which we all must fight for survival, validation, meaning, attention, and affirmation. The promise of a full and satisfying life only increases our antagonism and places us in a more precarious position. In response, we tend to assume one of two postures toward the Responsibilities of Self-Belonging: Affirmation or Resignation.[19]

THE WAY OF AFFIRMATION

Some people seem to thrive in a hypercompetitive society. They accept their Responsibilities of Self-Belonging and capitalize on them. "I *am* my own," they say. "I belong to myself. Society is sufficiently ordered for me to achieve my desires, express my identity, and become my true self. And wherever society is disordered, I can involve myself in the grand project of progress, so that if I cannot exactly become my true self, I can at least get closer and closer over time while laying the foundations for others to succeed where I was prevented."

Let's call this the posture of Affirmation. It is an endorsement of contemporary society as it is basically constructed, but more importantly, an affirmation of self-belonging.[20] Yes, life is difficult, it says. But if you apply yourself, visualize your goals, believe in yourself, and commit to perpetual self-improvement through technique, you can achieve a kind of mastery over life, at least in comparison to other people. You can be responsible for your own existence.

Note that Affirmation in the sense I am using goes beyond the "winners" Michael Sandel writes about in *The Tyranny of Merit*. These winners who affirm the justice of meritocracy say to themselves, "We can be self-made human agents, the authors of our fate, the masters of our destiny."[21] But the contemporary drive to be "self-made human agents" goes far beyond achievements in the marketplace or even social achievements. Sandel is right to observe a particular anthropology behind the affirmation of meritocracies, but I want to argue that it is part of a larger affirmation of the Responsibilities of Self-Belonging, which also includes spheres of identity and belonging and meaning that do not neatly fit in his account.

This mode of living takes the form of meticulous daily planners, highly controlled diets and exercise, a confident gait, leadership systems, five-year plans, personal assessments, and action items. The affirming have heard the promises made by society, accept them as legitimate, and intend to cash them in for as long as they can. The system basically works, they feel. And where it doesn't work, they can be part of the sacred effort to perfect it by ending injustices, inspiring individuals, and overcoming nature. Theirs is a life of Total Work, self-improvement, and measurable successes, of momentum, movement, adaptation, progress, and self-reliance.

Busyness feels satisfying to the affirming. They may even feel a sense of moral justification when they are exhausted and overwhelmed. There is a rightness to it. That's not to say that they exactly enjoy being busy all the time, but it does feel less distressing than rest. Knowing that they have productively used every moment of the day to improve themselves and their world and move toward some larger goals keeps away most of the guilt of life and fear of inadequacy. They must work hard so they can play hard, but there is nothing in-between.

Everything must be done at full volume, at peak efficiency, at full speed. There is no rest because rest is defeat, it is wasted time. Play is work in a different key. Just as with work, there are always ways to improve the way you play. Like the rest of us the affirming watch TV, but only while they exercise or message friends or answer emails. They may be constantly on their smartphones so that they can network and keep up with the news, but they're just as likely to be committed to mindfulness and self-discipline, which makes them more productive and well-balanced. Whether they use technology to improve themselves and accomplish goals or shun it for more organic, analog methods of self-improvement and accomplishment, they believe that society has provided them adequate tools (techniques) to become their best self, and that life is about becoming your best self. Such a life takes courage, but the payoffs tend to be highly rewarding, for a time, for some people.

Although she does not use the term Affirmation, Petersen beautifully describes this mood in her article on burnout. When she was younger, society's promotion of individualism, self-reliance, and positive thinking shaped her thinking: "I never thought the system was equitable. I knew it was winnable for only a small few. I just believed I could continue to optimize myself to become one of them." Once in college, these messages translated into the religion of work described by Thompson: "Things that should've felt good (leisure, not working) felt bad because I felt guilty for not working; things that should've felt 'bad' (working all the time) felt good because I was doing what I thought I should and needed to be doing in order to succeed." To work is to feel your life justified existentially; to pause from your labor is to risk a life of failure.

The spirit of Affirmation can take many different forms. I'm not only speaking of upper-class, highly educated White men, although it is certainly the case that those from privileged backgrounds find it much easier to believe that the system works. While wealth, race, sex, age, and other factors do incline or disincline someone toward Affirmation or Resignation, you can find Affirmation in all classes.

The prophets of Affirmation take many forms, from self-help gurus to megachurch pastors, email newsletters from self-described "neo-stoics," economists, teachers, politicians, and cognitive scientists like Steven Pinker, who remind you of the tremendous benefits of liberal democracy, the Enlightenment, and man's capacity to evolve and live a more satisfying, less painful, and more moral existence. Nearly all advertisements appeal to

Affirmation: you can improve your life if you buy this product or service. Not coincidentally, many of the loudest voices promoting Affirmation have a direct economic incentive for doing so.

THE WAY OF RESIGNATION

While contemporary western society appears to work well for a great many people, the grind of constant competition is unbearable for others. It's one thing to have to compete within your small town for the attention of a marriageable woman or for a good job. But once the competition goes global, as it has with economic globalization and the internet, and the tools of competition rapidly expand in both quantity and quality, and the stakes are existential, at some point you may conclude that there really is no competition *for you*. The fix is in. The teams were picked and you didn't make the cut. And since you cannot seriously compete, you may as well take your ball and go home. It is actually a more *efficient* use of your time to cut your losses. The alternative is the "sunk cost fallacy": continuing to invest time and resources into a hopeless cause.

This is the posture of Resignation. The resigned recognize and feel the Responsibilities of Self-Belonging just as much as the affirming, but they only recognize them in resignation: "I am only ever my own," they say. "Although it promises to, society will not provide me with the tools I need to achieve my desires, express my identity, and become my true self. The system is broken. The cards are stacked against me. But I can perhaps still discover moments of pleasure that make life worth living."

The resigned are often wrongly accused of not taking life seriously enough, of not growing up: a failure to launch, an inability to accept responsibilities, and so on. For at least a decade this is how some lazy pundits have described millennials and now describe Generation Z. The standard explanation is that a generation raised on positive self-esteem and participation trophies is too fragile and sensitive to exist as adults in the "real world."

My experience teaching millennials and the following generation has taught me that this is far from true. When a young person stops coming to class, binge watches *Friends* for thirty-six hours, and can't seem to get out of bed, it's almost always because the student cares too much, not too little.

They don't choose to tap out of life because they think winning is meaningless. They tap out because they are taught that winning means everything and they cannot envision any path to winning.

If you live in a hypercompetitive society where you know you cannot possibly compete against those with biological or economic advantages, why bother playing the game? Don't we call it the definition of insanity to do the same thing over and over and expect different results? In such a situation, opting out is quite rational and efficient.

Rather than failing to accept responsibility, the resigned have reasonably concluded that the best way for them to accept their Responsibilities of Self-Belonging is to find an alternative space to pursue existential justification. If I cannot compete in graduate school, I might be able to compete in a video game. If I cannot win the love of a desired spouse, I can find a sense of belonging in porn or romance stories.

Seen this way, the resigned are actually very self-reliant. They rightly see that their only true obligation is to make their own life meaningful, not to meet some broader cultural norm of success. According to the logic of our contemporary anthropology, the young man who chooses to work a menial job and devote all his passion to the cultivation of a digital avatar (in a fantasy community, or a sex and gender lifestyle community, or a video game, or a YouTube channel) is no less successful in fulfilling his Responsibilities of Self-Belonging than a highly driven entrepreneur.

DRIFTING BETWEEN TWO POLES

So far, I have described these two modes of living in the modern world in binary terms: there are the winners and losers, the affirming and the resigned. But they're better understood as two poles toward which we're all pulled. Few people spend their entire life in a spirit of Affirmation or Resignation. Most of us shift from one to the other based on life experiences and personality. Some go through adolescence resigned and blossom into Affirmation in college. For others, the structured systems of high school and college—such as grades, athletics, and social clubs—make it easy to be affirming in their youth, whereas the business world's diversity of metrics and volatility leads them to Resignation.

Some people are affirming in one area of their life but quite resigned in others. You might be resigned to singleness because alienated modern living makes dating difficult, but you might also be affirming in your career or your physical fitness or your social justice work. This is why I describe these as *postures* or *spirits*. You may be inclined toward one or the other, but they're not personality types and they aren't fixed states of being.

Of the two, I believe Resignation by far has the strongest pull at our moment in history. Modern people who devote themselves to self-improvement and personal excellence always eventually find themselves in the place of Resignation. You can be affirming only until you are resigned. One day you're too old to play the game, you no longer have the competitive edge, your beauty fades, circumstances turn against you, or you just grow bored. Such realizations may come all at once in an overwhelming revelation that leads directly to an existential or midlife crisis. Or they may come in smaller, niggling ways, like nightly reminders of your inadequacy. It may be more accurate to think of Affirmation as a temporary denial of Resignation. Sometimes the only difference between Affirmation and Resignation is the use of antidepressants. But in either posture toward the Responsibilities of Self-Belonging, the responsibilities remain unquestioned.

Resignation has the greater pull on us because the anthropology that shapes our society presents no actual ends for human existence, no purpose, only an increasing number of means. Justifying your existence is not a definitive action, it is an ongoing process. You're always journeying and never arriving. If you're responsible for meaning in your life, you can never cease the labor of creating and sustaining moments of significance. If you're responsible for defining and expressing your identity, you can never cease expressing, never cease discovering and fine-tuning your identity. Because your personhood is irreducibly complex, there is never an end to your searching. If you are your own, you can never stop evolving and progressing and perfecting yourself through technique. The perfectibility of human life through rational methods of efficiency is the bedrock of modern public values. If you are your own and belong to yourself, you belong nowhere and everywhere at once. You will perpetually struggle between your autonomy and the desire to surrender to a larger community of belonging. Resignation is the natural posture of a people with no ultimate ends to pursue.

This is precisely why one of the most common experiences of modern life is fatigue and burnout, and why Ehrenberg identifies "inadequacy" as the defining feature of modern depression: "Becoming ourselves made us nervous, being ourselves makes us depressed. The anxiety of being oneself hides behind the weariness of the self."[22] We experience life as weariness in part because we suffer from the anxiety of being our true self. It's not just that work is a "rat race"—all life in the modern world is a rat race. Often the only thing that separates people who affirm their self-belonging from those who resign themselves to it is the quality of the tools they use to cope—their self-medication.

● ● ●

The binary tension of existentialism is that on one hand, autonomy grants the individual godlike powers of self-creation, even as on the other hand, autonomy damns the individual to eternal self-preservation, as we saw in our earlier discussion of the contemporary anthropology and how society tries to equip us to live according to it. In the postures of Affirmation and Resignation we again see the binary at work, but now we can see how these contrary ideas overlap with the major modes of modern life. If we try hard enough, we can affirm our self-belonging and find pleasure in our radical freedom. But eventually it exhausts us all and we resign. I discovered this by teaching Sylvia Plath.

A STORY OF SELF-BELONGING: *THE BELL JAR*

The first time I taught Sylvia Plath's 1963 novel, *The Bell Jar*, I did not expect my evangelical college students to resonate so deeply with Esther Greenwood's despair. But I should have, because one of the reasons I love Plath's novel is that she accurately depicts a common experience of early adulthood, one that I experienced: the movement from Affirmation to Resignation in the face of the overwhelming Responsibilities of Self-Belonging.

The novel begins with its protagonist, Esther Greenwood, at the height of her success, a college student with a prestigious summer internship at a major woman's magazine in New York. She laments that although "I was supposed to be having the time of my life," she feels empty.[23] Coming from a small town and growing up poor, Esther understands that her story is a testament to what I have been describing as the promise of contemporary society: "Look what can happen in this country, they'd say."[24] Through hard work, willpower, and intelligence—through the affirmation of her Responsibilities of Self-Belonging—she had made something significant of her life, and this was only the beginning! However, Esther doesn't interpret her coveted internship as a sign that society had fulfilled its promise.

Rather than feeling fulfilled and empowered by her success, she feels tired and out of control: "I wasn't steering anything, not even myself."[25] Like Charlie Brown at Christmas, she knows how she's supposed to feel but she can't manage to feel that way. Where Charlie Brown is depressed by the phoniness and commercialism of the holiday, Esther is struck by the failure of society to fulfill its promise. Her success is not good enough. She is not good enough, despite doing everything right.

One reason my students find Esther's story so compelling is that her attitude toward school is similar to their own. Like Esther, they have been taught to see education as the primary space for them to establish their identity and value, to make something significant out of their lives: "All my life I'd told myself studying and reading and writing and working like mad was what I wanted to do, and it actually seemed to be true, I did everything well enough and got all A's, and by the time I made it to college nobody could stop me."[26]

Contrary to many criticisms of the younger generation, young people in college tend to be achievement-driven and goal-oriented. Since elementary school, students are taught to see high school as one long test for college, and college as one long test for the good life. Because of Advanced Placement classes, many of them had a GPA well above 4.5 in high school and begin college expecting their excellence to continue. Some of them come to the immediate and unsettling realization that they are not as exceptional as they thought they were. A few will go all four years excelling at everything they do. But even those who are highly successful eventually feel like impostors, like Esther.

Early in her internship, the editor-in-chief of the woman's magazine "unmasks" Esther in a meeting by asking her what she plans to do for a career.

In my experience, asking a college student, "What do you plan to do after college?" is the fastest way to induce a panic attack, unless they have an answer preplanned, in which case they probably aren't answering the question so much as rehearsing a speech.

Esther is surprised by her own answer. "'I don't really know,' I heard myself say. I felt deep shock, hearing myself say that, because the minute I said it, I knew it was true."[27] Then the editor informs the young woman that if she wants to be an editor in New York, she's going to have to learn French, German, Spanish, and probably Russian to stand out among the competition.

It is the combination of these two revelations that sends Esther into a downward spiral of depression and suicide. First, she does not know what career she really wants to pursue, even though she has many good options. Second, even if she were to commit to a career in editing, she would probably fail. The competition is much fiercer than she anticipated, and despite working determinedly her entire life, she just isn't good enough. She thought she was ahead of the competition, now she's learned just how far behind she has always been.

On the surface, neither of these problems may appear serious to you. If you are not currently in the position to decide what the rest of your life will be like, choosing a career doesn't seem all that difficult. Pick something that you enjoy doing and pays well, we're told. But the more options that are available to us in life, the harder it is to be confident in your choices. And a society that assumes that we are our own and belong to ourselves must give us as many options as possible so that we have the freedom to be who we want to be. So the options are always growing.

Still being quite young, Esther could have tried to learn foreign languages to prepare for a career in editing. She could have continued her commitment to Affirmation and bravely faced the fear of the unknown, but it feels pointless to her now, and she slips into a deep depression marked by inaction. She no longer wants to leave her hotel room. Ehrenberg argues that modern depression is largely defined by feelings of inadequacy and fatigue, and that is what we see in Esther.[28] When Esther returns to her room after the meeting, she discovers that she no longer really cares to be a good intern: "I wondered why I couldn't go the whole way doing what I should anymore.

This made me sad and tired."[29] When students learn how brutally competitive the world is and how little all their intense efforts have amounted to, it doesn't surprise me that some of them stop trying.

● ● ●

Like Esther Greenwood, my students have options—lots and lots of options. And they tend to be *good* options. On the whole, each generation has more career opportunities available to them than the previous generation. Executive positions that were exclusively held by White men thirty years ago are increasingly open to women and people of color. Online job listings have expanded access to global job markets. These are positive changes to our society.

My students tend to be high achieving, high performing, highly driven young people. They have been trained from childhood to figure out the system, compete, and excel, like Esther. They have grown up in a meritocracy. They have been admonished to be self-reliant, to face and overcome their fears, and to believe in themselves. They have been inspired to pursue their dreams. The secret to a good life, they are told, is discovering what you love and doing it for the rest of your life. And our society has provided so many career choices that all my students have to do is discover that one perfect career and be good enough to get hired. But if you spend any time really thinking about that, it's actually quite terrifying. At the center of Plath's book is an image that powerfully captures the tremendous terror of trying to choose the one right life.

Esther visualizes the challenge of choosing her life path as trying to decide among a tree full of plump, ripe, delicious figs. Each fig sits at the end of its own branch and calls to her seductively. Among her options are a stay-at-home mother, an editor, an Olympic crew gold medalist, a professor—the branches and the figs seem to go on forever, a receding horizon of exciting and fulfilling options.

So far, the image seems attractive. Like my students, Esther has a lot of options, sort of. But then the image takes a decidedly dark turn and Esther pictures herself starving to death, unable to choose, unable to move until all the figs rot and fall to the ground.

If she chose one fig, she would lose all the other figs. And they are all so attractive that she can't fathom saying no to any of them.[30] Between learning that the world is far more competitive than she had believed and her realization that she desires multiple exclusive lifestyles, Esther falls into despair. She moves from a posture of Affirmation to one of Resignation, from believing that society has essentially given her all the freedoms and tools she needs to belong to herself to believing that the game has already ended, and she never really had the freedom to pursue her desires.

This is, quite literally, a first-world problem. But it is a problem, and a remarkably intransigent one. Historically, and still in many parts of the world, "career options" were not a thing. Women rarely had the agency to choose anything but motherhood. Men only had a limited number of jobs to choose from. Clearly the explosion of career options that arose after the Industrial Revolution was a good thing.

For example, I would make an absolutely terrible farmer. But I'm not too bad at teaching composition and literature. Liberal democracy gives me the freedom to seek out a career that I'm good at and that can provide some benefit to society. Trust me, we are all better off if no one is dependent on me to grow crops. But we should be honest about the particular challenges of this freedom without taking anything away from the dramatic revolution in labor that has continued to expand options for individuals.

● ● ●

As Esther discovers, the more choices you have, the more anxiety you experience. When there are two kinds of cereal, it is not too difficult to choose between them. You compare prices, ingredients, nutritional value, and taste. At most, a handful of variables make up your evaluation. But what if we expand the shelves to include not two kinds but ten kinds of cereal, each with at least one off-brand version. Deciding between twenty boxes of cereal is much harder.

However, you don't spend much time deciding, do you? Why not? Because functionally you don't actually have twenty options. Over the years you have tried different types of cereal and made decisions about whether or not they can be included in your pool of cereal options. Or maybe you decided that you'll avoid cereals that market to children. Special K for you. Or perhaps price cuts down the options from twenty to five. Most likely it's a combination of these criteria, but when you walk down the aisle your mind filters out 90 percent of the cereal boxes. You technically see them, but in your imagination, they are not live options. If they were, you'd spend thirty minutes deciding between them.

In the case of minor life decisions, we can usually avoid the choice paralysis that affects Esther by reflexively limiting our choices to a manageable number so that our conscious mind is not burdened and overwhelmed.

That's all fine and good when we're talking about cereal and the stakes are low. But what if you had to buy one endlessly replenishing box of cereal that you would eat from for the rest of your life? Or what if you could only change your cereal at a tremendous cost: you lose 75 percent of your friends and you must move 100 miles away. Oh, and everyone you meet will judge you on your choice of cereal. Under these conditions, choosing between options is not a matter of prudence, but an existential burden. You can no longer reflexively rule out most of the available cereals. Everything remains a live option. And all of a sudden, a first-world privilege (having options) doesn't feel so freeing. That is the pressure felt by Esther, my students, and most people living in the modern West. Our lives are our own responsibility, it's our own fault if we make nothing of ourselves, and the easiest way to make nothing of ourselves is to choose the wrong career. Everything hangs in the balance.

● ● ●

The father of sociology, Emile Durkheim, discovered this surprising quality of choice in his book *Suicide*, the first sociological study of what inspires suicides in Europe. Durkheim observed that, contrary to what we would expect, poverty does not tend to increase the number of suicides in a community—but a fast-growing economy does. Durkheim concludes that one of the primary causes of suicide is not suffering but disequilibrium. When societal values rapidly change, including economic values, people lose the ability to clearly evaluate their lives.[31]

For example, when practically no one could afford a personal computer in the 1980s, owning a computer was not part of most people's expectations. They did not perceive owning a computer as a reasonable possibility, so they never felt inadequate for not owning one. When you don't have the option to buy something, you are much less likely to feel anxious about not buying it. You know your peers will think nothing of the fact that you don't own a computer. None of them own one either! At times you may briefly fantasize about being rich, but such daydreaming is strictly an exercise in imagination, rather than visualizing a goal.

But when the price of personal computers dramatically drops, it enters the realm of possibility for you, and you begin to judge yourself based on whether you own one. And even if you confidently make the choice not to buy one, your peers will still judge you. Now imagine that prices drop on all sorts of things all the time, and your regular experience is that your quality of life (measured in material goods) is perpetually shifting upward.

For modern western economies, a rapid expansion of consumer options is the normal experience. What used to be remarkable or a sign of middle-class status is very rapidly trivialized. Standards are never settled. Everything is always in flux, a condition that philosopher Zygmunt Bauman calls "liquid modernity."[32] Rather than a solid sense of what the good life looks like, we are left with ever-shifting values as our choices multiply.

The basic principle that Durkheim discovered was that at a certain point, increasing choice actually decreases satisfaction, sometimes precipitously: "Unlimited desires are insatiable by definition and insatiability is rightly considered a sign of morbidity. Being unlimited, they constantly and infinitely surpass the means at their command; they cannot be quenched. Inextinguishable thirst is constantly renewed torture."[33] As Esther Greenwood stares up at the tree, she sees an unending number of good choices. We might say, using Durkheim's language, that Esther has unlimited desires for her future, which makes her insatiable. Sometimes referred to as the "malady of the infinite," insatiable desires, Durkheim warns, are a "sign of morbidity"—and sure enough, Esther imagines herself dying from the inability to choose.

It is not merely that she has an infinite number of figs to choose from (she describes them receding upward beyond her vision)—it's that each choice represents a mutually exclusive good life. And this is what probably moves my students the most.

If life is one massive competition and your career is the primary field of action, then choosing a career is a monumental task. And like the declining price of toys and electronics, globalization and the internet have massively expanded the types of jobs available to people. What if they choose the wrong career? What if they choose the wrong spouse? What if they choose a career that's so demanding they can't find a spouse or have kids?

It is these last few anxieties that trouble Esther the most. She desires a career of some kind and she doesn't want the burden of children, but she also wants to be free to enjoy sex. Contemporary readers may find this dilemma confusing. Don't most young adults enjoy career freedom and consequence-free sex? What has changed since the 1960s is that birth control has liberated women and men from becoming parents, which is a natural consequence of sex. I apologize if this is news to you.

Esther's desire for sexual freedom and a fulfilling career is denied again and again by a fiercely competitive and sexist world. Part of Plath's point is that while Esther is not socially free to enjoy sex outside of marriage, people excuse the promiscuity of men. This is an old problem and a significant one. For all the traditionalist criticisms of women who abandon motherhood for a career, historically, men have made a practice of abandoning fatherhood for a career. Soon after her daydream of the fig tree, Esther is sexually assaulted on a date. She then attempts suicide, leading to electric shock therapy and a long stay in a sanatorium.

The turning point of the novel comes when Esther is fitted for a diaphragm. As she climbs onto the examination table, she thinks, "I am climbing to freedom."[34] To exercise this freedom, and to exorcize her virginity, she finds a young math professor to sleep with. The experience is horrific, leading to vaginal hemorrhage and a trip to the ER. But once she gets the math professor to pay for the medical bill, she claims, "I was my own woman."[35] And later she concludes, "I was perfectly free."[36] Despite the novel's reputation for being depressing, Plath ends on a fairly optimistic note. Esther confidently walks into a meeting with psychologists at the sanatorium to determine whether she is fit to return to normal society. Now she is free to pursue her desires without fear. Her freedom specifically means that she is her "own woman." In other words, she has again come to affirm her Responsibilities of Self-Belonging.

•   •   •

While I love Plath's novel, this conclusion always leaves me disappointed because it feels contrary to the spirit of the rest of the book. In all the previous pages Esther deals honestly and painfully with the Responsibility of Self-Belonging. I have yet to find a better image of the responsibility to justify and define yourself than Esther's fig tree. But Esther's solution doesn't actually resolve the problem of infinite choice that she so clearly experiences. A diaphragm allows Esther to enjoy two figs: sexual relationships with men and a career. But most of the figs, most of the beautiful and attractive lives that she agonizes over, which drop shriveled to the ground, are *other careers* that she still cannot have. If her conflict was between only two figs, the diaphragm would be a solution. But her choices were endless. The difference between picking one fig out of an infinite number or two figs out of an infinite number is functionally nothing ($\infty \approx \infty - 1$). She still can't be all the things her heart desires. She can't even be a handful of those things. And that means there is a very good chance she'll mistakenly choose the wrong career.

Plath's novel accurately presents a common dilemma for young westerners, but her resolution falls flat by her own standards. The Esther Greenwood that narrates the first half of the novel would have left the sanatorium and regained her confidence—her commitment to Affirmation—only to be reminded of all the desirable and unattainable figs that remain on the tree and the unreasonable competition that guards each of them. Then she would have slipped back, inexorably, into Resignation. Tragically, in her own life, Sylvia Plath was unable to attain the freedom and self-ownership her protagonist seems to achieve at the end of *The Bell Jar*, which makes it difficult for me to read the conclusion as anything other than the illusion of freedom.

•   •   •

Why is it that my students identify with Esther Greenwood? Esther is an atheist in the 1950s. My students were born after 9/11 and were mostly raised in conservative evangelical churches. Their foundational beliefs and experiences differ profoundly from Esther's. Many of the tensions Esther felt (for example the tremendous social pressure to get married and have children) no longer have the same power in American culture, even among evangelicals.

While the professed beliefs of my students and Esther Greenwood differ dramatically, they share the common experience of living in a society formed by the idea that we are our own and belong to ourselves. My female students are less likely to be pressured into marriage or motherhood than female college students seventy years ago, but their increased freedom does not lessen the Responsibilities of Self-Belonging. The stakes of justification and identity formation are still tremendous. They feel the same burden to make something significant with their lives and to create an interesting and valued identity through their life choices. They have the same exact sense that they are responsible for their own existence. Globalization and the internet have only increased competition by introducing more players into the game. Esther's fig tree has grown exponentially.

Anne Helen Petersen has also seen this career anxiety in millennials:

> Students internalize the need to find employment that reflects well on their parents (steady, decently paying, recognizable as a "good job") that's also impressive to their peers (at a "cool" company) and fulfills what they've been *told* has been the end goal of all of this childhood optimization: doing work that you're passionate about.

While Petersen does not define what students mean by "passionate," from the context it seems to refer to a desire for meaning and justification and identity. A good job doesn't just pay your bills; it fulfills you, shapes your identity, and justifies your presence in the community. Esther's despair is alive and well in the twenty-first century.

Young people, even many evangelicals, find themselves shifting from Affirmation to Resignation, from self-confidence in their own powers to establish and solidify their lives to despair over their inadequacy and lack of agency. And to cope with the intense personal demands of Affirmation or the despair of Resignation, each of us learns to self-medicate.

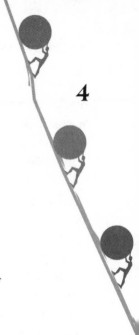

4

WE ALL
SELF-MEDICATE

Everything can be treated, nothing can be cured.

ALAIN EHRENBERG, *THE WEARINESS OF THE SELF*

A S SOCIETY FAILS TO FULFILL ITS PROMISE, as it fails to provide techniques adequate enough for us to meet our Responsibility of Self-Belonging, we require new techniques to cope with the stress, anxiety, exhaustion, and inadequacy. We cope when we use methods to lessen the felt burden of the Responsibility of Self-Belonging without actually challenging the responsibility. If you look closely enough, you'll discover that most people in western societies have adopted certain evolving practices that help them cope with life.

The burden of our responsibility may take any number of psychological, emotional, physical, or spiritual forms—anything from a feeling of inadequacy brought on by a hypercompetitive and increasingly demanding society to cognitive fatigue from the constant flow of information designed to equip us to make rational decisions, or the physical lethargy brought on by the suspicion that the cards are stacked against you.

A posture of Affirmation runs you ragged. You become consumed with self-improvement and Total Work, and whenever you pause from your toil you feel anxious and guilty. You can only conceive of "peace" as either exhaustion from Total Work or momentary satisfaction while working.

A posture of Resignation leaves you aimless and dispirited. You live with the meaninglessness of it all, the impossibility of ever doing anything that matters or is good enough to please your parents or those you admire or to impress your peers and draw positive attention to yourself.

In both modes, it's difficult to get out of bed. The Affirming struggle to get out of bed because they're exhausted from trying to satisfy the inhuman demands of the world. The Resigned struggle to get out of bed because they're exhausted from their awareness of the inhuman demands of the world.

For all of us the Responsibilities of Self-Belonging, whether consciously accepted or unconsciously absorbed from culture, are experienced as perpetual inadequacy. Your life is never justified, you are always in the process of validating your existence. Your identity is never secure, you are always in the process of discovering and proclaiming and defining who you are. Meaning is never given; it is always being reinterpreted or reasserted. Values are never certain; they are always being renegotiated. And belonging is never attained; it is always dislocated.

Society promises to provide us with the means to live full and satisfying lives through self-belonging, but these tools only increase our burdens by giving us new ways to work toward an unachievable goal. Social media offers to help us create and express our identities by giving us ever more tools for self-expression and promotion, but these tools only become more things for us to do. Technology always claims to be optional even as it becomes impractical to reject.

The distinction between tools to facilitate self-belonging and tools to cope with our inability to belong to ourselves blurs the more we look at it. Do we take antidepressants to become our "true self" or to cope with our failure to become our true self? Do we shop for clothing to express our identity or as a form of therapy? Rhetorically and in marketing, strategies for self-actualization and coping often appear the same, using the same sales appeal and the same language of empowerment. The more similar they appear, the less likely we are to notice that coping mechanisms are not actually effective tools for self-actualization. When we categorize both antidepressants and personal fashion as means of becoming more truly ourselves, we can no longer see how the former may be used to cope with the failure of the latter to communicate anything true or meaningful about ourselves.

It takes an active effort to overlook the implications of coping. Once you begin looking for examples of coping mechanisms, you quickly discover that our society is shockingly frank about how intolerable modern life is without some kind of "medication." The most vivid example I've seen of this came when my state, Oklahoma, legalized medicinal marijuana in 2018. Set aside the legal and civic debates about legalization for a moment and consider how marijuana was advertised. Driving down I-40 into Oklahoma City, I was greeted with billboard after billboard advertising dispensaries. The rhetoric varied slightly, but the dominant message was: "Are you unhappy? Try marijuana!"

One sign used sad and happy face emojis to show the effects of CBD (the store also sold medical marijuana). Another billboard asked if you were anxious. One featured a relaxed elderly couple in sunglasses, with the tag line: "Live your best life."[1] The ads appear to be effective. Although Oklahoma's marijuana law is not a recreational law, in practice there seems to be very little barrier to getting a medical card. By one account, one in thirteen Oklahoma adults has a medical marijuana card.[2]

The marketing and demand for medical marijuana reflects a society that finds life without drugs unbearable, or at least very unpleasant. It is difficult to look at these ads and not come away with the conclusion that our lives are not working for us. The rapid growth of dispensaries reflects a society that has given up, but that frames its resignation in terms of mental health. But if we live in a habitat that is not built for humans, we shouldn't be surprised that we need a little help to put up with our cage.

I use the phrase "self-medicate" because it describes not only what is traditionally understood by the term (the use of some substance to treat the symptom of an illness without the supervision and approval of a medical doctor), but also supervised medication. Since prescribed medication is very often elective medicine, it can be a form of self-medication. And the legalization of medical marijuana is a perfect example.

On July 25, 2019, some Oklahomans were "self-medicating" with marijuana, according to the traditional use of the phrase. On July 26, Oklahoma's law legalizing medical marijuana took effect and those same Oklahomans could now get a medical card so that they would no longer be "self-medicating." They were now "receiving treatment."

What changed between July 25 and July 26, 2019? In theory the only difference is that a licensed professional now decides who has a medical need for cannabis and who doesn't. But in practice, if you experience anxiety, you can get a card. There are plenty of affordable doctors who will meet with you through a virtual appointment to prescribe the drug. Traditional physicians may still be hesitant to prescribe marijuana, but a whole market of weed doctors has cropped up.

The real difference between those who "self-medicate" with marijuana and those who have a legal prescription is paperwork. It may be that prescriptions help curb excessive use of drugs (there is some debate over how well weed doctors monitor their patients), but the *purpose* of the medication remains the same: for those not suffering from diseases, medical marijuana makes life more tolerable. And in that sense, everyone who uses it, legally or illegally, is medicating themselves.

There remains a stigma around medical marijuana use—a suspicion that it isn't a legitimate drug and people who suffer from real medical cases of anxiety should use antidepressants or anti-anxiety medications. We don't think of someone with a prescription for Prozac as self-medicating. They are rebalancing themselves so that they can be more fully themselves. Thankfully, for the most part, psychiatric medication has lost its stigma. We conceive of antidepressants like blood pressure medication. You expect that many of your friends are on some kind of SSRI or related medication. But that is not the case with medical marijuana.

I fear that the demand for psychiatric medication (which continues to grow) is not much different from the demand for cannabis or alcohol or pornography or video gambling or online video games. Life is intolerable. We think of the use of some medication as a sign of weakness or immaturity, a sign of inadequacy, while other medications are a sign of someone who is taking a proactive role in improving their mental health. But really there's not a whole lot of difference between the person who relies on Xanax to get through life and the person who relies on marijuana or alcohol or whatever. One is socially acceptable, the others are not. One requires some wealth, education, advocacy, and health insurance. The others are more easily accessible. And while it's probably easier to be a high-functioning user of Zoloft than marijuana, both can become a dependency. Both can be self-medicating.

Once you step back and start thinking about how many ways contemporary people work to cope with modern life through self-medication—instead of only being critical of "socially unacceptable" forms like illegal drug use—you realize that a massive portion of our economy is devoted to coping mechanisms. And most of these mechanisms lead to some form of addiction. We can begin with the widespread use of antidepressants, but most people use a myriad of tools to get through their days. We need a myriad of tools because none of those society provides for us to cope with the Responsibilities of Self-Belonging are sufficient to the task. As Ehrenberg notes, "Depression and addiction are the two sides of the sovereign individual, the person who believes herself to be the author of her own life."[3]

• • •

In my previous book, *Disruptive Witness*, I explored the uses of distractions in the contemporary world and some of the reasons we are so addicted to them. There I focused primarily on our discomfort in confronting life's big questions. Many of us would rather divert our attention with social media than examine our lives.

I stand by this analysis of our culture of distraction, but since writing *Disruptive Witness* I've thought more about the way distractions are also used by people who are self-reflective and who do consider life's big questions. For these people, something else motivates their tendency toward distraction. It seems to me that "staying busy," including the use of technological and entertainment diversions, is a common way contemporary people cope with the stress of living in an inhuman environment. If you feel helpless to improve your circumstances, then you might as well not think about them.

Consider a parent staying home with their children for the summer.[4] There is nothing inhuman about caring for your children. It's one of the most human activities possible. But the layout of modern cities and the decline of communities have made it much harder to find human conditions to care for children. Given suburban sprawl, the parent is likely to be physically and emotionally isolated from other adults. The decline in birth rates may mean that the children don't have other kids to play with in their neighborhood, which was unimaginable to me as a child.

As a result, the parent is forced to focus entirely on their small children, which is wonderful for a few hours a day, or all day for a couple weeks. But when your social world is almost entirely made up of small children for months at a time, it takes an emotional and spiritual toll. Humans were not made to live in isolation. We can do it, particularly when there is a noble reason for the isolation, but it's not how we were designed. Even introverts need the company of peers who care for us. We were made to commune. Social media provides a simple, constant, disembodied, and addictive lifeline to other adults. Scrolling through Instagram for hours each day is unhealthy and unproductive, and it distances me from my children, but it is the kind of tool for coping with life that society provides.

Perhaps that example was more annoying than persuasive to you. I can imagine some readers thinking, *Well, it sounds like this stay-at-home parent needs to stop whining and be more intentional with their children!* Or, *If this parent can't handle parenting, they shouldn't have had kids to begin with!* Or, *Maybe they should look into babysitters,* and so on.

The point of this example is not that parents who are stuck at home with their kids are helpless to change their situation. Even if the parent did change their circumstances, there are a thousand other ways society alienates people from each other. Most likely, the parent hasn't even considered that there is something wrong with the structure of society that has led to their loneliness, depression, and dependency on social media to get through the day. After all, suburban sprawl *feels* normal. Instead, the parent will either blame their spouse, their children, or themselves. And maybe their spouse could be more considerate about sharing parental duties. Maybe their children could be more grateful and kind. Maybe the parent could be a little less self-absorbed. But even if all of that is true, it still doesn't change the fact that the way we live so dramatically separated from each other, locked in our homes, is bizarre and dysfunctional.

So we cope by diverting ourselves. In the artificial world of social media, an adult can feel as if they are trying to fulfill their Responsibilities of Self-Belonging, even though they know there's an emptiness to their actions. Our stay-at-home parent might turn to posting selfies on Instagram between putting out fights between the kids as a way of feeling like they're accomplishing something by expressing their identity. Or the parent might enter a political debate on Twitter, defending a cause they believe to be righteous. Their online activism gives them a sense of significance, a kind of fleeting justification in an otherwise mundane day. Or the parent may lose themself in romance or thriller novels. Or the parent might find themself wrapped up in some sort of low-stakes competition online that gives them a trivial victory in a hypercompetitive world. When the rest of the world feels like a tooth-and-nail fight for supremacy, when it feels like everyone is always jockeying for position or fame or power or attention, low-stakes competitions can help us cope by giving us small fields of victory.

Think of it this way. If you are crippled with anxiety over the prospect of having to find a good and meaningful job, playing *Fortnite* lets you exercise your competitiveness without actually risking much—except your time. The same could be said for fantasy football and a million different mindless mobile games. Then there is also the highly competitive nature of social media with very public records of the popularity of individuals and their posts. Again, all of these things are "tiny and meaningless and—sad-making," but they help us get through the day by diverting us from higher-stakes competitions. In the end, the man who self-medicates through counseling, antidepressants, exercise, and shopping therapy is just as desperate to cope as the man who self-medicates through *Fortnite* and the NFL and marijuana. The only difference is that one form of self-medication is socially acceptable and the other is stigmatized.

EVIDENCE OF DESPAIR

Not everyone feels that the Responsibilities of Self-Belonging burden us to the point of intolerability. You may have read the previous section and felt as if you were reading about an alien culture.

I recognize that we don't all consciously use coping mechanisms to get through the day, but I also think it's accurate to describe our collective reliance on self-medication as a societal illness. The fact that so many people go about their days without breaking down could be interpreted as evidence that our contemporary society is working out pretty well for us. We might also cite the many technological and medical advances that make our lives easier and safer. For scholars like Steven Pinker, these advances along with the measurable growth in life expectancy and quality of life are objective signs of the success of the Enlightenment project.[5] And it's true that humans have accomplished amazing things over the last three centuries.

So how can I seriously claim that Americans in 2021 "struggle to get through the day" when our daily tasks require less effort than ever? Doing laundry, checking the weather, commuting to work, and preparing meals take less labor and less time than in the past, yet Americans are depressed. Pinker blames our pessimism, our inability to see how wonderful our lives are, on psychological and sociological causes. We tend to be ungrateful. We focus on the negative. The media and cultural critics take a critical posture toward progress and that is why they cannot admit that things are getting better—or so goes Pinker's argument.[6] But this logic fails to account for the incredible complexity of life.

It's not only possible, but common for an advance in one area of culture to have an unanticipated negative consequence in another. That doesn't mean that progress is never good, but that it's possible for two things to be true at the same time: the mundane tasks that once occupied most of our days are easier, faster, and cheaper to complete, and the structures of our contemporary world bring new and inhuman burdens upon us. To bear those burdens, we turn to activities that fill the time we gained from labor-saving technologies.

Despite needing far less time to get daily tasks accomplished, most people discover that their days are packed. Rather than leisure, that extra time goes either to increased productivity or to self-medicating in one way or another. So, yes—in many ways our lives are easier. But in other ways we carry burdens that drive us to addiction and violence and depression. The reality of progress in some areas of society does not absolve us from the responsibility of observing and correcting disorder in other areas, even if that disorder comes from the progress. The progress we have made in travel, for example, does not give us the right to ignore the environmental and communal costs of that progress.

● ● ●

Another reason you might think I'm exaggerating about contemporary despair is that we're really quite good at hiding our suffering. Our communities rarely ever require us to be vulnerable.

When you live in close community and have obligations to others that transcend your personal preferences or emotions, eventually you have to be vulnerable and make them aware of hardships you're facing. That doesn't mean you have to open up to everyone you know about every personal problem you have. It's healthy and appropriate to be discerning about who you trust with your personal life. But if we were truly living in communities that included obligations to one another, we would eventually have to say something to somebody when we are depressed or anxious or addicted or whatever. The environment would make vulnerability a necessity, not an option.

In the modern world, public vulnerability is always a choice, and therefore it takes on an overwhelmingly performative quality. Here's what I mean. When communities (like churches, neighborhoods, clubs, and so on) are voluntary and "liquid," they become places we *visit* rather than dwell. So when a church community or a group of friends or neighbors pressures us into vulnerability, we can retreat to our homes or smartphones. You don't have to stick around and share your burdens with anyone, ever. One day you may "break" or be "exposed," but you still don't have to share.

The result is that our moments of vulnerability are often carefully cultivated and prepared for public consumption to maximize attention and develop our image. Consider the difference between a close friend confronting you about a distressing change in your behavior and an Instagram post announcing that you have been diagnosed with a mental illness. If that friendship is solid, it will be difficult for you to hide your suffering. At some point those close to you should recognize that something is wrong and intervene. But if our friendships and communities are highly conditional and, as Bauman describes it, "until further notice,"[7] it isn't difficult to avoid uncomfortable vulnerability. When we're vulnerable with our suffering, it tends to be a calculated, self-conscious public performance.

When necessary, or when it's to your advantage to make your suffering public, you can make an announcement on your own terms and so manage your image. Even if you choose to be in relationship with someone who can honestly ask, "How are you?" and to whom you would owe a similarly honest reply, there are many ways to manage your suffering so that others remain unaware. Society provides coping techniques such as psychiatric medication, therapy, meditation, exercise, breathing methods, optimizing productivity in the home, and so on. Each of these techniques have their value, but they can also be used to shelter us from being vulnerable with those closest to us.

Given how easy it is to avoid vulnerability in the contemporary world, we can't assume that just because people around us haven't shared their trauma and suffering, they are okay. You are better off assuming that everyone you meet is bearing some unspoken burden.

• • •

I suppose my own anecdotal experiences could be distorting my understanding of the modern human condition. But I don't think so. My observations have been far too consistent over several decades and different locations and classes of people. Most people, including people who appear to be well-adjusted, successful, and happy, have sorrows and traumas and fears and disorders that you cannot imagine, that you've never heard of or thought possible, and which, if you did learn of them, would forever alter your perception of humanity. That has been my experience.

What surprises me is that I keep being surprised by the depth and breadth of human suffering. Many years ago, a coworker and close friend of mine experienced a terrible breakdown—self-doubt and self-loathing mixed with anxiety, depression, and hopelessness. But it wasn't until a few years later that he told me what he had gone through. Here was someone I worked with daily, someone I prayed with and looked up to, and he was barely hanging on the whole time, and I never knew. I didn't even have a suspicion.

Not a hint. And what's really crazy is that years ago while he was breaking down, I was nearly gone myself. The details of my experience are irrelevant here. But when I told my friend what I had been struggling with when we worked together, he was just as shocked. He had no clue how dysfunctional I had been. Almost no one did. Almost no one ever does, unless we make it part of our public image.

After more than twelve years in the classroom, I've heard story after story of abuse, mental illness, and death. At this point, I expect that in a classroom of twenty-five students, at least two of them will have experienced some kind of sexual abuse, and others will have experienced physical or mental or spiritual abuse. And there's nothing abnormal about my students.

Life is much, much more trying than we publicly acknowledge. A lot of people struggle to get out of bed every morning. Some are only functional because of intense psychiatric medications and therapy. Some are only functional because they don't hold still long enough to bear witness to their own suffering. Some only appear functional. So if you read this chapter and come away thinking, *Our society basically works. Most people in America are well-off and happy*, I'd suggest that a lot of people you know who appear to be happy routinely wonder why life is worth living. Just because you don't notice millions of depressed people doesn't mean that we're okay. We aren't.

Two recent books have told the story of our current mental health crisis. In *Lost Connections*, Johann Hari explores America's troubling relationship with psychiatric medications, particularly antidepressants:

> One in five U.S. adults is taking at least one drug for a psychiatric problem; nearly one in four middle aged women in the United States is taking antidepressants at any given time; around one in ten boys at American high schools is being given a powerful stimulant to make them focus.[8]

At some point we have to accept that the widespread usage of psychiatric medication is indicative of *more* than biological problems. Something else is at work. Hari's book tries to get to the bottom of why we're so anxious and depressed. His findings suggest that we have "lost connections"—with ourselves, the world, our work, nature, meaning, and so on.

A much more alarming account of our mental health crisis is *Deaths of Despair*, written by the economists Anne Case and Agnus Deaton. The impetus for their study was the rise in suicides and the increasing death rates among middle-aged White Americans. They note that one of the few constants of the modern world has been falling death rates, but that in recent years this trend has reversed in America. For the first time since the First World War, life expectancy in America has declined year-over-year.[9] Case and Deaton ascribe this anomaly to suicides, alcohol-related deaths, and drug overdoses among middle-aged White Americans, particularly men without college degrees: "All the deaths show great unhappiness with life, either momentary or prolonged. It is tempting to classify them all as suicides, done either quickly, with a gun or by standing on and kicking away a chair with a rope around the neck, or slowly, with drugs and alcohol."[10] Much of the book is devoted to explaining the forces behind this "great unhappiness with life" among White Americans without college educations. Like Hari, Case and Deaton point to work that is less meaningful and fulfilling and the decline in social institutions and communities. They also point to the decline of religious belief and the rising cost of healthcare.

While Case and Deaton are largely correct to identify these as causes, I suspect that if we didn't focus on *death* as the metric, we would find that this "great unhappiness with life" manifests itself in other alarming ways. One demographic copes through extremely self-destructive behavior, but there are other ways to harm the self and even more for coping with "great unhappiness." A well-paying job might make it possible to insulate yourself from some of the harmful effects of meaningless work through therapy, self-care, and distractions, but if most people are still struggling with despair—and I think Hari's figures on psychiatric medication usage suggest they are—something deeper is going on.

To identify these deeper causes, we need to turn to the work of French sociologist Alain Ehrenberg and his extensive study of the history of depression in the West, *The Weariness of the Self*. In great detail, Ehrenberg charts the way depression—its causes, meaning, and treatment—has changed over the twentieth century. His startling conclusion is that we have largely moved from understanding depression primarily as a symptom of inner conflict, often driven by feelings of guilt for violating societal or religious norms, to understanding it primarily as a symptom of inhibition, driven by feelings of inadequacy.[11]

But why do we feel inadequate? Why are we afraid to act in the contemporary world? Ehrenberg's answer is precisely what I have been describing as our contemporary anthropology: "The ownership of the self has become our lifestyle; it has been sociologically integrated into our mores and is at the very heart of our intimate sovereignty."[12] But this sovereignty has not liberated us. Contrasting the modern condition with the dream of individual sovereignty he finds in Nietzsche, Ehrenberg writes: "The individual, free from morality, creating herself by herself and aspiring to the superhuman, . . . is not our reality. But, instead of possessing the strength of the masters, she turns out to be fragile, lacking in being, weary of her sovereignty and full of complaints."[13] The title of Ehrenberg's book reflects this diagnosis. We are weary of trying to be our own sovereign selves. We have radical freedom to remake our identities, but it has come at a great cost: "If moral constraints have grown lighter, psychic constraints have taken their place. Emancipation and action have stretched individual responsibility beyond all borders and have made us painfully aware that we are only ourselves."[14] Elsewhere he refers to this as the "illness of responsibility."[15]

To cope with these feelings of inadequacy and inhibition, societally we have relied heavily on antidepressants, which were once conceived of as tools to help people deal with specific inner conflicts for a period of time. But now they are prescribed long term as a way to readjust individuals to the modern world:

> Today's psychiatric reasoning legitimizes the prescribing of antidepressants to any person suffering from any sort of incapacity. . . . The prescribing of molecules with a wide spectrum of effects responds to an increase in today's normative demands; the difficulty of confronting them can be costly to an individual caught up in a world where professional, family, and emotional failure can add up quickly. Such failures can lead to social rejection much faster now than in the past.[16]

While there are absolutely many valuable and even important uses of antidepressants, Ehrenberg's history suggests that at least in terms of society at large, something other than biological illness is at work behind the widespread use of these medications. The demands of contemporary society, based on a specific notion of the human person, drive us to develop medical techniques to cope. So humans are forced to adapt to their own inhuman environment. At the root of our Resignation and our Affirmation is the belief that we are our own.[17]

BURNOUT, EXHAUSTION, FATIGUE

Despite the exponential growth in the number and complexity of coping mechanisms, most of us live with fatigue. Being worn out isn't the exception; it's the rule. We may even find ourselves guilty or confused when we aren't worn out. Countless times I have found myself feeling happy and well-rested and a doubt immediately enters my head: *Shouldn't I be doing something else?*

This is part of what Pieper means by a society of "Total Work." As Ellul describes it, "[Modern] leisure time is mechanized time and is exploited by techniques which, although different from those of man's ordinary work, are as invasive, exacting, and leave man no more free than labor itself."[18] Even when we think we are on vacation or relaxing, the spirit of our action is still *efficiency*. Vacation becomes a project that must be completed on-time and under budget. Even when we try to "veg" by scrolling through Instagram, playing a mindless video game, or watching episode after episode of a mediocre sitcom, the pace of the entertainment is frenetic. Images change rapidly and we get bored easily. Our rest is rarely restful. It is an active rest, a rest without silence or stillness, a rest marked by the overwhelming responsibility to make better use of your time.

You can come to an end of this anxious "rest," however. Eventually you become so aware of all your responsibilities, all the tasks that need to be completed, all the promises you've made, all the best practices for your health or to be a good ally or whatever, that you just sort of seize up. The demands for action are so great that your only recourse is *in*action. In my experience this looks like feeling so overwhelmed by my to-do list that all

I can do is stare at my computer screen. It's no wonder that so many Americans regularly feel exhausted or fatigued.

● ● ●

If you listen closely to the way we speak, you can find evidence of how burned out we are. Take the way people say, "I just need to," as in: "I just need to finish my taxes," or "I just need to cut down on carbs," or "I just need to read the Bible more," or "I just need to be less distracted while I study," and so on. Without realizing it, this phrase has crept deeply into my consciousness. I say it to myself throughout the day like a prayer to ward away the evil spirits of perpetual inadequacy.

Usually it happens when I'm reminded of some obligation that I've been putting off in order to deal with other obligations. Maybe I get an email asking whether I intend to select a health insurance plan this year, or I remember that my car's oil needs to be changed, but because I'm on the phone trying to figure out why I was overcharged for internet access, all I can say is, "I just need to get this bill sorted out, then I can deal with the health insurance."

On its own, it's not such a bad thing to say. It shows that I'm focused on the task before me. But it's never "on its own." There's always *one more thing* that "I just need to" do. And they aren't just chores, either. I find myself using the phrase to describe self-improvement goals: "I just need to memorize peoples' names when I meet them," or "I just need to not raise my voice when my kids misbehave."

The logic of this phrase is the same deal-making logic of an addict: "After this hit, I'll quit." Both "I just need to" and "After this I'll quit" use a laudable but insincere goal to justify continuing a self-destructive lifestyle.

For the addict who swears, "After this I'll quit," recovery is just pretense to excuse the addiction. For the Total Work addict who swears, "I just need to," a life of order and balance and peace is just a pretense to excuse more striving—and striving without rest is self-destructive. In both cases the goal is genuinely good, but as long as the addict makes deals with himself, recovery is never really an option. And so long as we tell ourselves that we "just need to" do one more thing, rest is never really an option. It's always tomorrow.

● ● ●

Let me give another example of how we experience burnout. Recently, I needed to be tested for a virus. I called the local clinic to make an appointment, but the receptionist informed me that I could not make an appointment over the phone with a human—I had to schedule one online. To streamline the process, the clinic sent me all the paperwork I would have normally filled out in-person, such as my medical history and health insurance information. The paperwork concluded with a series of legal documents I had to sign, waiving rights, releasing liability, acknowledging risks, and so on. The system made this signing experience extremely simple. All I had to do was digitally sign my name once and then click "accept" to apply the signature to each document.

But when I came to these legal documents, I immediately grew anxious. I quickly signed my name and clicked "accept" until I was done. I read nothing. Not a single word. I have no clue what I agreed to. But it was clear that the online system didn't *expect* me to read anything. It was designed to make these legal formalities as painless and efficient as possible.

Presumably, these documents were at least somewhat important, otherwise they wouldn't require them. And presumably my actual consent was important because I was supposed to put my name on each one of them. But I was overwhelmed. I was sick, after all. And I was filling out a form on my phone rather than talking with a human being at the clinic. My kids were arguing in the next room. The system invited me to just click "accept." And I knew that however important these documents might be, I had to sign them anyway. If I read them and discovered something objectionable, there was nothing I could do about it. There was no one there to ask. There was no one to negotiate with. No one to explain. So I signed in a kind of resignation, feeling helpless before the legal requirements and technological machinations of the system. I needed this test. The clinic only took appointments online. And the online form gave me no option but to accept.

Again, this example might just sound like a first-world problem or a middle-class problem, but there's something of a common experience here. The particular circumstances are unique to me, but the burden of living in an absurdly draconian, litigious, and bureaucratic world is not unique to me. If I weren't trying to get a medical test, I might be fighting to submit the proper forms to qualify for government aid or spending hours on the phone trying to figure out medical bills. There's always something. We experience a million such little indignities, all of which loudly proclaim that we are objects, instruments, or figures, that our humanity is far less significant than legal liability and efficiency. And so we feel overwhelmed and helpless before the machine. How could we not?

I'm confident that right now there's some form I should have filled out, some bill I should have already paid, some maintenance that should have already been done. These are tools to make our lives easier (forms, billing, and maintenance) and to increase efficiency—but there seems to be no reclaiming of time.

Technology expands to fill up the time it saves us. Technique increases efficiency (by definition), which allows us to perform more and more intricate techniques—which tend to use up the time that technique liberated. The easier it is to collect and manipulate data, the more data we can collect and manipulate to improve efficiency. We might cover more ground, but we don't seem to run any less than our ancestors. And if you never stop running, does it matter where you are going?

The Sisyphean tasks of bureaucracy overwhelm and exhaust us, but we are also drained by the inhuman shape these tasks take. For example, technology makes it possible for corporations to have an almost entirely speculative existence. I purchased my home insurance policy from an insurance broker over the phone. He searched a database of providers using my information. He found a policy that I agreed to and my bank pays through my escrow. I have never talked to anyone from this insurance agency. They have never talked to me. They are legally required to compensate me up to a particular amount in the event that certain misfortunes happen to my home, which they have never visited or even seen. The upside to all this is that I get to "shop around" for the cheapest rates available.

When so many of our commercial interactions have this kind of disembodied character, it is psychically draining. It's exhausting to have to trick an automated phone answering system into connecting you to another human. It feels like a test to see if you are worthy enough to warrant actual attention. And the reason companies use automated systems is that it's more efficient, and some customers will give up long before they get to talk to a human representative. You feel inhuman because the state and the market view you as a Case or Account Number, and you fear that no matter how hard you work to stay on top of things, there will always be some obligation you're forgetting. And one day you'll receive a call or an email or a letter announcing your delinquency. It's a terrible weight to walk around with.

Once you accept that we are all our own, it's reasonable to promote efficiency at the cost of humanity. And the natural outcome of that prioritization is that we all feel exhausted for being treated inhumanly.

TECHNIQUE AS THE SOLUTION TO TECHNIQUE'S PROBLEMS

Society promises us a good, full life if we accept our Responsibilities of Self-Belonging and dutifully use society's tools to meet those responsibilities. But these tools consistently let us down. We can never meet our Responsibilities of Self-Belonging, so the tools leave us to continually strive for a promised life that is unachievable. To cope with the burden of our responsibilities, society creates other tools that divert our attention or suppress our anxiety. Ellul writes, "It is necessary to protect man by outfitting him with a kind of psychological shock absorber. Only another technique is able to give efficient protection against the aggression of techniques."[19] Inevitably, these tools require more from us—and then they fail. But rather than question the premise of society's promise, we blame ourselves and turn again to society for another method, better training, or another tool to help us. When it also fails, we wonder if maybe we just didn't try the right method or tool, and so on.

Technique promises a better world but produces only a more efficient world with different problems. Technique is then used to solve the problems that technique unintentionally created, which only produces new unintended consequences. The further it goes, the more absurd it becomes and the more helpless we feel to stop it.

• • •

Consider social media moderation. Social media is a marvel of technique. With it we can efficiently communicate with family and friends, engage with celebrities, read the news, discuss important issues, promote businesses and charities and causes, and express our identity. At every turn, social media makes the work of communicating more efficient.

When I meet someone new, I am often tempted to immediately look up their Facebook, Instagram, or Twitter profile. This helps me remember their name, keep the contact alive, and get to know them without the hard work of spending time with them. If the purpose of meeting new people is to develop relationships or "connections" or to "network," then social media is far and away easier than business cards or Rolodexes.

Similarly, social media makes the sharing of family photos more efficient. Facebook allows me to immediately share baby pictures with everyone I care about, even my high school friends who I don't have time to call or text but who I want to remain connected with.

The reason I can immediately share baby pictures with everyone I care about is that no one has to approve what I post. I can upload whatever images or videos I want and they are immediately available. Certain content—copyrighted works, pornography, terrorism, violence, and so on—can be removed if it gets flagged by other users. But Facebook cannot have a human being check each post before it goes public.

The platform is efficient *because* nobody has to approve my posts. If they required moderators to approve each post before it went live, then they would have to charge for the service, and if they had to charge, many of my family and friends would not join, and that would mean that it would *no longer be an efficient way to share baby photos.* The efficiency of the platform depends on its being a highly open platform.

Social media's efficiency also creates social pressure for people to adopt it. You may not like the idea of Facebook, but if the only way you're going to see your niece's new baby is through a cross-country visit or a Facebook profile, you will choose the profile. Technique has tremendous power over our societal norms. When there's a more efficient method available, it's difficult to resist adopting it, and the difficulty just increases over time.[20]

Because Facebook is hard to resist, more people adopt it, making it even more efficient. But its efficiency depends on being an open platform, which means that explicit and illegal content will get posted. The users who post illicit content know that eventually their content will be flagged by other users and pulled from the platform, but this doesn't discourage them from posting because they know there will be a delay between when the picture or video goes up and when it gets reported and removed. If all content had to be vetted before it was publicly available, most delinquent users wouldn't bother trying to post illicit content. The thrill of shocking other users would be gone. But vetting all content would make the platform inefficient, and thus defeat the whole purpose.

The result is that social media companies are forced to contract small armies of content moderators to check each flagged item and judge it according to the evolving community standards of the platform. That means men and women spending hours of a day at a cubicle staring at images of rape, murder, child abuse, animal abuse, torture, terrorism, and so on.

Human beings were not made to watch image after image of such graphic content.[21] Even most first responders don't have to face that amount of evil each day. So a technique that was developed to make our lives easier and more fulfilling (sharing images on social media) has the unfortunate side effect of giving some people PTSD.

This is precisely what is happening in nondescript business parks around the world. There have been a number of chilling exposés of these contracted social media monitors over the years, all of which are widely read by horrified social media users everywhere. Companies make promises to improve the working conditions, of course, but there's no meaningful way to improve working conditions when the work involves watching rapes and murders.

To treat the trauma inflicted on their employees by the technique of social media moderation, the contracted companies introduce coping techniques: counseling, yoga, wellness breaks, and so on. These methods were almost certainly chosen with great care—and great legal counsel—for their ability to reduce anxiety (and liability) in the workplace with as little cost as possible.

Of course, the best way to reduce workplace anxiety in these companies would be to not ask employees to stare at traumatizing images, but that solution is unthinkable, or at least unspeakable. Because to speak that solution would be to place *some value higher than efficiency.* It would require social media users to do without the efficiency of easily shared images. It would require the social media companies to forgo profits. And anyway, if Facebook didn't offer users easy ways to immediately share their photos, then some other platform would, so why fight it? Instead of accommodating technology to fit human needs, these human content moderators are forced to accommodate the demands of technology. They are asked to adapt to what is inhuman.

The reports about these contracted moderation companies are grim. In one investigation, The Verge found that employees at a Facebook moderation office in Phoenix, Arizona, were developing drug habits to cope.[22] They turned to dark humor. They suffered panic attacks. They had sex with each other as a form of "trauma bonding." All the while, social media companies keep these employees at arm's length by hiring them as contractors, not full-time employees.

I have no doubt that social media companies will try new techniques to address these problems. At some point there will probably be artificial intelligence sophisticated enough to accurately moderate images and eliminate the need for constant human exposure to filth. But given the track record of techniques, I suspect such AI will also introduce new, unanticipated problems. In any event, the human capacity for imaginative evil will always be one step ahead of AI.

Society develops techniques to equip us to fulfill our Responsibilities of Self-Belonging and live the good life. Techniques, by Jacque Ellul's definition, value efficiency above all else. Efficiency is not a human virtue. It's not a traditional virtue at all. It's a metric for machines with clearly defined purposes—but not for humans. Inevitably, technique's reliance on efficiency produces tools that are highly effective and profitable while also being dehumanizing in one way or another. Sharing photos online aids us in defining and expressing our identity and interpreting meaningful moments in our lives. But it comes at the cost of thousands of people's exposure to the worst that humans have thought and said and done. Pornography aids us in feeling a sense of belonging and justification, but it comes at the cost of dehumanizing other people and instrumentalizing sexual intimacy.

According to the logic of our contemporary anthropology, the key is that these people *chose* to be exposed—they chose to take the job as a moderator—and if it's a choice, it is their responsibility, not ours. And if the pornographic entertainers choose to use their bodies and intimacy as a tool, it is their responsibility, not ours. We are all only our own and we can only belong to ourselves.

Maybe the worst part about all this is that these societal tools for self-belonging never come close to delivering on their promise. They just offer more promises. Our identities are never expressed enough. Our lives never quite feel meaningful enough. We never feel justified enough, or as if we truly belong. We "just need to" keep trying. When our efforts exhaust us or the new techniques to fix the problems of the old techniques fail, we move from Affirmation to Resignation. In the case of social media moderators, this looks like a move from yoga and group counseling to drugs and alcohol and unemployment.

But so long as our foundational understanding of what it means to be a human goes unquestioned, so long as we blame our problems on natural or biological limitations, societal injustices, or personal weaknesses, our only recourse will be more techniques.

Thank God we are not our own.

5

YOU ARE NOT
YOUR OWN BUT
BELONG TO CHRIST

ONCE WE ACCEPT THAT our contemporary anthropology is fundamentally flawed and produces an inhuman society that can never
fulfill its promises, we're left to cast about for an alternative. If we are not our
own and do not belong to ourselves, whose are we? To whom do we belong?

These questions make all the difference. Since at least the early twentieth
century, the predominate existential question for those in the West has
been who am I? But the better question is whose am I?[1] Who is this being
to whom I belong, how do I belong to them, and what are the implications
of this belonging on my life?

Historically, the Christian church has answered these questions by first
looking at a claim the apostle Paul makes in 1 Corinthians 6:19-20:

> Do you not know that your bodies are temples of the Holy Spirit,
> who is in you, whom you have received from God? You are not your
> own; you were bought at a price. Therefore honor God with your
> bodies. (NIV)

The context of these verses is a longer admonition against prostitution and
other forms of sexual immorality. The apostle Paul could have given many
other reasons for Christians to flee from sexual immorality. He might have
argued that prostitution is almost never truly consensual and is therefore
inherently violent and abusive. He might have argued that visiting prostitutes

will lead to illegitimate children and broken marriages or that such practices spread diseases. He might have argued that it is simply impure or that it should be socially unacceptable. He might have argued that sexual promiscuity is actually just a misguided attempt at suppressing personal insecurity. He might have even argued that faithfulness in marriage is important as a practice in self-discipline and integrity. But none of these reasons make it into Paul's letter. Instead, he grounds sexual morality in our *belonging*.

From the Garden of Eden, humanity's fundamental rebellion against God has been a rebellion of autonomy. Adam and Eve were given a clear law and chose to become a law unto themselves. The history of humanity has followed this example. When their son Cain murdered his brother Abel, God cursed Cain but promised to protect him from those who would seek to harm him for being under God's curse (Genesis 4:8-16). Yet despite God's promise, as Jacques Ellul observes, Cain built a city to protect himself.[2] It seems that Cain did not trust God to keep His word, choosing to rely on the power of walls to keep him safe instead of God's promise. Ellul points to this as the foundation of the spirit of human cities: self-reliance and autonomy.[3]

At its core, the impulse to build cities is the impulse to protect ourselves, to be self-sufficient, to provide for all we need to flourish as humans: "The city for Cain is first of all the place where he can be himself—his homeland, the one settled spot in his wandering. Secondly, it is a material sign of his security. He is responsible for himself and his life."[4] Cain's city is a claim that he is his own and belongs to himself.

In this sense, building a city is not merely a way to protect a community. It is an attempt to reject God's provision. If God exists, then we are not autonomous. If He does not, then we are alone with ourselves, whoever that may be.

Whom we belong to makes all the difference in the world. If we belong to ourselves, we are radically free—with all the accompanying glory and terror. But if we belong to God, then our experience of belonging in the world has limits that we have not freely chosen. And some of those limits will defy a value system based on efficiency and measurable harm.

Let us suppose, for example, that "joining yourself to a prostitute" (as Paul describes it) were a measurably efficient way of meeting your sexual needs in a sexless, dysfunctional marriage. It is cheaper than couple's counseling and less emotionally and cognitively taxing than working things out or separating. Let us also suppose that modern prostitution were free of violence and coercion, lost all its social stigma, was tolerated by your spouse, and was perfectly safe (and maybe even a net positive) for your health. By these standards, according to the contemporary anthropology, we would be forced to admit that the individual is free to enjoy prostitution. Some would even go so far as to say that any discomfort or guilt the spouse might feel is a form of self-hatred, a refusal to recognize and embrace the freedom of self-belonging—a failure to allow yourself to be happy.

But if Paul is correct and we are not our own, we do not have the freedom to use another human being's body as a tool to consume intimacy like we consume any other mass-produced product, regardless of how efficient and safe it might appear. Because our limits are not determined by inefficiency or measurable harm or even the law, but by the one to whom we all belong, God. We retain the agency to violate that limit, but doing so violates the reality of our right relationship to our neighbor and God.

●   ●   ●

Belonging necessitates limits. The question is to whom we belong. If we belong to ourselves, then we set our own limits—which means we have no limits except our own will. If we belong to God, then knowing and abiding by His limits enables us to live as we were created to live, as the humans He designed us to be.

Christians must be particularly careful here. Accepting limits is not the same thing as accepting that you belong to God. It's possible to obey many of God's limits and still deny that you belong to Him. There's nothing contradictory in personally choosing to live by a Christian sexual ethic while still believing that you are your own and belong to yourself. Scoffers might say that anyone who limits his or her sexuality because of some set of ancient, arbitrary tribal purity laws is a fool who's missing out on a great deal of fun and self-expression. But if these limits are freely chosen, they're still fundamentally an expression of autonomy. And that's how one can so easily belong in the contemporary church and strictly follow Christian sexual teachings while still being in absolute rebellion to the reality that you are not your own but belong to Christ.

Christian ethics, like any morality, can be treated as a lifestyle option. After moving to a particular religious part of the country, you may choose to adopt traditional Christian views on sex, greed, and honesty. You enjoy the sense of stability they provide and benefit socially from aligning with the community's values. Or maybe after a series of irresponsible and harmful life choices you find yourself at rock bottom and decide that your life needs some kind of structure, and Christian morality provides you with that structure. Or maybe becoming a parent changes your view of the world. It is not uncommon for parents to begin attending church so that their children are taught "good values."

When you choose to follow God's laws out of personal preference, you will eventually discover a breaking point where your desire for experiences or self-expression comes up hard against an ethical law. And at that moment, you can choose to abandon Christianity as an inadequate or antiquated lifestyle, find a more inclusive style of Christianity, or you can accept that Christianity was never meant to be a lifestyle and with the aid of the Holy Spirit deny your desire. Only if you truly belong to someone else does the latter option make any sense. If you belong to yourself, then it is foolish and perhaps even abusive to deny yourself. But if "you are not your own," it matters what you do with your body. It even matters how you do something as personal and intimate as making love.

Paul's words in 1 Corinthians make a claim about who we belong to and what it means to belong. It is no coincidence that throughout the Old and New Testament, adultery and idolatry are so closely linked. Idolatry is betraying your belonging to God. Adultery is betraying your belonging to your spouse and to God. For those who are in Christ, our bodies are the temple of the Holy Spirit, so we don't have the freedom to use our bodies any way we like. But the same Spirit that indwells us and limits us also enables us to live righteously and humanly.

This is a radically antimodern position to take, so much so that you may have felt uncomfortable even in this brief discussion of Paul's words. And that's okay. As we continue to consider what it means to not be our own, I'd ask you to remember the previous chapters. Remember that our current anthropology is already profoundly inhuman. Autonomy offered us freedom and gave us alienation. What could contingency offer us?

HOW A FIVE-HUNDRED-YEAR-OLD GERMAN CATECHISM CAN HELP US

In 1563, the theological faculty of Heidelberg University in present-day Germany released a new catechism aimed at educating lay believers about the basics of the Christian faith in a series of questions and answers. The catechism was meant to be a memorable way of understanding key doctrines of the church, and so each question and answer was meticulously cited with passages from Scripture. The catechism begins in a remarkable place:

> Q. What is your only comfort in life and death?
> A. That I am not my own,
> but belong with body and soul,
> both in life and in death,
> to my faithful Saviour Jesus Christ.
> He has fully paid for all my sins
> with his precious blood,
> and has set me free
> from all the power of the devil.
> He also preserves me in such a way
> that without the will of my heavenly Father
> not a hair can fall from my head;
> indeed, all things must work together
> for my salvation.
> Therefore, by his Holy Spirit
> he also assures me
> of eternal life
> and makes me heartily willing and ready
> from now on to live for him.[5]

By beginning with a question of "comfort in life and death," the Heidelberg Divines (the formal name for the authors) frame the essential doctrines of the Christian faith in existentialist terms. The question assumes that the reader feels *dis*comfort both at the prospect of living and the prospect of dying. It assumes that life requires some comfort to make it tolerable. This assumption follows the central biblical theme of "shalom" or "peace" as a basic human longing.

We may be tempted to bracket off this first question as the product of an unenlightened and undeveloped civilization. Europe in the sixteenth century did not have the benefits of the industrial, scientific, or information revolutions. They lacked democracy, civil liberties, and the tremendous wealth that would be generated by the free market. Of course they needed comfort!

Our own time has no less need for comfort than theirs, despite the astounding improvement in our material conditions over the last 500 years. Contemporary people are obsessed with means for coping with life. We don't self-medicate because our lives are wonderful, but because we need comfort to continue living. And many of the innovations we might point to as evidence for society's progress are themselves comforts that we use to get through the day. A good percentage of the other innovations that have defined the shift from the sixteenth century to our own day have done more to create further discomfort than to alleviate it.

No, the need for comfort in the face of life is not restricted to a particular moment in human history. It is a part of the human experience. But it is the case that the need for comfort manifests differently at different periods. Where people may have sought comfort to cope with the horrors of plagues and perpetual wars in the sixteenth century, the contemporary person struggles to cope with a loss of meaning, identity, and purpose.

Similarly, the need for comfort in the face of death transcends time periods. It may be that in the Renaissance people were more inclined to fear "what dreams may come," as Hamlet laments, whereas modern people fear the end of existence. It may also be that our fear of death is considerably *less* than that of earlier periods of Western civilization. For one, we are much better at extending our lives and distancing ourselves from the reality of death. If you are in the middle class and therefore less susceptible to deaths of despair, it is not at all difficult to avoid seeing a dead body or attending a funeral until you are decades into your life. Death is simply not present to contemporary people in the way it was for nearly all of human history. The experience of death is largely a choice for many of us until it ultimately isn't.

But this only means that the anxiety of death, the fear of sudden and eternal nothingness, shifts to an anxiety of living. Am I living a full and satisfying life? Is it enough? In that way, our avoidance of death only accentuates the anxiety we feel in trying to live adequate lives, when inadequacy means a failed life.

"THAT I AM NOT MY OWN"

You may be *un*comfortable with the phrase "I am not my own," because it brings to mind images of slavery, control, and authoritarianism. And yet the catechism refers to it as a source of *comfort*.

Part of our unease with the phrase stems from being raised in a culture that treats autonomy as sacred. We idolize rebels, free thinkers, and mavericks. Our modern myths are stories of rejecting traditional expectations to discover your true, pure identity. As we have seen, in the contemporary anthropology, to be fully human is to be autonomous. Society reinforces these claims in its structures, values, and practices. But there is another very good reason why we flinch at the phrase, "I am not my own."

●   ●   ●

The turn toward autonomy in the West was prompted, in part, by horrific abuses of authority, hierarchy, religion, and tradition. When the king, the priest, and the banker all openly collude to rob and oppress you for their personal gain, which they declare to be their divine right, you begin to doubt the entire idea of authority. Why wouldn't you? Between systemic abuses in the Medieval Catholic Church (see Dante or Luther on the subject) and a nobility whose way of life largely depended on brutal living conditions for serfs, there were plenty of reasons to embrace not only liberal democracy with its political freedom for the individual, but also what we might call metaphysical liberalism—the holistic belief that you are your own. There is a historical progression from political to metaphysical autonomy.[6] Whether this progression is inevitable is a separate question. The reality is that as, or soon after, individuals in Europe begin to attain political liberty, they also begin to think of themselves as free from other sources of authority: God, the church, tradition, cultural norms, family, nation, biology, and so on.

Abuses of authority have clearly not waned since the Middle Ages. Perhaps we have fewer institutions or individuals claiming authority over us (though I'm not sure how we could *measure* such a thing), but we still face daily examples of the abuse of authority.

Liberal democracy and metaphysical liberalism have created legal freedoms and liberated us from spiritual, moral, cultural, and psychological pressures to conform, but the authorities we do retain seem to have only shifted their methods of abusing powers. Instead of tightly regulated state and church laws that limit our behavior, we have an expanding number of institutions that use modern psychology, microeconomics, and mass communications to "nudge" us toward certain behaviors—to incentivize and pressure us to act in particular ways, often without our knowledge. The most obvious example is the way that smartphones "nudge" us to pay attention to them with sounds, vibrations, and rewarding interactions. Health insurance companies "nudge" us to eat healthier, governments "nudge" us to graduate from high school and read to our kids, and corporations "nudge" us to desire and consume products. Instead of the Roman Catholic Church's Magisterium definitively declaring God's revelation, we have a scientific community that interprets and declares what is *fact*.

Because the way our lives are limited by external forces has changed so dramatically, I'm not convinced we can confidently say that modern people are *more* free than medieval people. But we can say that modern people *feel* freer and are more skeptical of authorities, whereas medieval and ancient civilizations were more inclined to believe in the appropriateness of hierarchy and authority.

Our default posture toward authority has changed. We tend toward skepticism. So when we hear the phrase "I am not my own," our revulsion is partially a reaction to real and significant abuses of power that we have experienced in our own lives and that have occurred throughout history. When other forms of law oppress us, we quite naturally retreat into autonomy, or self-law.

•   •   •

For many contemporary people, the phrase "I am not my own" calls to mind not government overreach, manipulative advertising, or the unreliability of the scientific project, but traumatizing spiritual, emotional, physical, or sexual abuse at the hands of authority figures. Teachers, ministers, politicians, coaches, doctors, and employers regularly get caught abusing people under their care. And one of the ways abuse is perpetuated is by grooming victims into believing that they are not their own.

Before we can go on to consider how the belief that we are not our own can reorient us toward our true anthropology, we must acknowledge and address the very real danger of this idea. Once we accept that we are not our own, we are vulnerable to those who would take advantage of us. But then again, autonomy is no real protection from abuse or oppression either.

Despite the widespread acceptance of autonomy, the modern world does not lack for abusive authority figures. Contemporary abuses of authority may be less overtly coercive, but they remain coercive. In other words, autonomy does not get rid of abuses of authority, it just changes their appearance.

Regardless, we cannot ignore the fact that "you are not your own" has been and will continue to be used by abusers to control their victims, whether a cult leader, an abusive spouse, or an oppressive government. Any time you accept that your life does not exclusively belong to yourself, you open up the opportunity for evil people to take advantage of you in new ways. I want to offer a general response to the problem of abuse and address more specific difficulties as they arise later in the book.

•   •   •

Every abuse of authority involves an authority figure who desires his or her own good at the expense of others. When a government pressures its citizens into fighting an unjust war by appealing to patriotic duty, it is willing to exchange the good of its citizens' lives for increased power or wealth. When a cult leader uses shame to coerce his female followers into abusive sexual relationships, he does not desire their good. And when an abusive husband asserts control over his wife as if she were his possession, he actively opposes her personhood.

In each case the one in authority treats the other person *instrumentally*. The citizen is a tool for achieving the goals of the state. The female follower is a tool for the cult leader's pleasure. The wife is a tool for her husband. Instrumentalizing human persons is one of the defining features of our contemporary anthropology. When we are all our own, we have no obligation to think of each other as anything more than tools for our personal gain. But in the counter anthropology I am recommending—the idea that we are not our own—we seem to find the same instrumentalization at work. Perhaps the counter anthropology is inhuman too? Not quite. Rather we should say that all abusive forms of authority treat people as less-than-fully-human and do not desire their good.

The problem with rejecting individual sovereignty is not that it inevitably robs you of your personhood. On the contrary, we have already seen how the sovereign self leads to the inhuman conditions of the modern world. The danger of rejecting individual sovereignty is that if we belong to anyone who does not actively and truly desire our good, we will be abused. The reason autonomy *feels* safe is that we think we can trust ourselves to look out for our own well-being, whereas others will always look out for their own well-being over and against ours, to some extent or another. I know that I will take care of myself, but if I submit to your authority, I expect that eventually, despite even your best intentions, you will use me in harmful ways to benefit yourself.

A government agency may claim to exist to serve citizens, but once I have to apply for unemployment, it quickly becomes clear that to the agency, I am just a Social Security number, a data point, an opportunity to increase efficiency and contribute to quarterly performance goals. I may receive genuine help from an employee, but only despite the agency's indifference.

A ministry may claim to exist in order to disciple and care for people in need. But occasionally the ministers appear to be more interested in being *seen* helping people than actually helping anyone. At least, that's what it feels like when you look at their social media posts and branding.

A spouse may claim to be devoted and faithful, but eventually their self-interest will win out. In fact, in an honest relationship, most of your married life will be made up of navigating and prioritizing, sacrificing and defending your interests and your spouse's. Even in marriage, where you would hope two people could set aside their egos and genuinely desire the good of their spouse without reservation, it only occurs, if it ever occurs, in brief flashes.

•   •   •

Humans are incapable of completely, unreservedly desiring the good of someone else. Eventually our selfishness or desire for self-preservation pits us against the good of others, no matter how selflessly we try to live. Our hearts deceive us. Our bodies betray us, which is one reason why personal autonomy is so attractive. At least I can trust myself to look out for my own interests—or could that, too, be part of the way my heart deceives me?

Do we actually desire our own good? If we were honest with ourselves, we'd have to admit that on average we aren't much better than anyone else at desiring what is truly good for us. We regularly desire and pursue self-destructive experiences and goals. I know what I need to do to care for my body and yet I regularly do the things that will harm me and fail to do the things that will benefit me. It is not a coincidence that self-destructive behaviors are almost always simultaneously attempts to self-medicate and cope with modern life. Sometimes we only recognize how we have sabotaged ourselves long after the fact, when we can no longer protect ourselves or change our fate. We are uniquely capable of self-destruction and self-abasement. Humans can treat themselves as objects for their own dehumanization all while justifying it as self-expression and liberty. It would be impressive if it weren't all so terrible.

Where does this leave us? If we cannot trust ourselves to desire and pursue what is good for us, and we certainly cannot trust other humans to desire and pursue our good, what remains? To whom can we safely belong? To whom can we trust our existence without fear of abuse?

We need to belong to someone who is perfectly able to desire our own good while desiring their own good, someone for whom there cannot be a conflict between our good and their good (John 3:16; Romans 8:28; 2 Peter 3:9). We need to belong to Christ.

"BUT BELONG, BODY AND SOUL, BOTH IN LIFE AND DEATH, TO MY FAITHFUL SAVIOR, JESUS CHRIST"

What does it mean to belong to Christ? What are the Heidelberg Divines describing when they say I "belong, body and soul, both in life and death, to my faithful savior, Jesus Christ"?

First, there is a common grace way in which all people (and all of creation) belong to Christ. This is not what the Heidelberg Divines had in mind, but it is no less true, and it will be helpful for how we understand the Christian anthropology.

Because we were intentionally created and are sustained by a living and loving God without whom we could not be, we belong to Him. We see this principle at work throughout Scriptures. For example, in Exodus 19:5, God tells the Israelites, "All the earth is mine." Our existence in this world is contingent on God's active work of creation. You might think of this as a kind of existential belonging. It is a true kind of belonging, one radically different from the contemporary anthropology we have been exploring in previous chapters.

But the Heidelberg Divines had in view a second, much more significant kind of belonging to Christ. Through Christ's death on the cross for our sins, His resurrection from the grave, and the indwelling of the Holy Spirit in our bodies, we have been drawn into a unique, covenantal relationship with Him.

In 1 Corinthians 6:20, Paul uses the imagery of an ancient slave market to describe the way Christ has purchased us at a price. The implied price is Christ's death on the cross. We are not told who the old owner was, but we might imagine it was ourselves—enslaved to our passions.

In the Roman concept of slavery, purchasing a slave was legally equivalent to purchasing a human "thing" (a "*res*" as numerous commentators note).[7] These slaves lacked legal status as a person. With very few exceptions, slave owners had absolute control over their slaves and their slaves' bodies. To be enslaved to a man of high social standing was considered an honor and could result in a fairly comfortable life, but the fact remains that legally, they were human "things."

Depending on how closely we read this metaphor as analogous to our belonging to Christ, we may find it troubling. For example, the idea that

God has absolute control over us rings discomforting to modern ears. More troubling to me is the lack of personhood behind the idea of human "things." Here is where I believe the analogy reaches its limit. If these verses meant that by belonging to Christ we become subhuman, human "things," then Christ would be at war with His own creation, His own image. And that is certainly not the case. So how should we interpret this passage?

We are slaves to Christ like ancient peoples were slaves to Roman owners in that we belong to Him without remainder. He is not a leader we follow. He is not an employer we rent our labor to. In accepting Christ as Lord, we acknowledge that our belonging to Him is true and *good*. But unlike ancient slave masters, Christ's ownership over us does not entail the defacement of our humanity.[8] And this is a unique property of Christ's use of power in contrast to any human's. The power dynamics of human slavery require that the owner dehumanize the slave in order to achieve dominance. In that sense, people cannot enslave people they view as fully human. They can only enslave people they view as former or conditional or marginal people.

God's ownership of His children is categorically different because our humanity is no threat to His sovereignty. On the contrary, He *designed* us to worship and belong to Him *as* people. If God wanted subhumans or mere things to serve Him, He would have only made trees and animals. But He didn't. He made us. And unlike any other belonging imaginable, when we belong to Christ, we belong *without* effacement. In fact, our belonging ennobles us, making us co-heirs with Him of the heavenly kingdom.

Another way of understanding how we belong to Christ is that through His sacrificial death on the cross, He freed us from bondage to sin and we are now joined with Him. When I "join" my friends for lunch or "join" a conference call, there is no sense of union involved, only communion. I commune with my friends over lunch. But to be joined to Christ is to be united with Him in His death and resurrection.[9] Just as He died for our sins, so we are dead to our sins. Just as He rose from the dead, so will we. While we are exhorted to follow Christ, our union with Him goes much further than a kind of mimicry. We are united to Christ when we are baptized into His name and His Holy Spirit indwells us. In a mysterious but real way, our personhood is united with Christ's and our identity is altered so that when God the Father turns His face upon us, He sees His Son and His Son's righteousness.

To belong to Christ, then, means dwelling with Christ rather than trying to exist apart. As we have seen in the previous chapters, none of us can effectively live apart. The Responsibilities of Self-Belonging are cruel and impossible. All of us, without exception, belong to Christ as His creation. All of us owe Christ our love. All of us need His mercy. But not all of us *accept* that we are His creation or that we need His mercy.

Those who deny Christ's lordship and mercy continue to belong to Him: it is objectively the case that He made them and preserves them, even when they vainly devote their lives to creating and sustaining themselves. Their identity is grounded in their personhood, even when they run themselves ragged seeking to cultivate a public image. Their experiences have meaning, even if they think they are entirely subjective emotions. Injustice and evil and beauty and goodness are real, discernible values, even if those who deny Christ believe them to be arbitrary assertions of power. And their place in the cosmos is known by the one who made them and gives them breath, even if they feel as if they were floating through empty space.

A Christian anthropology asserts that all these things are true about human beings, but our longings are met in union with Christ when we accept our belonging to Him. That is precisely where we find comfort in life and death.

HOW SHOULD IT CHANGE THINGS?

Our justification before God. If you are not your own but belong to Christ, then there is nothing you can or must do to justify your life. The whole project of actualizing, validating, fulfilling, vindicating, establishing, or justifying your existence is built on the faulty premise that your existence is something that needs justification and that you are capable of providing that justification on your own.

When someone says our lives don't need to be justified or that we don't have to prove ourselves, they usually mean something like, "You are special and important just the way you are." But special how? Important to whom? The only possible answer according to our contemporary anthropology is "special because only you are you" and "important to yourself, because you are the only voice that matters." And we find ourselves right where began—with the Responsibilities of Self-Belonging.

It turns out, "You are special just the way you are because you are you" is merely a metaphysical way of pulling your existence up by its bootstraps. But when I say that your life does not need to be justified, I mean something entirely different. It's not that your life is existentially validated because you choose to see it that way. No, your existence is good and right and significant because a loving God intentionally created you and continues to give you your every breath. Your life is significant whether you choose to see it that way or not, which is almost the opposite of the responsibility to self-justify.

●   ●   ●

Everyone feels the need to account for their existence—why am I alive and why does it matter? As Ernest Becker notes, each person must account for the radical miracle of their own face, a face that represents a consciousness, a personality, a name, history, experiences, relationships, memories, and so on—in other words, a face that represents total personhood: "One's own face may be godlike in its miraculousness, but one lacks the godlike power to know what it means, the godlike strength to have been responsible for its emergence."[10] But if Christianity is true, then your being in the world is fundamentally good because the Creator made you and sustains you and you are made in His image. You are existentially justified because your existence is not random. You were intentionally created. You are intentionally sustained. In Christ we live and move and have our being (Acts 17:28). The only persons who would actually need to justify their existence are those who were not intentionally created by a loving God. To be alive is to have a justified life, a life of purpose.

Our desperate efforts to justify our existence are striving after a state we are already in. But that doesn't mean we no longer feel the need to justify ourselves. The felt need remains and even intensifies as society grows increasingly secular and the Responsibilities of Self-Belonging weigh on us more and more.

Knowing that your life is justified because God made and preserves you does not mean that you will always feel purposeful or need to prove you're worthy. If I had to guess, I'd say that Americans in the evangelical church are not much better at accepting their lives as a gift from God than their secular neighbors. I witness much of the same ambition, the same fight for validation, the same fear of inadequacy driving people in the church and outside the church—in my own heart.

●   ●   ●

Which raises a question: Why do we feel the need for existential validation when our existence is always already good? If Christianity is true and we are not our own but belong to Christ, and therefore our lives are justified by virtue of our creation and preservation, shouldn't we feel confident in our existence? Our restlessness and insecurity could be interpreted as signs that the contemporary anthropology was correct all along: we are our own and are responsible for our own lives.

One theme we will discover in every implication of accepting a Christian anthropology is that things are still pretty terrible out there. Almost everyone else you meet will continue to believe that they are their own and so are you. Almost every institution will treat you like an autonomous individual, subject to instrumentalization and valued according to efficiency. Almost every store will still have self-checkout lines. Instagram will not suddenly disappear when you realize that you belong to Christ. There is no magic here, only a confused, desperate, anxious world, and God. There is only technique, dehumanization, self-medication, and Christ's love. There is only the freedom to accept the truth about your existence, even when it doesn't change the world or fix all your problems.

I understand this might be a disappointment. You might feel you've been tricked into reading this far with the expectation that I'd offer some clear steps to make society better or to improve your life. I hope you won't return the book or leave a bad Amazon review.

No matter how much we consciously affirm that our existence is already justified through God, virtually every other voice we interact with will tell us, "No. Keep striving. You haven't done enough. If you quit now, your life will be a waste. Do something else to make it worthwhile." At its best, the church will be a sanctuary from this idolatrous babble, and here, if nowhere else, you should find other souls who will remind you that your life is not a quest for significance or self-actualization, but an act of joyful participation in God's grace. In the liturgy of church, in sacrificially serving each other, in reminding each other that we are not our own, and in coming to the Lord's Table we can push back against the contemporary anthropology as a community. Too often churches in America fail to live up to this standard, even though we have the resources in our tradition and theology to correct the lie that we are obligated to justify our own lives.

The other main reason we strive to justify ourselves despite already being justified is that autonomy is easier to accept than contingency upon God. It's not easier to *live with*, but it is easier to *accept*, because limits feel stifling. They require a denial of the self. Dependence is humbling and it's just easier to affirm yourself. The problem is if you go down the road of affirming yourself, you don't get to choose when to stop. You have to go on affirming yourself forever. It's a hell of a burden. But it's one we all readily take on and then suffer under. It's the same sin that seduced Adam and Eve. It's the same lack of faith that drove Cain to build a walled city rather than trust in God's promises, which brings us to the other sense in which a Christian anthropology changes our pursuit of justification.

●   ●   ●

Even if I accept that my existence in the world is a good thing, I'm still left with the question of whether or not my actions are good. Even if God's creation and preservation provide us existential justification, the need for moral or theological justification remains. Is my life good? Yes. But have I *lived* a good life? Am I a good person? Well, that's another matter. And we desire justification in both senses.

If we are not our own but belong to Christ, then there is a moral judge outside of ourselves, beyond the shifting moral fads of society or the positive affirmations of our neighbors. There exists a lawgiver, someone who can define what it means to live righteously, who can judge our actions and intentions, and most importantly, who can look upon us with approval and say, "You are righteous before my eyes."

The burden of acting rightly is uniquely human. This is one place where the existentialists were quite right. We have radical freedom to act. Every moment of our lives is made up of hundreds of small choices. Some of them seem unconscious, but virtually all of them are the result of some choice we have made to cultivate habits or attend to desires. We are born into this world and the fact that we are alive is good—but what should we do with this life?

The more you meditate on it, the more you realize that you have almost godlike powers to affect the world. Your choice to smile at a grocery store checker rather than ignore her (a simple way to love your neighbor) could have resonating effects beyond your wildest imagination. A simple lie can become a wildfire, devouring people and relationships whole. Each of us has the ability to break someone's will and crush their dreams. There are countless ways you can *legally* destroy another human being. Verbally abuse them until they give up on life. Play with their emotions and then mock them publicly.

Once you honestly begin looking at what humans have the power to do with their actions, it can be terrifying. We make so many choices in life. There are so many ways to sin and cause harm without ever knowing it. There are so many ways to hate God and our neighbors.

We are very good at making excuses for our actions and avoiding an honest account of who we are, what we have done, and how we have harmed other people. But if you take the time to truly consider these questions, you will discover that the consequences of sin are utterly out of your control.

Our belonging to God gives us a specific set of laws for determining right actions, which in their simplest form amount to loving God and loving our neighbor. From these two laws, humans can know what it means to act rightly in any circumstance. And the more we grow in wisdom and understanding, the better we can discern and address sin in our lives. Compared to the moral uncertainty of the contemporary anthology, belonging to Christ gives us the tremendous comfort of a beautiful and clear moral horizon. We know how we ought to act.

•   •   •

But the other result of growing in our understanding of sin is that we discover how sinful we are. We discover that our being in the world, which itself is good, inevitably involves hurting our neighbors and sinning against God and man. The goal of living righteously is clear, but the task itself is crushing. Kierkegaard describes this as living transparently before God. To stand before an all-powerful, all-knowing, and perfectly righteous God can be terrifying, and to live before such a God without trying to hide our sins is even more overwhelming.[11]

If you haven't done so already, go ahead and try to really live righteously—even for five minutes. If you're doing well, you may avoid some common social sins like being openly racist, and you may manage to restrain your more overt forms of lust or greed or hate. But try, just try to not lust in your heart—ever. Just try not to envy your neighbors' house or well-behaved children. Just try not to feel a fleeting desire for violence when someone cuts you off in traffic.

As with the Responsibilities of Self-Belonging, some people respond to the standard of righteousness with Affirmation and others with Resignation. The affirming believe that they have enough guidance about right and wrong and enough discipline and willpower to be righteous. The affirming may also give into a kind of despair, believing that while they cannot attain righteousness, they are obligated to ceaselessly try harder. If they just have a little more self-discipline and perhaps better technique, maybe they can purify themselves, perhaps God will look upon them in love. They continue to seek God's face through disciplined righteous action.

The resigned consider their own hearts in light of God's law and cannot imagine ever drawing the assurance of God's face. Upon that face they can only see a shadow of judgment and damnation. Either the severity of their sins or their personal delight in sin inclines them to see righteousness as a task for other people. They may give up all hope of righteousness. If we are not our own but belong to Christ, then we do not live in moral chaos, but if God's law is so severe that we can never be good enough, perhaps moral chaos is preferable to damnation.

Because of the weight of sin, we cannot look upon the face of God and live. Yet neither can we live without God's face approvingly turned toward us. That is our bind.

Both postures assume that our righteousness is determined by our actions—if we simply discipline ourselves and develop the right techniques, we can be good enough, or at least better than the next guy.

The reality of standing before a totally just God drives others to deny their personhood, to believe that they are something other than human: something self-established and self-defining. But this only leads to despair, as we have seen in the previous chapters. It doesn't ever make them less than human. It doesn't mean they are no longer before God. It only means that they must struggle every moment to deny their createdness, their miraculousness, their humanity, their belonging to God.

Recall the tension we saw between the exhilaration and the terror of belonging to ourselves. We find a similar tension here in standing before God. Before Him we have love and belonging, but we also have absolute justice. Who can stand before Him? But there is a difference in these tensions. The tension in our contemporary anthropology can only be resolved by the individual choosing to focus on one side over the other. So you choose to think about life as a grand adventure rather than an impossible burden. But nothing actually changes.[12] The tension we feel in standing transparently before God is resolved through Christ. Not us. Not our storytelling. Not our words of affirmation or positivity. But objectively, in time and space, Christ's death resolves this tension.

If we belong to Christ *through* His sacrifice on the cross, the nature of our desire for righteousness changes. We don't receive God's loving affirmation, "Well done, good and faithful servant," by acting righteously. Rather, when we acknowledge that we are not our own but belong to Christ, when we accept that Christ died for our sins and seek to live before Him, God looks at our face and sees the beauty and righteousness of His Son. And the judge of all assures us that we are loved, accepted, and adored. We live before a personal God, not the mechanical god of proceduralism or efficiency. The relentless, impersonal, litigious, crushing force of progress and self-improvement is ended in Christ. The demands of universal benevolence, which asks us to carry the world on our shoulders, are resolved in Christ and His providence.[13] In this way, we are not only able to stand transparently before God without fear of condemnation, but we are only truly ourselves when we do.

• • •

These two kinds of justification—existential and theological—are deeply intertwined. When you come to realize that your existence is justified because you were created and are sustained by the love of God, then you will also come to acknowledge Him as Lord. So consciousness of existential justification ought to lead to gratitude for the gift of life and, therefore, to theological justification. Anyone who is spiritually justified knows, or ought to know, that Christ sustains them breath by breath, which is the greatest sign of existential justification.

A Christian anthropology describes our natural state before God, our neighbor, and the created world. Fundamentally, we are not our own. Rather than rebelliously insisting on our radical freedom, a Christian anthropology invites us to assent to the goodness of our belonging in Christ, which is what it means to enter into a covenant with Him. Then our belonging takes on a very specific trajectory. Because we belong to Him, God uses all things to work together for our good, for our salvation, for our growth in union with Him.

Our identity before God. If you are not your own but belong to Christ, then the entire modern project of identity formation and expression is a sham. That means a major portion of our economy is based on the myth that we need to be someone unique. Expressive individualism is the logic guiding many modern industries, like entertainment, fashion, and social media. These are massive corporations generating billions upon billions of dollars in revenue each year from people who feel an overwhelming burden to be seen so that they feel real and significant—people who have been lied to.

The truth is that you are always your person, created by God with your face, your name, and your consciousness. While being a unique person, you have always existed in relation to others, primarily to God, but also your neighbor, and the created world. There is no version of your self that can be extracted from these relationships and your history and your body. You are inexorably embedded in space and time.

There is no image for you maintain because you were made in the image of God. There is no identity for you to discover or create because your identity was never actually in question. It felt like it was because we live in liquid modernity, but that feeling isn't reality. And there is no need for you to express your identity to make it more solid or to compete in the ever-growing marketplace of images because your personhood doesn't need affirmation from other humans to make it valid.

If some of this sounds familiar, it's probably because you've heard it in the form of self-help, pop-psychology, or positive self-esteem advice. You may have been told by an earnest high school teacher that you don't have to try so hard, or you don't need the approval of others. Maybe your favorite pop star or actor encouraged you (along with the rest of their fans) to love yourself just the way you are.

But as we saw with existential justification, secular assurances that we are "all right" always turn out to be based on our own will, our own effort, and our ability to assure ourselves that we are all right because we believe we are all right. Your identity is secure only insofar as you feel it to be secure. No one outside of you can truly affirm your identity. Really the best we can do is remind one another that we each individually have the power to declare that our identity is good. In other words, your identity is a creation of pure subjectivity, sustained and affirmed by subjectivity. But identity always calls for external affirmation, a witness, which is one very good reason why modern people are perpetually in an identity crisis.

On the one hand we are completely dependent on ourselves to determine, create, and affirm our own identities. On the other hand, identity *requires* some kind of external recognition by its very nature. To have an identity, there must be another being outside of you who can see your face and say your name. The gift of your life assumes both a giver and a recipient. But once we begin to rely on other people to recognize and affirm our identity, it becomes uncertain, shifting according to the whims of other people. I think this is why most of us roll our eyes whenever we are encouraged to "accept" ourselves or "believe" in ourselves or "be whoever we want to be." They are empty self-esteem slogans that don't reflect the reality that we need some kind of external affirmation. Self-affirmation simply doesn't satisfy. We need a witness.

• • •

There is a Christian version of affirmation that also fails to ground our identity. Christians will sometimes speak of their identity in Christ as a response to feelings of insecurity or an identity crisis. You may hear a ministry encourage you not to "find your identity in your work" (or beauty, or wealth, or education, or whatever the idol may be) and instead to find it in Christ.[14]

There is an important truth here: in liquid modernity, we will try all sorts of means to hold together our identity. As Zygmunt Bauman points out, liquid can only be temporarily forced into a shape, just as our identities can only be temporarily solidified in liquid modernity.[15]

Imagine yourself as four ounces of water. You are infinitely malleable. Others may try to impose a shape upon you, but you are fundamentally liquid. You may pour the water into a glass (an identity) in order to give it form, but the water doesn't actually *become* solid unless you freeze it.

It is true that modern people, stuck with selves that are more like water than ice, tend to obsessively try out different cups and glasses to give form to our lives. You might "find your identity" in being physically fit or in advocating for a particular social justice cause or in a theology or a style of music—all different kinds of glasses and cups.

The danger for Christians who urge others to find their identity in Christ is that most modern people have a secular understanding of identity, one rooted in that contemporary anthropology, where identity has more to do with lifestyle and image than personhood. "Christ" becomes just another, better identity. You're still pouring water into a cup, you just had to find the *right* cup.

There are a number of serious problems with this advice. For one, what exactly does the Christ-identity look like? Certainly, being a follower of Christ gives you a set of morals and a community. We may go so far as to say that Christianity offers us an entire worldview. But morality, community, and worldview are not *identity*. They can contribute to our identity, but they are not our identity.

An identity necessarily includes a name and a face. I *am* O. Alan Noble. There may be other O. Alan Nobles in the world, but to address *me*, you must call my name and look at my face. When you do, you refer to the person (with a consciousness, body, and history) who has had certain experiences, carries certain memories, and can be said to hold a "biblical worldview."

But when you address me, you are not addressing my worldview or morality or community or even the sum of all those things. It turns out, all the "identities" I have tried on, all the cups I have poured myself into, aren't actually solid identities at all. If Christianity is merely a different cup, even if it is a superior cup, then my "identity" in Christ is no more than a style of living.

When we encourage people to find their identity in Christ, what we too often mean is that all the other cups we choose to pour our identity into are idols that can never give us the solid identity we desire. This is true, but it's equally true that if we consider Christianity just a different cup, then it is no better. In fact, it can become just as much of an idol.

●　　●　　●

The kind of affirmation of personhood I am speaking of in the Christian anthropology is radically different from secular affirmation and from calls to "find your identity in Christ" that do not challenge the modern conception of identity.

If you are your own and belong to Christ, then your personhood is a real creation, objectively sustained by God. And as a creation of God, you have no obligation to create your self. Your identity is based on God's perfect will, not your own subjective, uncertain will. All your efforts to craft a perfect, marketable image add nothing to your personhood. The reason the opinions of others don't define you isn't because your opinion is the only one that counts, but because you are not reducible to *any* human efforts of definition. The only being who can fully know you and understand you without reducing you to a stereotype or an idol is God.

This does not mean that you don't have a "true self." You do. But it is just not one that you are burdened with creating. We live as our true selves when we stand transparently before God, moment by moment, as Kierkegaard reminds us: The self's task is "to become itself, which can only be done in relationship to God."[16] This means knowing that we are spirit as well as body. It means living in light of eternity without the effacement of earthy life. It means knowing that we are a miraculous creation, a pure gift from a loving God. It means that we have limits, we have duties, obligations, and commandments that we must obey. It means we are contingent and dependent upon God. Anytime we imagine ourselves to be autonomous, anytime we, like Cain, strive to be utterly self-sufficient and deny the hand of God in our lives, we are not merely in sin; we are in denial about the way things truly are. In Kierkegaard's view, this denial is fundamentally despair. Our contemporary drive to be authentic can find its fulfillment in the active choice to recognize our belonging to and before God.

In Rowan Williams's book *Being Disciples: Essentials of the Christian Life*, the Anglican theologian captures the Christian understanding of identity:

> You have an identity, not because you have invented one, or because you have a little hard core of selfhood that is unchanged, but because you have a witness of who you are. What you don't understand or see, the bits of yourself you can't pull together in a convincing story, are all held in a single gaze of love. You don't have to work out and finalize who you are, and have been; you don't have to settle the absolute truth of your history or story. In the eyes of the presence that never goes away, all that you have been and are is still present and real; it is held together in that unifying gaze.[17]

Human identity assumes and requires an external person who can acknowledge and affirm us, who can say our name, look us in the face, and tell us it is good that we exist. It can't be a generic statement or a platitude either. When we see someone wearing a T-shirt that says, "The World Needs You!," nobody seriously feels acknowledged and affirmed. When a famous YouTuber tells his young, emotionally vulnerable viewers that they are "all beautiful just the way they are," they only feel affirmed if they fantasize about him saying those words to *them*, personally, face to face. The fantasy quickly fades, however. Like a dying fire, it requires constant attention and fuel to keep it alive. Which is one reason YouTubers and celebrities who target insecure teenagers tend to have obsessive and addicted fans.

To know that we are okay, we need acknowledgment and affirmation from someone who knows us. We desire to be truly known and loved for who we are—not for the image of ourselves that we have created, not for the image of ourselves created by other people, and not for us as a generic human with certain inalienable rights or potentials, but ourselves as we really are. That's why I have been emphasizing the importance of your name and face.[18]

It is no coincidence that one of the most common blessings in the Christian tradition includes the image of God looking at us in the face. In Numbers 6:24-26, the Lord gives Moses a blessing for Aaron and his sons:

> The LORD bless you and keep you;
> the LORD make his face to shine upon you and be gracious to you;
> the LORD lift up his countenance upon you and give you peace.

The repetition of "you" and of the Lord turning His face upon our face stresses the personal nature of the Lord's blessing. The God of the Bible is a God who loves nations and peoples and persons. It is only in God that we can find someone who can know us without any deception and love us still. Our identity is grounded in the loving gaze of God. When we stand transparently before God, abandoning our efforts of self-establishment and confessing our sins and accepting His grace, we feel that loving gaze upon us.

● ● ●

If the metaphor of the liquid self and the glass identity is the analogy for our flawed contemporary anthropology, what is the alternative? What metaphor describes the Christian account of the human person as a person with an identity?

We must begin with the fact that our personhood, our "self," is not actually liquid, so we don't need to find a solidifying identity to give ourselves shape and definition. Certainly, we will *experience* our identity as liquid because our society tells us it is, but it's not true. As Rowan Williams points out, we experience our identity in bits, incomplete and fluid. But that is not the objective truth about us.

You will continue to doubt your identity. You will continue to question who you are and who you ought to be. Advertisements will continue to cultivate your insecurities. Our cultural stories will continue to portray an identity crisis as the archetypal conflict in our lives. Social media platforms will continue to pressure you into perpetual, anxious self-expression. The ideal life will still feel like a self-created and sustained identity. The conspiracy to promote a false anthropology will continue to permeate our society. But you can name it and remind yourself and others that it is a lie—a damnable lie. Perhaps that is small comfort, but I don't think so.

In *Back to the Future*, Marty McFly watches in horror as one by one his family members slowly fade from a photo. He alters history and their existence fades away. This is how some of us feel about our lives. Our image is conjectural, speculative, subject to fading away, being canceled, growing irrelevant, or blending in until we are utterly indistinct from everyone else. Life is the process of keeping our image sharp, definite, and compelling, of drawing the gaze of others to bear witness to our image. The Christian anthropology upsets this idea of identity completely. Your true identity is not a publicly projected image that requires regular maintenance, upgrades, and optimization.

Your identity is who you are before God, your personhood, your existence in the world. Our tendency is to conceive of our life and our identity as related but separate things. We have life in the sense that we are not dead. But we have valid identity in the sense that we have successfully defined ourselves against everyone else. In this way, our identity is dependent on continually competing with and presenting ourselves against others. But if the Christian anthropology is true, our identity is acknowledged by a living God and there is no need for me to compete in order to feel real. It was never my standing out that made me real, it was only my standing before God. My identity has always been secure precisely because I was created by God—the same God who bears witness to my life.

Our meaning before God. If we are not our own but belong to Christ, then meaning is not a story we make up to dramatize our lives. Meaning inheres in creation and in our experiences, and when we rightly interpret the world, even if only in glimpses, we partake of a truth that transcends us.

The love I feel for my family is not merely a feeling, but recognition of the goodness of family, the goodness of each of their individual lives, and the beauty of our intimate community. "Family" means the earnestness of

a handmade Father's Day card from my oldest daughter, Eleanor. It means
the way my son, Quentin, talks fast when he gets excited baking banana
bread with me. It means the knowledge that when my youngest daughter,
Franny, snuggles with me, she feels as safe as she will ever feel in this world.
It means making my wife, Brittany, laugh when the stress of life is unbearable.
It means taking much longer to write this book than it might have because
I took breaks to read to my children. "Family" means a constant effort to
remind each other of the love and grace of God.

Each of these truths that give meaning to my particular participation in
"family" has an objective reality grounded in the character and revelation
of God in His Word and creation. And if I didn't see these experiences as
meaningful, it wouldn't matter. They would go on meaning, go on being
significant and part of God's ordered universe, whether I noticed or not. But
I am blessed when I do see them.

Does it actually matter whether this experience has a reality beyond my
emotions? Do I actually lose something significant if my interpretation of
"family" is purely a product of my mind? A lot rests on this question. For
many modern thinkers, meaning is only something one *feels*. They admit
that our society is experiencing a "crisis of meaning."[19] And virtually no
one doubts the benefits of meaningfulness. People who feel that life is
meaningless are drawn to suicide and other self-destructive behavior.

But if all that matters is that you *think* or *feel* that your life has meaning,
society can just discover ways of increasing those feelings. Ellul believes
that this is precisely what society does. In order to retain productivity, the
modern worker "must be made to feel a community of interest; the idea
that his labor has social meaning must be instilled in him."[20] What is important is the "feeling" and the "idea," not the reality. For these thinkers,
the crisis of meaning raises the question: What methods (techniques) can
we use to feel meaningful? And the answers are almost always the same:
find community, be vulnerable, connect with nature, find a job that gives
you agency, take care of your health, and so on.

We don't like to think of meaningfulness as just a thing in our heads, but
as long as we don't consciously remind ourselves that meaning is utterly
relative, then it's not so bad. If you tell me that my interpretation of "family"

is just something I'm feeling in my head—that it isn't reflective of truths about reality, but just the result of personality, chemical reactions in the brain, evolutionary drives, and so on—I may be tempted to punch you in the face. But if we embrace our feelings as "meaningful to us," and avoid thinking about them as a useful myth, we might be able to get many of the social and interpersonal benefits.

● ● ●

Let's apply a mental exercise I call "the drug test." It's useful for revealing the inner logic of any solution to our contemporary crisis (loss of meaning, value, or belonging, an identity crisis, etc.): a drug is developed that gives users the emotional and biological sensation of meaningfulness. The physical side effects are trivial. Is anything lost?

Consider work. One of the challenging aspects of living in the contemporary West is the feeling that your labor is pointless at best and harmful at worse. Think about how many products are not just unnecessary but also pointless. If you could wave a wand and all copies of a certain movie were gone, would the world miss anything? Think about how many items in Walmart you could snap your fingers and wish away leaving no one the worse for it and many people better off. Much of our economy is devoted to the design, production, and sale of things that are completely forgettable, meaningless, or even harmful.[21]

In a way, it's a testament to the efficiency of the industrialized world that my kids can bring home a "gift bag" from a birthday party filled with five plastic toys that they will fight over but never enjoy and that will be thrown away (hopefully) within three days. Someone designed those toy dinosaurs. Someone built the factory and the machines to manufacture them. Someone ran the factory and machines. Someone advertised the toys. Someone transported them. Someone stocked them. And when they get thrown away, someone may ship them *back* to their country of origin where they will rot for a thousand years in a landfill. In the end it would save everyone a lot of trouble if the manufacturers took them directly to the landfill. Our society is so efficient that we can mass produce junk. The best that can be said for it is that at least the designer and factory worker and everyone else along the way had a source of income.

But work is more than just providing sustenance. We long to know that our labor means something, that it does something good in the world, that it has dignity. We don't all need to be doctors or nurses, but we want to know that our labor matters. The thought that our labor might just be part of a global shell game is, frankly, very depressing. Many people suffer from the feeling that their work is meaningless.

Back to the drug test.

Let us imagine that the new drug makes you feel as though your job matters. Thanks to various new techniques, the price of the drug is cheap enough, and the increase in productivity for workers who feel important is great enough, that the store owner pays for workers' prescriptions. You still sell plastic toy dinosaurs that children will briefly fight over before they are unceremoniously tossed in a landfill, but now it *feels* important. Physiologically, when you make a sale you feel a sense of accomplishment and pride. Your eyes light up. You feel less fatigued. You smile. Is this wrong?

The drug test is not entirely hypothetical. For one thing, the pharmaceutical industry is massive and the demand for medications that address specific maladies (attention, anxiety, sex drive) is only increasing. While I doubt there will be a magic pill that makes work feel meaningful for people, it's not difficult to imagine a pill that removes inhibitions and anxieties that accompany working a meaningless job. We already have those pills: antidepressants.

For another thing, even when critics of overmedication offer solutions to our crisis of meaning, they focus on creating the conditions under which we are statistically more likely to experience the *feeling* of meaningfulness. Sure, it's probably better for people to rely on social conditions and environmental changes than on medication to *feel* meaningful, but both strategies are fundamentally the same. Both treat the sensation as the thing itself.

Whether the factory owner improves the lighting, puts up inspiring posters, and calls employees "associates" so that they feel like manufacturing toy dinosaurs is meaningful work, or whether he uses medications to accomplish the same thing, the work itself can stay the same.

Our society will only get better and better at modifying our perceptions and emotions without modifying the conditions that give rise to our emotions. If I am my own and belong to myself, and if meaning is only ever a construction in my head used to make life bearable by giving it the semblance of order and direction, then there's no significant reason I shouldn't just use a pill or some other technique to give myself the feeling of meaning. But here's the thing: it matters to me that my job actually is meaningful. It matters to me that the joy I feel being with my family reflects a deeper truth about existence. I'd rather feel purposeless in my job and know it is purposeful than feel purposeful and know it is really purposeless.

If I am not my own but belong to Christ, then the meaning I experience in life has an objective existence when it rightly reflects the truth about God and creation and my neighbor. The safety my daughter feels when she snuggles with me reflects the transcendent truth that God Himself cares for her. Even if I'm too busy playing on my phone to realize the significance of her sigh of contentment as she pulls my arm around her on the couch, that moment still speaks of the nature of reality. God willing, I will attend to that nature, choosing to be present in the moment and thanking God for the wisdom it provides. But even if I don't, it's still there and it is still fundamentally good. When I brush the hair from my wife's face as she's sleeping, and I feel the warmth of her skin and know that she is present with me in bed, that her personhood is distinct from my own but joined with mine in marriage, that her face is the face of one I love and who loves me in return—that is real. And if you can replicate that feeling with a drug or with emotional or psychological manipulation, I'd rather feel nothing at all. Either my experience of meaning reflects in some shadowy way the real being of the world, or I am of all people most to be pitied.

Our values before God. If we are not our own but belong to Christ, then the values that give shape to our culture and personal lives rightfully place limits on us. There remains a personal dimension to morality, but it is always grounded in the existence of another, namely, God as revealed in His Word and creation. In some ways, these limits will chafe, not because they are unjust or inhuman, but because any limit to our absolute freedom is costly. It requires a denial of self, which is the opposite of our contemporary anthropology.

Our personal preferences in beauty, justice, goodness, and so on must conform to the perfect standards of God. But those standards also give us the ground to act courageously, to sacrifice ourselves, to delight in beauty without doubt, to enjoy the good gifts of this life as good gifts. Most importantly for our own moment in history, our belonging to Christ means that efficiency cannot be the guiding value of human enterprises.

We saw in 1 Corinthians 6:19-20 how the apostle Paul uses our belonging to God to determine how to honor God with our bodies in sex. This may be the most uncomfortable part of a Christian anthropology for contemporary people. Of all human experiences, sex feels most securely in the domain of the private individual. The idea that our sexual expression ought to be formed by someone outside ourselves feels like a violation of our individual sovereignty. As Charles Taylor notes, "For many people today, to set aside their own path in order to conform to some external authority just doesn't seem comprehensible as a form of spiritual life."[22] It seems particularly incomprehensible to conform to an external standard of sexuality.

But this is mistaken. Sex has always been formed by someone outside of ourselves. By its very nature, sex involves the self-giving of a man and a woman. Only if sex is conceived of as a technique for personal pleasure or power can we reasonably say that it should be entirely private and free from external limits and obligations. And sex as personal pleasure or power is a perversion. It is an impoverished form of physical love, "tiny and meaningless and—sad-making."

Sex is only truly good when it is an act of self-giving, entered into with a desire for the good of a spouse within the sanctity of marriage. Rather than better sexual techniques, our sex should be defined by prodigality—a kind of joyfully over-abundant self-giving, unrestrained by productivity or performance, always in excess of what is strictly necessary. In marriage, a man and wife are not their own but belong to each other in a dim but ecstatic shadow of our belonging to God. Just as our self-giving in commitment and devotion with love creates the foundation for sex, so too does our givenness and our commitment and devotion to God in love create the foundation for our lives.

In chapter three I argued that contemporary pornography is the epitome of the modern condition. Pornography is the only space where we are told, "Yes, you may" to any desire. But as we saw, infinite desire is a malady, not a gift. It leaves us empty, addicted, and feeling inadequate. To accept that we are not our own is costly too. If "Yes, you may" (for a price) is the sexual law in a pornographic society against which we begrudgingly permit a few exceptions, "No, you may not" is the sexual law in creation, against which God has sanctioned a few beautiful exceptions.

The anthropology of "you are not your own" is not easy or free from sacrifice. By some metrics it is the less efficient way of living. There will come times in your life when you will be obligated to deny some pleasure, some intimacy, something or someone genuinely lovely because you are not your own but belong to God, and through Him, to your family and your neighbor. It may even be the case that after years of marriage you meet someone else who loves you more and with whom you would have a more pleasurable life and compatible marriage. There are a lot of beautiful, fascinating people in the world and anyone who says otherwise is a fool.

But to stand before God, we do not have the freedom to abandon our responsibilities and promises when love grows cold or friendship becomes difficult or parenting is too much or caring for your elderly parents is embarrassing. We should not submit to abusive relationships and there are biblically legitimate grounds for divorce and separating yourself from certain relationships. But you are not free to pursue any desire you have. It doesn't matter how badly you want it, how good it feels, how much you are missing out on, or how supportive our contemporary society is, we must accept our responsibilities to God, the church, our family, and our neighbors.

For some of us, our obligations to others will require us to tolerate loneliness, to accept abstinence for a season or a lifetime, to live where we don't want to live, to work a job we don't enjoy, to give up comforts we love, to let go of honorable dreams and passions, to physically suffer, to forgo thanks and recognition, to lend money without expecting repayment, to allow our rights to be infringed upon. In one way or another, we will be called to the renunciation of our desires in affirmation of God's grace and providence, but never in resignation. Renunciation in affirmation, not resignation.

I mentioned earlier in this book that I have watched in mourning as more and more friends and acquaintances abandon their spouse and children for a more "satisfying" or "authentic" relationship. There are many ways to abandon your obligations. Some fathers abandon their children by working all the time. Some people abandon their friends when friendship is costly. Some treat their church as a social service provided for a certain amount of tithe rather than a living body of believers united with Christ. Belonging to God sets limits on our lives. Sometimes they are hard limits to bear. It is not easy to stand before God, even with grace. Moment by moment we must set aside our sinful desires, even the ones closest to our heart, to live sacrificially. I do not want to lie to you. This is a difficult life.

●　　●　　●

What have we gained if we are relieved of the Responsibilities of Self-Belonging only to come under the yoke of self-denial? Freedom. When the yoke is not self-righteous legalism but rightly ordered love, denying yourself the fulfillment of desires gives you the freedom to delight in the goodness before you.

Esther Greenwood was radically "free" to choose any fig on the tree, but that only made it impossible for her to choose at all. You are radically free to delight in the gifts God has given you without the anxiety, regret, dread, or paralysis of infinite choice. Part of that delight comes directly from the contingency of those gifts, from the fact that God gave you a particular gift at a particular moment in your life. And because He gave it to you, it is good. You don't have to worry or wonder or daydream about all the other figs or women or friends or talents or careers or experiences or children or whatever that you *don't* have. They don't matter.

This is a radical idea. So much of our culture is focused on making us feel discontent and inadequate. We live in a perpetual state of "I just need to" because our hypercompetitive society cultivates in us an addiction to self-development and because people buy more junk when they think they need more junk. If you are your own, it makes sense. You'll need to keep acquiring to fill yourself up and give your personhood some weight in the world. But even though you can acquire a lot of things and experience a lot of pleasures, you aren't actually free to love them.

Love requires presence. Love cannot be always looking ahead or to the left or right. Why is it that when someone stares intently into our eyes and says they love us we feel a chill? Your body recognizes that this "I love you" means something different from others. When they stare into your eyes, they are attending *to you*. They are giving their presence to your presence rather than rushing ahead to the future.

Love requires us to be still and take joy in the goodness of this moment. And if we are not our own but belong to Christ, that's exactly what we are free to do. You don't have to prove anything. You don't have to acquire more. You don't have to weigh your options and consider what you might be missing out on. You are free to be present and attend to the gift in front of you whether it's your spouse, your child, a song, a pleasant talk with a friend, or the wind in the trees.

Of course, this is not efficient. Efficiency demands that we always pursue the best option available. It asks: Can you use this time more productively? Is this the best person you can marry? Can't my child do better than this? Is this the best career for me? Is looking at this tree a good use of my time when I haven't emailed my manager yet?

But that's precisely the point. The reign of technique robs us of the gifts God gives us and leaves us in an inhuman environment. We aren't free to love anything because there's always something else. But if we are not our own, then there can be (and are!) higher values than efficiency, like love, gratitude, beauty, and goodness. Then it turns out that delighting in the gift you have is far more freeing than desiring any improper gift you can imagine.

When you don't have the "freedom" to view the unageing naked bodies of any type of woman whenever you like, you may begin to delight in the contingency of your wife, to love every inch of her aging body, which is sexually inaccessible to you most of the time because of the toils of everyday life. That doesn't make denying yourself easy, but it does make it human.

Learning to love your spouse's very human body, learning to delight in sex that is contingent on health and stress and feelings of security and love makes sex more human, not less. It submits sexual pleasure to human limits rather than submitting the human body to instrumental use. It's inefficient for the sake of love and beauty. As we saw in our discussion of pornography, it would be more efficient to turn to pornography when your spouse's body begins to age or when you desire something "new." It would be more efficient for you to just masturbate when your spouse is too burdened by life to be intimate. But to treat your spouse and yourself and your neighbor (in this case, all those whose pornographic pictures are available to you) as fully human rather than as tools, you must love them by denying those desires. Only if you are not your own does that sacrifice make sense.

And what is true of sex in marriage is true of the beauty of friendships, nature, our bodies, art, and all other good things in this life: when we reject efficiency as our meta-value, we are free to delight in the contingent, broken, aging, incomplete, and yet beautiful gifts God has given us.

●　　●　　●

The Christian alternative to technique is *prodigality*, which requires the faith to be still, to depend on God for your future. We live prodigally when we act according to love or goodness or beauty rather than primarily efficiency. The overflowing cup which God gives David in the twenty-third Psalm is prodigal. Strictly speaking, there is no need to fill a cup until it overflows. The expensive ointment Mary uses to anoint the feet of Jesus is prodigal. As Judas observed in John 12, a more efficient use of the ointment would have been to alleviate poverty. Our very lives are prodigal. God did not need to create us. But He did, and it was and is good.

This isn't to say that we should be inefficient for the sake of being inefficient. That is no less inhuman than being efficient for the sake of efficiency. Prodigality simply means a way of being in the world that takes for granted God's existence, goodness, and providence, freeing us from the Responsibilities of Self-Belonging so that we can joyfully attend to what is present. It is prodigal because from a contemporary secular perspective it appears to be wasteful; you are not primarily focused on whether or not you are "winning," "benefiting," or "progressing" through the action.

One model of this prodigality can be seen in Josef Pieper's short but brilliant work *Leisure: The Basis of Culture*. I've already mentioned Pieper's criticism of our culture of "Total Work," which he ties to the vice of *acedia*, a restless rejection of living before God. In the contemporary world, *acedia* is often justified through technique and progress. To resist an entire culture addicted to *acedia* and technique, Pieper calls us to leisure. While contemporary people are quite good at vacationing and amusing ourselves, we are terrible at leisure, in Pieper's sense of the word—because leisure is done in absolute trust in God and His providence: "Leisure is possible only on the premise that man consents to his own true nature and abides in concord with the meaning of the universe."[23] Put differently, we can only have leisure—true rest—when we can stand before God and accept that we are not our own.

For modern people, leisure will often involve intentionally choosing not to use all the conveniences, options, technologies, and powers available to us. In Ellul's language, "Man will agree not to do all he is capable of," which sounds like the opposite of being prodigal to most of us.[24] We may think of prodigality as lavishness or wastefulness, but Christian prodigality is the act of submitting efficiency under the influence of other, higher values. We may think of leisure as doing whatever makes us most physically comfortable, but Christian leisure is the practice of delighting gratefully in God's creation without regard for what is easiest, simplest, or cheapest.

Maybe sitting on your porch and reading to your children has been proven in studies to improve their vocabulary by five points (I just made that up), but to read leisurely is to read to them on the porch because it's lovely outside and you love your children and it's a good book. It may be that gardening reduces stress and helps the environment, but you garden leisurely when you enjoy the feel of the earth in your hands and the taste of fresh tomatoes and the beauty of a well-designed flower garden. In a business, prodigal leadership could involve paid parental leave because children are a gift from God, not because the benefit will attract better employees. It could mean closing on Sundays despite the dramatic loss in sales. Again, some of these things have "measurable benefits," but to act prodigally is to make decisions based on love, goodness, and beauty rather than efficiency or productivity or profit. Whereas we tend to feel reassured when we can justify our pleasure in terms of measurable benefits, Pieper warns, "It is impossible to attempt to engage in leisure for health's sake. . . . Leisure cannot be achieved at all when it is sought as a means to an end."[25]

To act prodigally also means that you have no need (or, ideally, no urge) to document your actions in order to prove your development to others via social media. Too often our motive for some activity is the benefit we will

accrue when others see us. Making a lovely dinner because it's lovely and
not to post it to Instagram is leisure. Watching a great film because it's great
and not so you can post your opinion on Twitter is leisure. From our contemporary society's perspective, there is something wasteful about these
actions. We want to know that there is a clear, provable benefit—otherwise,
like the older brother in the parable of the prodigal son (Luke 15:11-32), or
like Judas when Mary broke her expensive jar of perfume and bathed Jesus'
feet in it (John 12:1-8), we grow bitter at the waste.

If we are our own, we need to justify everything we do. We need to know
that we are optimizing and competing and improving. But if we are not our
own but belong to Christ, things can just be good. And that's enough.

•   •   •

A Christian anthropology explains my daily experience of meaning: that
it includes but transcends my personal experience, that the "feeling" of
meaning is not the same thing as meaning. A Christian anthropology makes
best sense of the joy I experience listening to beautiful music. It makes best
sense of the love I feel for other people. It makes best sense of my desire for
justice. Between the existence of meaning and validity of value, Christianity
makes best sense of the parts of life that mean the most to me. I know alternative explanations for the desire for justice I feel in the face of hor-
rendous human evil. I know how the pleasure of music can come from
specific musical intervals, cultural norms, and memories. And I know how
love can be explained through biology and evolutionary psychology. But
each of those explanations necessarily leaves me with an impoverished
version of some essential part of my life. In that way, belonging to Christ
does not negate or deny the good things in this world. Instead, it reminds
me that those good things don't just feel good. They really are good.

Our belonging before God. If we are not our own but belong to Christ, then
we are not free to belong wherever and to whomever we choose. We have
limits and obligations. But we also can never be lost. No matter how uncertain,
disorienting, and alienating the world may become, we can never be lost.

A defining feature of our moment in history is that we have tremendous
freedom to choose where we belong. Society provides us the technology and

laws to join and separate ourselves at will from family, place, community, religion, and so on. And if we are our own, it is only right that our commitments should be "until further notice" commitments. A Christian anthropology asks much of us because it denies us the modern liberal right to define our own communities and commitments. Our most significant commitments are not ones we choose, but those given to us: church, family, and place.

No one chooses who they will be born to or their family's history. They are given to us. And no parent should be able to choose the child that is born to them. They are given to us. We are given to each other. These basic, natural, familial bonds place obligations on us, regardless of our preferences. Though that is not to say that you should put up with abuse or blindly submit to your family's will for your life. Please don't hear that.

The particular way your obligations to family play out will depend on the circumstances and the specific shape of your relationship. But *that* you have obligations, that you *belong* to them in some basic way, is not a choice. It is a fact about the world. Most Americans are much more likely to err by denying our obligation to family than to suffer abuse because of those obligations. However, there are many exceptions to this general rule. A number of cultures in America still retain a high respect for family, and in those cultures the greater danger is in putting up with abuse in the name of family. We must use wisdom.

The same may be said for the body of Christ. To follow Christ, to acknowledge that you belong to Him and that He died for your sins, requires accepting the obligation of belonging to the church. And if you have been in a church long enough, you know that this commitment is not an easy cross to bear. People disappoint. It is much easier to cut and run when belonging is unpleasant, painful, or uncomfortable.

While belonging to the church, you will be hurt. You will have to learn to love people who look different from you, who have different interests, passions, and languages. You'll have to give sacrificially to support people who in a strict meritocracy don't "deserve" your compassion or aid. You'll have to submit to the right leadership of elders. You'll have to get over yourself and get out of your head. Maybe hardest of all, you'll have to do all this while rejecting the lie that it is your love and service that makes you righteous or important or justified. You are righteous because Christ is righteous. You love and serve because He loved and served you.

Like family relationships, your belonging to a particular church does not mean that you should put up with abuse or surrender your reason and discernment and will. God has given you a desire for justice and a mind so that you can name what is evil and make wise decisions. But even when sin and circumstances compel you to leave a particular local congregation (a decision that should only be reached with great fear and trembling), you still belong to the body of Christ, the universal church. You still have obligations to care for fellow believers, preach the Word, and commit to a local community of Christians.

To a lesser extent, we belong to where we live. Our contemporary anthropology tends to make us think of our surroundings as tools for self-development or improvement. If we are our own, then the natural world and the architecture of a city are valuable only if I can use them to get ahead. For example, it may be advantageous for me to care about the natural world so that the polar ice caps don't melt and send Florida into the ocean—but I don't fundamentally *owe* creation anything.

But if the Christian account of human persons is correct, where I am matters. By dwelling in a place, I am forming a relationship with it, one with bonds and obligations. I don't have the freedom to alienate or separate myself from my physical environment any more than it has the freedom to deny me. There may be situations that justify leaving home and recommitting to a new place, but like leaving a church or distancing ourselves from our family, we should approach such decisions with extreme trepidation and prayer. God has created us as mobile beings. There is nothing inherently wrong with moving for work. But if we belong to Christ, our default ought to be that we see ourselves committed to our families, friends, communities, places, and the church. This is where we belong, even when it is difficult.

Once again, the Christian anthropology does not lead to a pain-free life. It requires us to accept our place in the world. We can move and leave abusive churches and cut off destructive family members, but we should see each of these actions as a tragic diversion from the way things ought to be, not as an opportunity to express our individuality or become our true selves.

Belonging to a place does not just involve a commitment to the community and your neighbors, but also an effort to live in the natural environment. Ellul notes that one of the dehumanizing aspects of the modern world is that we live in an almost entirely artificial habitat:

> The human being was made to breathe the good air of nature, but what he breathes is an obscure compound of acids and coal tars. He was created for a living environment, but he dwells in a lunar world of stone, cement, asphalt, glass, cast iron, and steel. The trees wilt and blanch among sterile and blind stone façades.... Man was created to have room to move about in, to gaze into far distances, to live in rooms which, even when they were tiny, opened out on fields.[26]

Today it's possible to live in a specific space and be utterly ignorant and unaffected by the unique creational qualities of that space. But our belonging to Christ does not permit indifference to His mighty work of creation. This has ecological and architectural implications. Growing up in the High Desert of California, one of my most depressing, regular experiences was the sudden appearance of a suburban housing tract with its bright colors and green lawns, surrounded by high brick walls. And beyond those walls a vast expanse of desert spread with Joshua trees, juniper bushes, and jackrabbits. The "city" was alien to the land and I could *feel* its alienness, even as a child.

We may not be able to effectively stop the construction of houses alien to the land, or protect the environment from industry, or make our cities more walkable and natural, but belonging to Christ compels us to resist, to advocate for living among the beauty of God's mighty work of creation.

I fear that this section, like my discussion of values, will trouble many readers. I may be introducing you to obligations and commitments that you've disregarded in the past. Accepting that you belong to your family will almost certainly result in being hurt and taken advantage of by others. Accepting that you belong to the church will almost certainly make you vulnerable and cost you time and resources you could more efficiently use to advance yourself. Accepting that you belong to the place where you live will force you to care about your neighbors when it would be much easier to write the place off and move away. This last implication is particularly difficult for young people who have been brought up to believe that they are free to move wherever they like, to pursue whatever career they like. What would happen if we begin to encourage young people to consider the needs of the *immediate community* as they explore career options? It takes no small amount of courage and sacrifice to accept that you belong to other people and to serve them accordingly.

Although a Christian anthropology involves obligations that we do not choose, they are categorically different from the Responsibilities of Self-Belonging. As we saw in the previous chapter, the Responsibilities of Self-Belonging are by their nature, first, solely our responsibility; second, always inadequately met, no matter how hard we try; and third, used to justify our lives, which means success depends on overcoming an impossible task by ourselves.

But the obligations that naturally come from rightly belonging to people and places (whether we chose them or not) are not fulfilled in order that our lives are justified and we aren't alone. Because I belong to my family, I am free to serve them without the lie that my service makes me important or determines my place in the family. I serve *because* I belong, not *to* belong.

●　●　●

Belonging to God, the church, our families, our city, and our neighbors is difficult and limiting, but it's also comforting. Consider the way people use the phrase "We need you." When someone we know is plagued by suicidal ideation, we may find ourselves encouraging them by reminding them, "We need you," or, "The world needs you." Such a claim implies an obligation between us; it implies that we cannot decide to take our *own life* because we are *not our own.*

Why is it that we find the statement "We need you" to be so reassuring? After all, their need puts a burden upon us, limiting our freedom to exist autonomously. If other people need us, and if it *matters* that other people need us, then shouldn't we experience that need as a limitation? Indeed, in some cases that is exactly how we experience others' reliance upon us.

All parents feel this tension at one time or another—that their children's dependence on them radically limits their freedom. But I think these annoyances are the exceptions. For one, they tend to be fleeting. The parent who has bitter thoughts about his newborn restricting his social life or career will usually recognize the vanity and egotism of such thoughts. It may take looking at the sleeping child in her crib, or snuggling with her while she laughs, but proper relationships of dependence and obligation are not experienced as unjust limits to our freedom except in moments of personal failure.

If we really are our own, "We need you!" is just a way to manipulate people into feeling that they belong so they don't commit suicide. But if we belong to Christ, then it is true. We do need each other. Within the church, each of us needs the other members of the body of Christ. To a lesser but still significant extent, we also belong to our neighbors outside the church. We are called to love them and dwell with them in peace and seek their interests (Philippians 2:4). We "need" them in the sense that we share obligations with them, whether to a family or a city or nation. Belonging to someone beyond ourselves is a comfort.

●　●　●

To live in a high tech, ultra-mobile society of sovereign individuals and perpetually changing norms (liquid modernity) is to be haunted with disorientation and disequilibrium. Speaking prophetically about what the "death of God" would mean for humanity, Nietzsche's madman asked, "Whither are we moving? Away from all suns? Are we not plunging continually? Backward, sideward, forward, in all directions?"[27] Nietzsche saw that the loss of God as a foundational belief in Europe would result in disequilibrium because the old order of the cosmos would retreat only to be replaced by private order imposed on the world by each of us individually. We feel as if we are untethered, floating in space. Free to move but unable to touch the ground.

All bonds feel tentative and uncertain. Our place in the world feels speculative and subject to change. We wonder where we truly belong and how we can ever know that we belong. Our anxiety over belonging makes us highly sensitive to the flaws and betrayals and disappointments that attend all human efforts at community. We are not surprised when a friend betrays us, but it does cause us to question if we can ever belong safely anywhere.

A Christian anthropology does not protect from such flaws, betrayals, and disappointments. It can't. But knowing that we are not our own because we already, always, and rightly belong to Christ means that our place among creation is secure. We may not subjectively *feel* secure. We may doubt ourselves. And we will still struggle to live in a society that undermines commitment and belonging at every turn. But *objectively* we belong.

This objective belonging, which means belonging before and because of God, is completely different from Bréne Brown's everywhere-and-nowhere belonging.[28] For Brown, we belong anywhere we choose to be, but we also belong nowhere because we belong to ourselves and only in ourselves can we find the belonging we desire.

The nature of belonging, much like meaning and identity, is to belong *with* someone or something. To fit within a community requires there to be a community. If we stand alone in the wilderness, which is Brown's advice, then at best we can only ever belong to the wilderness.

But belonging to Christ means that there is always a being before whom we find ourselves. It means that no matter how disorienting society might become, no matter how dislocated we feel in a shifting world, the God of the cosmos knows us. He knows precisely where we are. This is not mere theological abstraction, either. Christ's body here on earth is the church. When you accept your belonging in Christ and His sacrifice for your sins, you are united with His body. You have a place, a role, a purpose within a community across space and time. Human institutions will come and go, communities will form and disintegrate, congregations will grow and wither—but your union with Christ remains secure.

THE PRACTICE OF GRACE

By now this is all starting to sound repetitive because we have stumbled upon a number of truths about life that our contemporary world had previously obscured. Not that these are new truths. Far from it. They are very, very old. Acknowledging a Christian anthropology has basically the same implication for each sphere of life: grace alone sustains us. When we accept the grace of God rather than denying it and striving for self-sufficiency, the basis for every major contemporary anxiety is removed. But because we continue to live in a culture that dogmatically asserts that we are our own and belong to ourselves, we will continue to experience these anxieties. So long as our society is built and maintained for a false idea of humanity, humans will chafe under the disorder. When you go against the grain of nature, you are bound to get splinters. You have very limited control over this disorder, but you have some control over your response, which should be gracious.

We are radically contingent on God for our creation and preservation. Our contingency upon God frees us to delight in creation as it is—and that includes ourselves. In that sense, life is the long practice of accepting grace. We may start with the common grace of creation, but that grace calls us onward to the truer, greater grace of God, the forgiveness of sins and our union with Christ. In accepting Christ's sacrifice for our sins, we acknowledge our need for redemption and our inability to redeem ourselves. In accepting our union with Christ, we acknowledge that we have never actually been autonomous.

Secular affirmation offers what claims to be unconditional hope, but in every case it depends upon us granting ourselves affirmation based exclusively on our own will, which never fulfills for long. We either submit to the tyranny of technique (total work, perpetual self-improvement, success, etc.) or we declare ourselves to be good by personal fiat. Both strategies devolve into Resignation at some point, when total work breaks us or when personal affirmations are revealed to be hollow.

Our radical contingency—the way of grace—does not free us from the obligation to live rightly, but it does change the terms of our ethical duty. Living rightly before God is a way of living honestly in the world, of being our true self. It does not justify your existence or define your identity. It is an outflowing of the truth, the practice of grace.

6

WHAT CAN WE DO?

A T THIS POINT YOU MIGHT EXPECT ME to introduce my "Five Steps for Changing Your Life by Accepting That You Are Not Your Own." But as this is a work of nonfiction, I won't be doing that.

It would be a relief if the problems described in the previous chapters could be fixed by simply changing the way you think about yourself. But the premise of this book is that the damage caused by our false anthropology is much greater than the sum of our individual beliefs. If everyone in America suddenly acknowledged that they are not their own but belong to God, we would still be left with systems, institutions, practices, and tools that are designed for the sovereign self, and it wouldn't take long before we found ourselves right back where we started. We cannot evangelize our way out of this problem. We cannot volunteer our way out. We need a miracle.

Our desire for a program of self-improvement, a personal method of accepting that you are not your own, is itself a symptom of the problem. We believe we can use technique to solve the problems of a society governed by technique—but as we've discovered, that does not work.

However, understanding our time can help us. When you come to see how contemporary anthropology shapes our desires, forms our society, and drives us to depression and despair, you are better able to resist its influence. There is tremendous power in the ability to rightly name things and calling the Responsibilities of Self-Belonging what they are—a lie—can be a great source of comfort. The burden to be someone, to live life to the fullest, to endlessly iterate and optimize and compete—when we observe these for what they are, it takes some of their power away.

But here's the thing: the housewife who can name and denounce the lie that meaningfulness in life is entirely tied to career success still lives under a government that perceives her as less valuable. She still lives with neighbors who believe the lie and judge her according to it. She still is exposed to endless techniques for improving her parenting or cooking or posture or sex life, each of which is a sign of her failure, reminding her that she can't measure up. She still shops at stores filled with poorly made plastic, disposable products that end up in landfills and were manufactured by people on another continent whose lives she cannot possibly imagine and for whom labor is rarely ever dignifying or human, a job only tolerable because it feeds their children.

Believing that you are not your own but belong to God truly is a comfort in life and death. It is our only real comfort—all others are derivative. But comfort is not peace. And so long as our society is premised on a false anthropology, we will live in deep tension. The lion remains in the zoo, even after he discovers that it is not his true home.

● ● ●

Living in a society governed by technique and inspired by a spirit of Affirmation, we know exactly what to do when we identify a problem in life:

1. Define the problem.

2. Explain why it exists.

3. Develop a targeted solution.

4. Implement the solution.

In the more advanced forms of problem solving, these steps are cyclical and we continually test our diagnosis and evaluate the efficiency of our solution until we've worked out the imperfections and "fixed" the problem.

I want to begin this chapter by inviting you to reconsider our default method of responding to problems. Many problems can be effectively addressed through careful analysis, evaluation, and action items. For example, this is roughly the method I would use to repair a leaky faucet or to write legislation to simplify our tax code. But some problems cannot be solved by gathering more data and developing targeted action items—not even if you constantly assess your strategy and fine-tune it with better data. That doesn't mean that we should lose hope of anything getting better or that we should cease doing good. It just means that we have to think of our role in changing the world differently.

● ● ●

I worry that someone will read this book and conclude that we just need to adjust our anthropology and then things will be fixed: that if we all recognize when we buy into the lie of Affirmation or the despair of Resignation, if we are honest about the ways we try to cope with life through self-medication, if we evaluate every way we might contribute to the instrumentalizing of other humans or the reign of technique, and if we all individually choose to live in accordance with the truth that we are not our own but belong to God—*then* we will be okay.

I am not saying this. The last thing I want to do is burden you with yet another way you are failing at life and another way to fix yourself and the world through self-optimization. Whether you find yourself among the affirming or resigned, you already feel that burden acutely. You may still delude yourself into thinking that you can manage the burden, but you are carrying it in one way or another.

Instead of a strategy for fixing society or for self-improvement, I am going to offer what I believe to be wise counsel. These recommendations are untestable and have no data to prove their effectiveness that I am aware of, although I'm sure such data exists. Data always exists.

GRACE

The place we all must begin is with grace for our neighbors and ourselves. The practices of our contemporary anthropology are not going to go away any time soon, and simply being aware that we live in a society that is unfit for humans will not make the inhumanity go away.

Therefore, we ought to expect that life will remain difficult—inordinately and senselessly difficult. In a rightly ordered and just society, the desire to self-medicate, which is so ubiquitous in our own time, would be dramatically reduced. Undoubtedly people would still find reasons to distract or numb themselves to their suffering and guilt, but not, I think, with the same obsessive fervor that animates so many people today. And certainly not with the massive market machinery that promotes and enables endless varieties of self-medication. But we don't live in a rightly ordered and just society and we should not expect that fact to change any time soon.

Instead, we must "wait without hope," as T. S. Eliot says.[1] This phrase, which we'll look at more closely in a moment, has occasionally been misinterpreted to mean that Eliot, himself a Christian, had no hope for the resurrection. But the hope Eliot tells his readers to wait without is false hope: a hope that demands results, an impatient hope, a hope that is pragmatic, a hope that rushes to action, a hope that cannot be still and know that God is God.[2]

This false hope naturally leads to bitterness. When we are convinced that we have the plan for redeeming the world and that we are the agents of that redemption (whether it be spiritual or political or physical), we won't have grace for those who aren't part of our movement or who aren't doing enough. The inadequacies of others become intolerable because redemption is just around the corner if those people would just get on board. When your neighbor fails to recycle, or they don't vote the right way, or they aren't as righteous as they ought to be, you grow bitter at them. It is because we wait without hope that we can have grace for our neighbors.

While we wait for Christ to return, coping with sin, injustice, suffering, and a society that is not built for humans will be difficult. In my own life, I've seen the ways I use sitcoms as diversions from the stress of life and jokes on social media to deal with the anxieties of parenting in a culture where everyone has advice and a better system. I've seen how spending fifteen minutes each morning coordinating my shirt, tie, slacks, socks, shoes, sweater, and pocket square is a way of exercising some measure of order and beauty on my days that so often feel frantic and stale.

Creation and cultural works help me to cope with the burden of contemporary life, just like everyone else. Ideally, I wouldn't need help with this burden. But I don't live in an ideal world, and neither do you.

What I know is that when I am exhausted from working and my kids are getting into fights and the AC unit breaks in the middle of summer, it is a good thing to ease my anxiety by making a pun on Twitter. It is pleasant to laugh at a well-made sitcom with my wife after the kids go to bed. It's even good to spend fifteen minutes coordinating my socks and pocket squares. Some methods of coping are inherently sinful, some are self-destructive, and some are addictive. But some of them are just less good choices. Not bad choices, but *as methods of coping* some of them are less good. If I were a better man, more spiritually and intellectually mature, maybe I'd only find comfort in poetry, prayer, contemplation, and walks in nature. Sometimes I do, but this society is brutal and there is no shame in finding joy in simple pleasures that ease the burden we carry, even if those pleasures are "less good."

I can hear you thinking, "Why would you choose a less good method to cope?" We can't consciously choose anything less than optimal without beating ourselves up over it. And this is precisely the danger, that we turn our rest into yet another task to master, another opportunity to compete and maximize efficiency.

In designing creation, God took our human frailty into account, and blessed us with a number of gifts that help make life tolerable. Understood rightly, these are ways that belonging to God is a comfort in life. For example, Ecclesiastes makes it clear that we can and should take comfort in the fruit of our toil, bread and wine, and the joy of sex with our spouse:

> Go, eat your bread with joy, and drink your wine with a merry heart, for God has already approved what you do.
>
> Let your garments be always white. Let not oil be lacking on your head.
>
> Enjoy life with the wife whom you love, all the days of your vain life that he has given you under the sun, because that is your portion in life and in your toil at which you toil under the sun. (Ecclesiastes 9:7-9)

In two prior passages, the Preacher of Ecclesiastes tells us that taking pleasure and enjoyment in toil and the fruit of our toil is a gift from God (2:24-25; 3:12-13). Simple, honest pleasures ease the strain of living. Similarly, the psalmist proclaims in his great litany on the wonder of God's creation that God created wine to "gladden the heart of man" (Psalm 104:15). This is a frank acknowledgment that in this life we will need to have our hearts gladdened, and that God uses His creation (grapes) along with human works (wine) to gladden us. In addition to bread, wine, and love, we might add dad jokes, running, an NBA playoff game, a good book, and listening to well-made music. None of these joys can justify our existence, define our identity, give life meaning, determine our values, or grant us belonging, but they can give us the comfort of pleasure. As gifts from God, they are good.

This is where Josef Pieper's theory of leisure can help us. Leisure is a kind of rest from labor that depends upon God and does not require any utilitarian justification. In fact, it cannot have a utilitarian justification and be leisure. Pieper goes on to explain that at the heart of leisure is divine worship.[3] Understood this way, these simple pleasures of life, which do in fact help you cope with the trauma of modernity, find their basis in the worship of God. When we delight in the good things God has given us, with gratitude toward Him and without any utilitarian justification, without any effort to "earn" our joy and pleasure, then it is a form of worship.

The Preacher of Ecclesiastes justifies his recommendation of pleasures to cope with vanity precisely because these pleasures are gifts from God. Moral pleasures are manifestations of God's providential grace to us, reminders that He is good and that our suffering is only for a time. They are reminders that the right order of things, the telos toward which we are moving if we accept Him as the Son of God, is love. In delighting in these gifts, we honor Him.

The inhuman nature of society does not excuse sinful behavior, nor am I absolving us of the responsibility to be discerning about our habits. All I am saying is that in a society that always demands more and more of us, God can use simple pleasures to comfort us, and that is good.

Once you accept that contemporary life is inhuman, that God gives us good gifts to comfort us, and that even when there are ideal forms of leisure it is still fine to take pleasure in simple gifts, it ought to humble you and give you grace for your neighbors and yourself.

This means that you should avoid judging people who are really into sports or exercise or who, in your opinion, spend too much time on social media. You probably have no idea what burden they are carrying. You almost certainly have no idea whether they are delighting in that gift in gratitude to God or out of selfish despair. Should they be mature enough to never binge watch *Friends* after a demoralizing day at work? Maybe. But we also shouldn't live in a society that treats us as inhuman tools. Sometimes laughing for a few hours, even at a corny sitcom, can remind us that *we* don't carry the weight of the world on our shoulders—a providential gift from a God who knows our weakness and suffering, a God who made wine to gladden our hearts.

When you feel that someone might be coping with life in ways that could distract them from God, dull their senses, or waste their time, go ahead and pray for them. When appropriate, recommend pleasurable gifts from God that are more restful and edifying. But focus on your own self-control. Work to make your community a little more human. Remember that you have your own coping strategies that are "less good." And just because your coping strategies might be more socially acceptable doesn't mean they are any better. Work to improve your own habits of coping (use Philippians 4:8 as your guide). But most of all, have grace for your neighbors and yourself, because God does.

A BRIEF WORD ABOUT PERSONAL RESPONSIBILITY

I suspect that some readers finished the previous section and are worried that I'm just making excuses for people, maybe for myself. Perhaps you wondered whether acknowledging the brokenness of society as a major source of our suffering just invites us to disregard personal responsibility.

One of the clearest divides in American politics is over the question of personal agency. Does each individual American citizen have the right and the ability to live the American Dream? Are our successes and failures the results of our own actions and mindsets, or the result of environmental and biological forces? Very few thoughtful people on the right or left actually believe that people have complete agency or are completely determined, although it may seem they do based on the political rhetoric we hear.

There is a tangential debate about agency with practical implications: how does a belief in agency or determinism affect our actions? Each side frames the argument differently. From the right: "If we tell people that their fate is largely determined by forces out of their control, then we are inviting them to give up on life and blame their failures on the system." And from the left: "If we tell people that they are largely responsible for their own fate, we are inviting failure and self-loathing, which will lead to them giving up on life when they blame all their failures on themselves." This argument has less to do with how much agency we actually have and more to do with the power of belief. Some people will argue that even though we don't control our own fate, we must tell ourselves that we do or we'll become resigned.

I'm not arguing for defeatism, but neither am I an advocate of Positive Thinking. Our society is inhuman in large part due to the near-universal acceptance of an anthropology that denies our nature. So engrained is this anthropology in our institutions, values, and practices that even if many of us were to consciously reject it, we would still live with the lingering effects for years.

America has spent over 150 years dealing with racism and it will probably take another 150 years, at least. But that does not give anyone the right to ignore racial injustice. It doesn't absolve anyone of personal responsibility to live righteously, but we also have no right to lie to people about the existence of racism just so they'll be more optimistic about their own agency. Similarly, we have no right to lie to ourselves or others about the disorder that's endemic in society just so we'll be more optimistic about our own agency.

More importantly, it doesn't mean we stop hoping for justice. Let's return to T. S. Eliot.

> I said to my soul, be still, and wait without hope
> For hope would be hope for the wrong thing; wait without love,
> For love would be love of the wrong thing; there is yet faith
> But the faith and the love and the hope are all in the waiting.[4]

This is no defeatism or determinism. On the contrary, it's the greatest possible form of hope: an absolute faith in God's faithfulness and His ability to bring justice and truth and beauty in circumstances where we can no longer imagine them.

I suspect this part of the book would feel much more satisfying if I lied to you, but I'm not going to. You will not save the world; you can't even save yourself. At best, you may see the corruption in society more clearly, you may be better prepared to deal with the indignities of the modern world, and you may make small, rear-guard advances for truth, goodness, and beauty in your sphere of influence. I hope you do! But if you can get over yourself and stop thinking in terms of efficiency, you can honor God and love your neighbor while having faith that He will set things to right. Don't let yourself ask, "Is this good deed making any real difference?" If it really is the right thing to do, the efficiency does not matter.

Your obligation is faithfulness, not productivity or measurable results. As Paul reminded the church in Corinth, "Neither he who plants nor he who waters is anything, but only God who gives the growth" (1 Corinthians 3:7). Or, as Eliot said, "For us there is only the trying. The rest is not our business."[5] And it isn't.

But the "trying" is no small thing. "Trying" and "waiting without hope" require courage and faithfulness. That they require more courage than Resignation is not surprising, but they also require more courage than Affirmation or "waiting with hope." It is not difficult to work courageously when you believe that your actions will turn the tide and bring about change. It is another thing altogether to act courageously without the expectation that you will change the world.

Such a courage is the paradox at the center of this chapter, this book, and the Christian life. In action we try to be self-sufficient, autonomous. Often, we act because we don't trust that we will be preserved otherwise. But our calling is to "be still and know" that God is God, and not *you* (Psalm 46:10).

It's not too difficult to *act* and say that He is God. We frantically work all week to take care of ourselves and on Sunday we sit in church anxiously going over all the things we still need to get done. When we sing, we say that He is God, but our hearts are committed to self-sufficiency. We don't actually *know* that He is God, we just act like it. This a religious form of Affirmation.

It's also not too difficult to be still and *deny* that He is God, which is a form of Resignation. We give up on the possibility of life getting better and distract ourselves with meaningless pleasures. The stillness of Resignation is actually *acedia*—the hopeless sloth that medieval monks referred to as the "noonday devil."[6] Once you accept that there is no God, you can rest in the meaninglessness of life and stop trying.

The hard thing is to be still *and* know that He is God. But that is the only way you can know Him. A holy stillness accepts that God is sovereign and rests in His goodness and grace. It accepts that you cannot save the world or yourself. A holy stillness leads to action, but an action in stillness.

Here is the paradox. In holy stillness we acknowledge God's presence and provision. In holy action we acknowledge our moral obligation to God and our neighbor. But because it is action in stillness, we don't entertain the lie that our actions can ever produce self-sufficiency. Stillness is resting in God's grace. Action is an extension of that grace and nothing more. Because we are not our own, we can be still. Because we belong to God, we can act in humility.

When you stand transparently before God it is impossible not to desire in love to obey Him, but it is also impossible to imagine that the world or even your own righteousness rests on your shoulders.

When we rest in God's sovereignty, we can honestly observe how society negatively affects us without making excuses for our sins or denying personal responsibility. When we rest in God's sovereignty, we can act to do good without deluding ourselves into thinking that we will save the world. When we rest in God's sovereignty, we can have grace for ourselves and our neighbors as we cope with an inhuman society that will only be saved by God.

WITH PALMS TURNED UPWARDS

What have we to do
But stand with empty hands and palms turned upwards
In an age which advances progressively backwards?[7]

In a beautiful poem on what we might call "the problem of the city," T. S. Eliot identifies many of the maladies that we have discussed thus far in this book: dehumanization, technique, alienation, the decay of communities, the emptiness of consumerism, secularization, the inhuman environment of the modern city, and so on. As one response to the problem of the city, Eliot writes the lines quoted above.

Through all these pages we have looked at what we could now describe, with T. S. Eliot, as a society that "advances progressively backwards"—a wonderfully paradoxical image. Our society hastens to advance and to progress. We learn to tolerate the injustices and insecurities of our own time only because we have faith that things are advancing and progressing and one day life won't be so bad.

But our "progress" has in many ways contributed to our inhuman environment. We have been progressing backwards. Yes, real progress has been made in some areas, on certain issues of justice and morality, issues of race and discrimination in America, for example. Simultaneously, we have made our social world less human in other ways. We treat one another as instruments to our personal ends. We are burned out from ceaselessly striving to meet our Responsibilities for Self-Belonging. And what makes it all but unbearable is that we *continue* to advance.

It feels as if this progress is unstoppable. We may observe that we are moving backwards. We may lament the inhuman conditions of work or the marketplace or the home. But we seem helpless to do anything to stop or even slow the "progress." People will continue to develop more efficient techniques and technologies. We will continue to adopt them to keep up. And we will continue discovering the unintended consequences of these developments after they have done their damage and we have already moved on to a new technique. This too feels overwhelming. You may even ask if this entire conversation is worth having if we can't start a revolution to entirely remake society.

These lines from Eliot suggest that we really only have one response to the inhuman conditions of our world: to stretch out our hands in supplication to God.

True supplication is not passivity or resignation. It is an act of dependence upon God, which always involves obedience to His will. When we reach out in supplication before God, we don't get to ignore injustice or the dehumanizing structures of society. But it does mean that our actions are done in reliance upon God. As Eliot says elsewhere in "Choruses from 'The Rock,'" our duty is to "take no thought of the harvest, / But only of proper sowing."[8] Supplication is a form of acting in stillness before God.

Every Sunday as a part of our church's liturgy, the pastor invites the congregation to stretch out our hands, palm upwards, to receive God's benediction. The benediction sometimes comes from Numbers 6:24-26, which asks for the Lord's face to shine upon us. As in Eliot's lines, our hands are empty because we offer God nothing. We are literally empty-handed. All we can do is receive the gift of grace. We have nothing to offer in return. We cannot reach up and take it. All we can do is be still and receive God's grace. But we do have the obligation to meet together as the church and to stretch out our hands.

From the world's perspective, this is supreme foolishness. The spirit of the world demands action and plans and agendas and movements and cannot abide stillness. But faithfully doing the good that lies before us while waiting dependent upon God for redemption is the most meaningful action you can take. And it's the only way we can righteously respond to the crisis of our time.

• • •

To understand how these lines from Eliot offer us the way forward, we need to return to Jacques Ellul. His conception of "technique" explains our society's obsession with efficiency, which he diagnosed in his work *The Technological Society*. One of the great tragedies of Ellul's book is that when you come to the end and have been largely persuaded by his thesis and troubled by his warnings, you discover that he offers no answers. For that, we must look to a very different kind of book by Ellul: *The Meaning of the City*.

In this text, Ellul traces the biblical concept of the "city" from Cain's first founding through the New Jerusalem. Based on his exegesis of Genesis, Ellul argues that the fundamental spirit of the "city" is rebellion against God:

Cain has built a city. For God's Eden he substitutes his own, for the goal given to his life by God, he substitutes a goal chosen by himself— just as he substituted his own security for God's. Such is the act by which Cain takes his destiny on his own shoulders, refusing the hand of God in his life.[9]

Notice that the spirit of the city directly corresponds to the contemporary anthropology we have been studying. Ellul sees the construction of cities as human efforts to belong to ourselves, to create an environment that denies the reality of God's provision, a space where it grows easier and easier for humans to act without acknowledging their contingency upon God. The city walls keep them safe from animals and enemies. The shelters and collective living reduce the threat of natural disasters. The importation of food and other supplies frees city dwellers from the whims of the natural world. And the progress of the city, its laws and buildings and economy, gives hope for tomorrow. From the beginning cities have worked for this autonomy, but the modern world makes it even easier to refuse "the hand of God" in our lives: "It is only in an urban civilization that man has the metaphysical possibility of saying, 'I killed God.'"[10]

Ellul uses the term "city" to refer to civilization broadly—both ancient walled cities and modern urban spaces, places where people live overwhelmingly surrounded by a humanly built environment. By that definition virtually everyone in the West lives in the city now. Between our hyperconnectivity, rural high-speed internet, and our reliance on transported goods and services, we experience that dependency on the city to varying extents certainly across the United States, and to a lesser extent, the world. And despite the change in distance and time, Ellul says, "The nature of the city has not changed, for the nature of the world does not change."[11]

Ironically, according to Ellul, a city that is built to stand apart from God does not make humans freer; it makes them less human. The city is "a world for which man was not made."[12] In our own discussion we've seen this principle at work in anthropology. To the degree that the contemporary anthropology centers existence on the individual person, it creates an environment that's actually less conducive to human life. Ellul ominously concludes, "The very fact of living in the city directs a man down an inhuman road."[13]

The city is seductive—governed by logic and technique, but rejecting critiques of its own logic. It is vampiric—it turns people into machines and merchandise and enslaves them. People are seduced by the city because it promises to meet their every need (and thus make them independent of

God) and enable them to meet the Responsibilities of Self-Belonging. But it only makes them less human:

> He is used, consumed, eaten away, possessed in heart and soul, and the city gives him new complexes, requires of him new reflexes, transforms his tastes and his mental make-up. The demons push him on with their enormous power, forcing him to find in the city the realization of his desire for escape and liberty.[14]

The problems created by the city are the very problems it promises to solve.

Although Ellul does not frame his study in terms of anthropology, he describes the same problem (the inhuman environment of contemporary society) and identifies the same basic cause (human efforts to live autonomously aided by technology). The modern city is a space constructed for humans who are their own and belong to themselves.

We might expect Ellul to offer some practical corrective, some strategy for redeeming the city. Or we might expect him to call for renewed evangelism so that over time, as individuals come to Christ and turn from sin, the city will become a more human space.

But Ellul eschews both of these popular evangelical solutions to social ills. Instead, he warns us,

> There seems to be no theoretical solution to satisfy this problem. There is no theological demonstration for one to follow. The answer comes with life, day by day, in the conflict between the world's necessity and the liberty given us of God, between the world's wisdom (which we can never totally set aside) and the folly of the cross (which we can never totally live out).[15]

It is this emphasis on day-by-day faithfulness that I find so compelling about Ellul. Our egotistical temptation is to think that what matters in life is what is big and visible and political. So we make grand plans and join national movements in hopes that we can make a "real" difference. And no doubt, some political movements can make a real difference. But for the most part the answer to the city is found in millions of tiny decisions to live faithfully even while living in the city.

But what does "faithfully" mean in this context?

• • •

Looking at two examples of redeemed cities in the Bible, Nineveh and the New Jerusalem, Ellul argues that the only meaningful response to the problem of the city, the only righteous action Christians can take, the only thing we are obligated by God to do, is to glorify God in the city where we live.[16] We are not called to save the city because we can't. Our social engineering won't solve the problem. Our justice initiatives won't stop the city from eating people. Our evangelism won't slowly convert the city into Eden. But neither can we flee. Ellul points out repeatedly that God has not called us to leave the city. So long as we can remain and glorify Him, then we are obligated to stay and live.

This is difficult to understand. When a scholar like Ellul so persuasively criticizes the roots of our civilization, we expect one of two solutions: revolution or retreat. Ellul emphatically says "No!" to both. It is not in our power to redeem the city. That is God's task. God convicted and converted the entire city of Nineveh (Jonah 3). God will establish the redeemed city of New Jerusalem. There are no action items for us to complete, no strategies or methods or best practices for converting an entire city, let along an entire society. It is an act that can only be accomplished by God's intervention. So, too, does the hope for a New Jerusalem seem foolish from a worldly perspective, a city free from sin and sorrow whose light comes from the presence of God Himself. Only God can establish this beautiful, holy city on earth. In our own efforts we can do nothing to bring it about. In other words, Ellul, like Eliot, calls us to stretch out our hands, palms turned upwards, to receive God's work of grace.

• • •

Our task is to wait, as Eliot says, "without hope," because whenever we pin our hope to a specific political or social goal, we end up hoping for the wrong thing: a finite human solution. Whether it's hope in a pro-life Supreme Court that will end abortion or hope in a perfectly equitable economic system or hope in a party or politician or policy, our vision for how to "fix" society will always come up short.

But if we belong to God, we can have faith that He is bringing about His justice and His redemption. We may end up like Jonah if we are not careful. Jonah hoped for the wrong thing. He had seen the violence and evil committed by the Ninevites against the people of Israel and hoped that they would not repent and that God would destroy Nineveh. When God instead brought about the repentance of the Ninevites, Jonah became bitter. Even after the miraculous repentance of an entire city, he could not imagine God's plan as good.

If we insist that our society be fixed through a specific political or social agenda, we may grow bitter when God righteously chooses to bring redemption in a way we could never have imagined. Jonah could not save Nineveh. He couldn't even love it. Neither could Jonah bring about God's judgment upon Nineveh. What he could do in response to the wickedness of Nineveh, and what we must do in response to the inhuman conditions of our society, is represent God in the city.

●   ●   ●

Retreat from society has a certain appeal among Christians. Why should we continue to live in a space that is increasingly inhuman, that systemically denies God's existence, goodness, and providence, and that consumes fellow humans as fuel for the furnaces of greed and lust? If we cannot bring about the redemption of the city on our own, then why wait for judgment? Why persist in a space that is antagonistic toward us?

If we are not our own, then our obligation is to honor God with our lives. He has called us to stay in the city and to work for its good—but mostly to pray. Through the prophet Jeremiah, God commanded the Israelites exiled in Babylon to "seek the welfare of the city where I have sent you into exile, and pray to the Lord on its behalf" (Jeremiah 29:7). Much like Jonah, I can imagine that the exiled Israelites were not particularly eager to seek the welfare of their oppressors' city. Babylon, too, was an inhuman city. They may have longed for Jeremiah to tell them to rise up against Babylon or flee into the desert. But our plans, even when they seem just and wise, are not God's plans. Jeremiah's prophecy comes with a promise from God: "For in its welfare you will find your welfare." Our presence in the city brings glory to God and is a light to our neighbors and a judgment on rebellion against God. When we act knowing that we are not our own, we resist the spirit of the city, which insists we be free from God and His providence.

We should not have delusions of grandeur that we will save society, and we cannot flee society, but Ellul warns us that neither can we "integrate." Our "participation cannot be total with no limiting conditions."[17] In Christ's High Priestly Prayer, before His capture and crucifixion, He asks the Father *not* to take us out of this world, but instead to "keep them from the evil one" (John 17:15). Given the power of the "evil one" over the world, it is only through God that we can be kept from him.

To avoid integration, we must first be able to see and reject the seduction of the city. The city's promise that it can enable us to fulfill our Responsibilities for Self-Belonging demands us to give everything over to making a name for ourselves, establishing our autonomy, and building a good life free from limits. It promises to help us achieve this through its laws, technology, social norms, and stories. But it is an empty and soul-sucking promise. So our first task is to rightly discern and reject the spirit of the city while praying for the city's welfare.

Rejection must begin very simply: make a practice of calling out the contemporary anthropology as it appears in your life. Whenever an ad invites you to feel alive through buying a product, whenever a film implies that you will not be fulfilled until you embrace your inner self, whenever an expert urges you to optimize your life, whenever you feel inadequate in the face of overwhelming competition, call it what it is. This is an outworking of our contemporary anthropology. It's a false conception of the human person that assumes that I am my own and am solely responsible for making my life matter. It is a lie. I am not my own but belong to Christ.

● ● ●

Perhaps this approach seems too passive to you. We need a data-driven solution with measurable results, someone might say. "Empty hands and palms turned upwards" is no strategy for change, which is quite true, of course. It's not a strategy for saving the world; it's faith in the one who created and preserves the world:

But how is such a thing possible? It is beyond human strength, and only at Nineveh is such a thing shown as happening, with God's intervention. But our task is not to spend time pondering this success, but to obey our orders, and by doing so we enter into combat with the power of the city itself.[18]

Our desire to find a proven strategy for perfecting society is another example of technique's power over our imagination. What God asks of us is *prodigal* action—to work to love your city, to make beautiful things, and to care for the welfare of your neighbors, even if there are more "efficient" means available. Waiting on God's work of grace, which defies our expectations as it did Jonah's, appears to be foolish. What a waste of time and energy! And yet it is precisely this resting in God's work, not our own, that challenges the spirit of autonomy.

Alternatively, you may worry that putting our hope in Christ to redeem the world will become an excuse for us to stop seeking justice. Why bother to pursue justice if only Christ can bring true justice? Again, I would refer us back to Ellul's admonition: "Our task is not to spend time pondering this success, but to obey our orders."[19] Or T. S. Eliot: "For us there is only the trying. / The rest is not our business." We don't get to calculate the effectiveness of faithfulness or love. We don't get to reassess our commitment to justice when we don't see change happen. If abortions increase and racial justice remains elusive and wars develop in new and even more dehumanizing forms, we don't get to stop doing good. We have received orders from God to "do justice, and to love kindness, and to walk humbly with your God" (Micah 6:8).

You may never see the fruits of your labor in this life, but it doesn't matter. God did not call you to be successful. He called you to be faithful. However, if you are responsible for your own existence, only tangible, measurable, immediate success can come close to satisfying you. And you will grow increasingly frantic to see your political vision fulfilled, your cause triumph, and increasingly intolerant of failures and of people who disagree with you.

● ● ●

We must find ways of living in the contemporary world that insist that we are not our own but belong to God—ways of living that testify to our radical dependence on God for our existence and preservation. The purpose of these ways of living is not to redeem society, as if that were in our power. As Ellul admonishes us, "Our task is . . . to represent him in the heart of the city."[20] As soon as we start prioritizing the most efficient ways to change society or the most psychologically effective strategies for evangelizing, we won't actually be representing *Him* in the heart of the city. We will be representing a fully integrated city-dweller who has accommodated Christianity to the sovereign self.

At that point, we may discover that it's more efficient to seek the "welfare of the city" through dishonesty and oppression. Far too many evangelicals have begun their work advocating for justice and righteousness in their communities or nation, only to abandon integrity for pragmatism when they don't see immediate results. Like the ancient Israelites, we may find ourselves supporting a candidate, policy, or party who promises to protect us if we will only "trust in oppression and perverseness" (Isaiah 30:12). Even if an oppressive leader, like Pharaoh, defends us for a time, it isn't true peace. True salvation or cultural renewal comes not through our actions but through our rest in God and quietness before Him: "In returning and rest you shall be saved; in quietness and in trust shall be your strength" (Isaiah 30:15). You are not likely to see a Christian political organization advocating for "rest" and "quietness"; it makes for an uninspiring (and, therefore, inefficient!) fundraising campaign. But it is what we are called to. The Christian who rests in God is not inert. They still obey the command to do justice, but they act in stillness, knowing that it is God who sustains and redeems.

We are responsible for being faithful to the truth that we are not our own but belong to God. Ellul describes this responsibility as truth-telling: "And this is where man's work lies—to help bring truth and reality together, to introduce somewhere in some small way, the victory won in truth by Christ into concrete existence."[21] Revealing the false promise of Self-Belonging and the goodness of our contingency on God is our work in the city. We testify to the reality of our true selves when we live transparently before God. For Ellul, the only time we can cease this work and flee the city is when the city will no longer permit us to glorify God with our lives.[22]

For some of us, there will come a time when society no longer tolerates our witness. We may find that society has no room for us when we stubbornly refuse to adopt techniques that dehumanize our neighbors, when we condemn the false promises of Self-Belonging, when our criticisms reduce profitability, when we affirm the existence of our neighbors because of their given created-ness and not their self-created identity. I'm not speaking of mere inconveniences or even a loss of some legal rights that might come from obeying God against society's standards. We can no longer stay within a society when the cost of dwelling in that society is disobedience to God, which is a high standard—much higher than some alarmed Christians in America realize. At such a time, we will face either martyrdom or exile from the city. But so long as we are able to glorify God, we must dwell in the city, pray and work for its welfare, and live as people who belong to God in a creation that also belongs to Him.

DWELLING IN THE CITY AND DESIRING THE GOOD OF THE OTHER

We are left with the task of living in a habitat that is not built for us. If Ellul is correct in his assessment, merely surviving in this inhuman habitat is not enough. We have a duty before God, to whom we belong, to represent Him, to be a faithful reality-affirming presence in a world that "advances progressively backwards." Accepting that Christ is the one who brings salvation and redemption, how do we live faithfully as people who are not their own but belong to Christ?

In belonging to Christ, we belong to His body here on earth—the church. Our decisions and actions ought to pursue the good of Christ and His church. The challenge is understanding what that means. In belonging to Christ, we also belong with our neighbors and the created world. Although we do not belong to our neighbors or the created world in the same way as we belong to Christ (adoption) or the church (family), God's commands to love our neighbor as ourselves and to care for His creation obligate us to seek their good.

We are united to Christ and His body through the Lord's Supper and baptism. We are united to our families through blood and shared history.

We are united to our neighbors through our shared humanity, our sin nature, our need for redemption, and our shared civic experience. Your belonging to your neighbor is a subsidiary kind of belonging: because you belong to Christ and He has commanded you to "do good to everyone" (Galatians 6:10), you have a deep obligation to care for the interests of your neighbor. Paul goes on to say that we must do good "especially to those who are of the household of faith," which may seem like an excuse to ignore the suffering of our non-Christian neighbors, but it is absolutely not.

You cannot desire the good of your non-Christian neighbor too much. It is not possible. However much you desire for your non-Christian neighbors to receive justice and know God's love and mercy and to be treated rightly as human persons made in God's image, you could always desire their good more. In contemporary America, our temptation is to care too little, not too much. Our tendency is to think of ourselves as totally independent of our street, neighborhood, and city. But we have an obligation to them. That obligation is subsidiary in the sense that it is a derivative belonging, rooted in and bound by our all-encompassing belonging to Christ.

We are not free to pursue whatever brings us the most personal fulfillment. We are not free to define our identity in any way we wish. We are not free to use people or creation as tools for our own ends. We are limited. But it is in embracing and respecting these limits that we testify to our belonging to God and oppose the false promise of Self-Belonging. Rejecting the Responsibilities of Self-Belonging that so onerously burden us actually frees us to desire the good of others.

Instead of desiring and pursuing our own good, we are obligated to desire and pursue the good of others (Galatians 6:10; Philippians 2:3-4). That "good" is not always measurable (but it can be, as in the case of poverty reduction or nutrition), and neither is it determined by the latest research or cultural trends. The good is defined by God. As we conform our hearts to God's will through prayer, the Lord's Supper, the Word, and regular gathered worship, we gain the wisdom and discernment to desire the good of others. It is a lifelong project and we will make mistakes. Our posture must be one of humility and selflessness, but if you are faithful, God will give you wisdom.

The good of others stands in stark contrast to "progress," "efficiency," "self-actualization," and so on. For one, when we desire the good of others, we cannot reduce them to abstract numbers or statistics or models. You cannot actually desire the good of an abstract principle or theoretical person.

Another difference is that the good of your neighbor or the environment may not be the most efficient outcome. For example, it might be more efficient (by some estimates) to legalize prostitution. It provides a service to many lonely people and enables people who may not have other marketable skills to provide for themselves and their families.

But to desire their good, we cannot sanction the instrumentalizing of their intimacy. It may be less efficient to increase the social safety net so that mothers without marketable skills do not have to turn to prostitution, but it is a way to desire their good. Perhaps you have a better proposal—I don't doubt that one exists. But desiring the good of your neighbor requires us to go beyond efficiency as the highest value.

Another difference is that when you desire the good of others and that good is defined by God, you will regularly desire and pursue goods that your neighbor does not desire. You know this in your own life. There are a great many things that each of us desires and pursues that are not for our good. Sometimes we know they are not good for us; other times we're convinced that we know best and only later realize our mistake.

For example, you may be in a relationship with someone who is bad for you. They encourage your worst impulses, or they abuse you in some way. You may recognize that he or she is "bad for you," but you stay with them because you desire them. Or perhaps your friends have all warned you that your girlfriend or boyfriend is a terrible person, but you're convinced that they are wrong until years later. If we are our own and belong to ourselves, it is difficult for anyone to say to another person, "I know what is for your good better than you do in this situation." The very idea reeks of pride and a violation of our freedom as individuals. But the fact is that quite often we don't do what is good for us. If we are not our own but belong to Christ, desiring and pursuing the good of our neighbors, even when they don't agree that it is their good, is our duty. It's a way to love them and glorify God.

•   •   •

Once you accept that you are not your own but belong to Christ, many parts of your life that once you took for matters of personal preference are revealed to be matters of God's will.

Consider marriage. If we are our own, then marriage is one of many possible paths to self-fulfillment. Children are an option with which you can accessorize your marriage, or not—like buying a home, opening a joint checking account, owning a pet, or choosing an Ikea bookshelf. For couples who feel a calling to be parents, it can be a satisfying and meaningful experience. But when children don't fit in with the personal goals of a married couple, we expect the couple to abstain from having children.

But if we are not our own but belong to Christ, then God's design for marriage and sex matters. By design, children are the natural fruit of marriage, as sex is the natural physical culmination of marriage. Marriage isn't just about the good of the couple. Wendell Berry reminds us, "Lovers must not, like usurers, live for themselves alone. They must finally turn from their gaze at one another back toward the community."[23] There are plenty of significant exceptions to this design. Many couples struggle painfully with infertility. Other couples avoid pregnancy because of serious health risks. But the exceptions don't alter the meaning of God's design. An essential part of what it means to be married is to pursue procreation. We may not *want* the meaning of marriage to be tied up with children, but it is, objectively. And when we embrace that design, we bear witness to the fact that we are not our own, that we depend on God for the provision and grace necessary to be a parent.

Parenting will cost you. It will demand energy and resources that you do not possess. While the love of your children will be a great source of joy, many hobbies, pleasures, and career opportunities will be lost. For mothers, your body is dramatically given over to the growth of the child. And that body will never be the same. It is a sacrifice. Having children at the peak of your youth also means that you might fall behind in your career. Without children you could more easily work longer hours—or you could travel or save for retirement. You could make love during the day without fear of the kids knocking on the door and asking why it is locked. Or you could use the bathroom without someone yelling for a glass of water. To be a parent is to belong to another person as guardian. It's a terribly inefficient and unproductive prodigal gift. Over and over again, in profoundly physical, emotional, and spiritual ways, you will not be free. But that's okay. You were never your own to begin with.

Single people and couples who are unable to have children will face different but no less substantial and important burdens in life, particularly if they actively desire the good of their neighbor. Life is not a competition to see who has it worse. There's plenty of suffering and sacrifice to go around once you seek the good of others. Nearly everyone in America has tremendous freedom to reject all obligations except for the Responsibilities of Self-Belonging. Parents can outsource their parenting and focus on their careers. Single people can neglect their family and neighbors in need. Childless couples can devote their income to luxury and travel instead of caring for the poor. But if we recognize and reject this false anthropology and begin to desire the good of our neighbor, then we are all free from the Responsibilities of Self-Belonging so that we can love others.

●   ●   ●

Or consider career choices. For many young people today, choosing a career is a nightmarish task that weighs on them throughout high school or college, waiting to crash down like Damocles's blade. Recall Esther Greenwood's anxiety from *The Bell Jar*. For people who believe that they are their own, competition is typically where we feel most validated and the most honored form of competition for adults is the marketplace. This pressure turns choosing the right career into an *existential* crisis.

In our quest to discover the right career, we turn inward, hoping to discern something about our personality and identity that will clearly point to an occupation. The focus of our decision-making process is ourselves. We consider our skills, our passions, our experiences. Other people figure into our planning only because they determine how marketable and competitive certain careers are. But their needs as people are unimportant. In some cases, we may even resent the fact that we have to think about whether a job is in demand. We'd prefer to be paid to do whatever work we find fulfilling, regardless of whether or not it is good for our neighbors.

In the event that our inner quest reveals that we're altruistic, we tend to look at jobs where we can feel like we're helping people, whether or not that's what our neighbors need the most. Even when we're altruistic, we're not encouraged to ask, "What do my neighbors need? What does my community need? What problem can I address?" Instead, we ask, "What is a job where I can help people?" And the answer is usually doctor, nurse, counselor, teacher, and so on. Of course, these are all honorable professions, but if we desire the good of our neighbor, maybe none of these are what our specific community needs. Is it really loving your neighbor if you become a doctor so you can help people, but then you have to leave your community to find a place that needs another doctor? Is that better than staying where you are and becoming a teacher at a struggling public school?

If you're a Christian, perhaps your desire to help people motivates you to become a pastor or missionary. But could it be that your city doesn't need another pastor? Maybe it needs someone working AC repair who mentors youth on the weekends. Could it be that a Majority World country doesn't need another missionary, but the indigenous churches there could use our financial support? When you perceive your life to be a hero's journey, even when you *try* to be intentional about helping others, there's a good chance you'll end up with a career that lets you *feel* helpful.

From a certain perspective, there's no meaningful distinction between feeling helpful and being helpful. As long as you feel helpful, you will experience the benefits of a more fulfilling life. You will feel that your life has meaning and purpose and so you'll be less likely to fall into destructive addictions and so on. But that's just the point. If we are not our own but belong to Christ, then it really matters if we are desiring and pursuing the good of our neighbors. It doesn't really matter all that much if you feel a certain way about it. Talk to any good public school teacher and they'll admit that they often don't *feel* like what they are doing makes a difference. But remember Ellul: our task is "to obey orders," not to measure success. And those teachers, if they are good teachers, are desiring the good of their neighbors. They are doing good, even when they don't see the immediate results.

A Christian anthropology should radically change the way we think about careers in the West. We still need to know our own skills and abilities, and we should consider what work we would enjoy doing and what is marketable, but because we belong to Christ, to His church, and to our family and our neighbors, we must also discern what our community needs. Those needs obligate us.

When you begin thinking in this way, it frees you from the burden of having to pick the one right career. Whatever job pays your bills and is honorable and serves your neighbors is a good job. It doesn't define your identity or justify your existence or even determine your purpose in life. It's merely a good thing to do today. Thinking this way also frees you from the tyranny of social hierarchy. Honest and skilled plumbers and mechanics and bus drivers do just as much to serve the good of their neighbors as teachers or bankers or pastors—and in many cases, they do much more for a lot less thanks.

●   ●   ●

Or consider rest. If we are our own and belong to God, we have the freedom to rest. We do not have to hold up the world or even ourselves—which is good because the Responsibilities of Self-Belonging are unbearable. Rightly practiced, a Christian anthropology should create people who are known for their ability to rest. Not an efficient "recharging" so we can return to work refreshed and more productive. Nor the conspicuous "fun" of travel or partying that gains its significance through social media posts. Nor a frantic "relaxation" that requires us to consume the right content ("Have you seen this movie? What about the last episode of_____?") so that we don't experience the fear of missing out. Nor "vegging" with its sense of hopeless exhaustion and incapacity.

Biblical rest is possible because we do not need to act to save the world or to justify ourselves. Because a loving God created and preserves the world, because He has promised good to all those who love Him, we don't have to be busy. We don't have to feel guilty for not being productive all the time, or for not using our leisure in the most effective way. Rest without anxiety or fear of falling behind or missing out is not only possible for us because we are not our own. It is required of us. Biblical rest is leisurely.

As we learned from Pieper, the inability to rest from your labor is a failure to trust God's provision and is the sin of *acedia*.[24] Culturally we valorize those who don't stop the hustle. Athletes who are "gym rats," Silicon Valley start-up employees who sleep under their desks[25] so they can work eighteen-hour days, 4.5 GPA high school students who are involved in multiple extra-curricular activities, and so on. Such a monomaniacal drive does not reflect the reality that God is sovereign and that our righteousness is in His Son, not our work.

●   ●   ●

To me, the most moving two verses in all of Scripture are Luke 10:41-42, when Martha comes to complain about her sister, Mary, who isn't helping serve a meal to Jesus:

> But the Lord answered her, "Martha, Martha, you are anxious and troubled about many things, but one thing is necessary. Mary has chosen the good portion, which will not be taken away from her."

Having had this same conversation with my children many times, I have to say that my impulse is to side with Martha. I also share Martha's habit of being "anxious and troubled about many things." But Christ's words to her cut me to the quick: "Martha, Martha."

By speaking her name twice, Christ draws Martha out of herself and her fear that if she didn't take care of everything the world would fall apart, or at least her corner of the world. I imagine that at the first sound of her name, Martha initially paid attention to Christ, but perhaps her mind still raced with all the things that needed to be done in the home. Martha was physically present with Christ, but spiritually all she wanted from Him was to order Mary to help. With the second mention of her name, I imagine that Martha's defenses fell down. Christ spoke to the Martha behind the Martha who believed that she was personally responsible for everything.

The essence of His response is that there is only one thing ultimately necessary: delighting in Christ. "Necessary" is a heavy word, carrying a sense of urgency and action. I am sure that Martha was convinced that serving in precisely the right way was "necessary," just as we have a long list of "necessary" things that must get done each day before we feel at peace. Perhaps Lazarus stopped her in the kitchen and said, "Why don't you join

Mary at the feet of Jesus?" And Martha may have replied, "I just need to finish this, and then I can." There's always one more thing we "just need to" do. Jesus subverts Martha's conception of what is necessary. The "one thing" doesn't require Martha to act, or at least not how we usually think of acting. Here again is an action in stillness. All that is necessary is to rest at the feet of Christ and delight in Him.

We are a people of Marthas, chronically unable to cease our work to delight in Christ. We feel safer when we have exhausted ourselves laboring for our own justification. And the sight of Marys—those who can rest—makes us bitter. But it doesn't have to be this way. By God's grace, as we continue to understand that we are not our own, we may begin to learn to rest.

RESISTING THE SPIRIT OF THE CITY

Whatever our presence in society looks like, whether we're in marketing or construction or community service, to represent Christ in the city requires opposing the spirit of the city, and that will come at a cost. When we live as those who belong to Christ and we treat our neighbors and this world as belonging to Christ, we will come into conflict with the spirit of the city. Evangelicals have long worried about persecution for their religious convictions (a fear that is not unfounded but is often exaggerated), yet I suspect we would face much more persecution, or at least discrimination, if we were to fully embrace our belonging to Christ, living it out in our commerce and politics.

When was the last time a Christian in the West was mobbed for pointing out that idols are just idols? Demetrius the Ephesian silversmith of Acts 19 stirred up a mob against Paul because Paul went around telling people that "gods made with hands are not gods" (v. 26). A significant portion of the Ephesian economy was centered on the Festival of Artemis and the sales of silver idols of the goddess. Paul came along and unveiled these idols as what everyone already knew them to be: statues made by silversmiths. Pieces of metal, not gods. Since they were simply well-carved pieces of metal, they could not fulfill their promises. Prayers and sacrifices offered to statues of Artemis were incapable of giving worshipers what they desired. Their idols were impotent. Like the little boy in "The Emperor's New Clothes," Paul merely observed what was self-evident, but no one wanted to see. Why? When a city's wealth is dependent on everyone believing a lie, then it's easy to believe—especially when that lie is also comforting.

The surprising thing should not be that Paul incited a riot, but that his experience is not more common. That should be cause for reflection among Christians. Our society is no less consumed by idols than Paul's. Our economy is no less dependent on idols. And our idols are just as impotent. They promise us peace, justification, identity, meaning, belonging, and wholeness, but only increase our inadequacies. Could it be that Christians have accommodated their faith to a society of silversmiths? Could it be that the reason Christians have such an easy time integrating into the modern economy of America is that in practice we agree with the idea that we are our own and belong to ourselves? While I think most Christians would theoretically reject the sovereign self, it is easier in our day-to-day experience to feel that we are our own than that we belong to God.

In place of dependence on idols or ourselves (which is really the same thing), Christians can resist the spirit of the city by openly and consistently acknowledging our radical dependence upon God. In his critique of meritocracy, Michael Sandel claims,

> The most potent rival to merit, to the notion that we are responsible for our lot and deserve what we get, is the notion that our fate exceeds our control, that we are indebted for our success, and also for our troubles—to the grace of God, or the vagaries of fortune, or the luck of the draw.[26]

Sandel lists three examples of who we might be indebted to, but we can only show gratitude to one of them: God. You cannot be grateful to "the vagaries of fortune" or "the luck of the draw." You can only acknowledge statistically improbability. Here we can see how a biblical anthropology offers "the most potent rival to merit." The good things we experience and possess in this life are gifts from God. Our gratitude toward God should be public and explicit and should result in generosity that appears radical from the world's perspective. Rather than seeing charity as a good work we perform out of our earned and merited success, we ought to think of every good thing we have as a gift from God that He has given us stewardship over in the expectation that we will in turn offer to others as a gift. We show compassion to our neighbors not because they deserve it, and not because it's technically possible they might deserve it. We show compassion because Christ had compassion on us when we did not deserve it. It is this posture of total dependence on God lived out in word and deed that can rival meritocracy and the city's spirit of autonomy.

● ● ●

What would it look like if we represented Christ "in the heart of the city," not as part of a grand strategy for saving our society, but as simple, faithful, anonymous acts of love? Prodigal acts that testify to our contingency upon God, of the goodness of our belonging to Him. I can only speak of the few implications that have occurred to me over the years, but there are many, many more. A great many of the prodigal acts are so close to me and so costly that my heart is loath to consider them. But this is where the body of Christ can serve, as we humbly remind one another that we belong to Christ.

We can begin by challenging ourselves with questions that reveal our complicity with the spirit of the city. We might ask ourselves:

- How does our presence in our community contribute to or distract from the humanity of our neighbors?

- How do our jobs or businesses encourage people to believe that they are their own?

- How does marketing contribute to the lie that we must discover and express our identity?

- What cultural idols are we overlooking for the sake of prosperity or comfort?

- Does this technology aid us in delighting in God's creation and loving our neighbor, or does it inculcate pride?

- In our daily conversations and actions, how do we compete for attention and significance?

- Can we do this task while desiring and pursuing the good of our neighbor?

- In our daily conversations and actions, how do we encourage others to pursue the Responsibilities of Self-Belonging?

- Can we rest, be silent, and know that He is God?

- Where are we elevating efficiency, productivity, or profit over beauty, goodness, or truth?

- Do we make a practice of leisure and invite our neighbors to join us?

- Are our churches known as places where people feast, prodigally delighting in God's good gifts with gratitude?

In asking these questions, we may discover that some occupations are inextricably tied to the dehumanization of others and should be rejected. Some markets are overwhelmingly premised upon making your neighbor feel inadequate. Some managing styles prioritize productivity above health or family life. Some technologies inherently treat people as tools for our pleasure. Some advances only advance us progressively backward.

NOT DOING ALL THAT WE CAN DO

Another way we can resist the spirit of the city is by altering the default way we think about what we are permitted to do. As we've seen in the previous chapters, the modern world places the sovereign individual at the center of the world, and one of the prime ways we experience this is in the endless choices we are offered in everything from politics to dining to identities. The very existence of all these options inclines us to exercise our freedom to choose. These choices make humans capable of more and more (think back to our discussion of our pornographic society, for instance). But for people who are not their own, our basic assumption should not be that we have absolute freedom to choose among all the options society offers us. The fact that we are capable of some action and are socially and politically permitted to commit an act doesn't mean we are free to before God. As Ellul admonishes us, we must "agree not to do all [we are] capable of."[27]

Where our society continually says, "Yes, you may. For a price!" we must learn when to say, "No, we may not, not for any price." As any child knows, self-restraint is difficult to even imagine when everyone else is giving in. But that is precisely the kind of witness we need to be.

For example, when a new technology is released, our default posture should not be adoption, but cautious discernment, judging the innovation by standards higher than efficiency. Ellul sees a model of this in the way the early church dealt with technology:

> Technical activity did not escape Christian moral judgment. The question "Is it righteous?" was asked of every attempt to change modes of production or of organization. That something might be useful or profitable to men did not make it right and just. It had to fit a precise conception of justice before God. When an element of technique appeared to be righteous from *every* point of view, it was adopted, but even then with excessive caution.[28]

Just making the decision not to adopt all the technology available to us, not to participate in all the entertainment made for us, not to exercise all our legal freedoms will testify to our belonging to someone greater than ourselves.

When we reject society's affirmation of our desires, we also resolve the problem of the "malady of the infinite," as described by the sociologist Emilé Durkheim. By not doing all that we can do, we are relieved of the pressure to meet greater and greater standards and acquire more and more goods.

Of course, choosing not to do all that we can do isn't inherently a meaningful defiance of the spirit of the city. Many people quite conspicuously abstain from foods, technologies, products, or services as part of a lifestyle of ethical consumption. It's entirely possible to treat ethical behavior, even ethical behavior that genuinely helps others, as a way to meet your Responsibilities of Self-Belonging. Perhaps you feel morally justified when you abstain from buying unethically produced goods, and fair trade assuages your guilt. But that isn't the same thing as accepting that you are morally justified because of Christ's death on the cross, and because you belong to Him you are not free to treat other image-bearers as tools or objects.

Not doing all that we can do when it isn't motivated by expressive individualism or self-righteousness forcefully asserts that the most significant limit on our actions is not material (What is available to me?), legal (What will the state allow me to do?), or natural (What can I physically do?), but divine (What ought I do in light of my belonging to Christ?). In a society that despises limits, we must be willing to accept limits for ourselves and encourage them for others.

POLITICAL FAITHFULNESS

In the West, particularly in America, we tend to turn to political solutions for any and all social problems. In this case, the disorder we have charted from our contemporary anthropology does have a strongly institutional quality. Our laws, regulations, rights, and citizenship are shaped by the belief that humans are fundamentally their own. So we have good reason to desire a political solution. If we resist the spirit of the city in our hearts and homes but passively permit its dominance in the political sphere, we cannot honestly say that we are glorifying God in the midst of the city. We are not living faithfully. We are not even really resisting the spirit of the city. We're just trying to save ourselves. And that is precisely what this entire book is opposed to: being responsible to and for yourself alone.

Yet I am hesitant to offer political solutions. My hesitancy stems not from the lack of good political options. On the contrary, there are too many options, because the modern state is incredibly vast. And herein lies the difficulty. There are millions of ways in which our government dehumanizes its citizens. Some of them are tiny, bureaucratic ways—a social safety net that utilizes forms that treat human suffering and difference as boxes to check. Some of them are massive—a criminal justice system that views human persons as units of social disruption that must be purged. The disorder is so great that I simply cannot offer you a roadmap to saving the state. Wiser people than I have tried and the momentum of a society governed by technique and a false understanding of the human person has gone on unhindered.

In 1979, Bob Goudzwaard published *Capitalism and Progress: A Diagnosis of Western Society*, in which he presents a diagnosis that is not altogether different from my own. An economist and Reformed Christian, Goudzwaard frames the problem in terms of the rejection of "norms" and deep faith in progress, whereas I have framed it anthropologically and focused on technique, but there is significant conceptual overlap. The final few chapters of *Capitalism and Progress* include several recommendations for systemic change, a number of which I believe continue to hold some promise. These recommendations include restrictions on the use of advertisements (both the amount and the method of persuasion), monitoring agencies for new technologies, dignified work (improved working conditions, more creative jobs, more worker control over corporations, and so on), and a focus on our responsibilities to the environment and our neighbor. They are bold and fascinating recommendations, but they would require massive changes to our global economy to be successful.

When he wrote *Capitalism and Progress*, Goudzwaard confessed to having "no ready blueprints" for the societal changes, and whatever changes were necessary would be extremely difficult to make (like "moving mountains") and would still not produce an "ideal" society.[29] Nevertheless, he believed that there was a window of opportunity for deep structural change as people in the late 1970s grew dissatisfied with the "progress-dominated and progress-plagued society."[30] Forty years after he wrote these words, I think we must admit what he titled the "available openings" for structural change have not led to a more human society. Instead, we discovered new and more efficient ways to adapt humans to an inhuman society (recall all the strategies for self-medicating we discussed). Our entertainment improved. Our medications improved. Our consumption improved. However heavily the Responsibilities of Self-Belonging weigh on us, we find ways to cope rather than get to the root of our disorder.

Although a Christian anthropology doesn't lead to a grand strategy for the political salvation of our society, it doesn't advocate for quietism either. Waiting without hope doesn't mean inaction, but action in rest, or more specifically, action resting in God's providence. When we have the agency to secure the good of our neighbor, whether through political discourse in the public square or voting or working as a politician or civil servant, then we have the responsibility to secure that good.

While I am even less optimistic about making deep structural changes than Goudzwaard was in 1979, I do not believe we have the right to resignation. This is part of the obligation of living before and belonging to Christ: we do not get to cease desiring the good even when we can't imagine how the good might be brought about. We must be faithful to do our good work wherever we are regardless of the results, so long as it is truly good work.

This could look like campaigning for a local ordinance or bond measure that will ensure that your community treats the homeless with dignity. Or it could look like an employee at the unemployment office who addresses people by name and looks them warmly in the face and smiles. It may mean opposing trade with nations that use slave labor, even if it dramatically hurts our quality of living. Along with Goudzwaard, I believe we ought to advocate for political, corporate, and personal policies and practices that place the spiritual, mental, and physical good of people and the good of the environment over the good of efficiency or progress or profit. The idea that we have a right to our current level of consumption, and that it is even a patriotic duty to consume, should be rejected.

To accomplish these goals, we ought to think about advocating for government at a human scale. It may be that governments beyond a certain size become hopelessly inhuman, driven almost exclusively by bureaucratic inertia, data, abstractions, procedures, and technique. Subsidiarity, pushing governance to the lowest, most local level possible for any given policy or issue seems like one practical step toward government at a human scale.[31]

Wherever you are in your community, whatever sphere of influence you have, you are called to desire and pursue the good of your neighbor because we belong to Christ, not ourselves. Self-interest is simply not an option for us.

While it is dangerous for us to imagine ourselves as saviors of the free world, it's also true that we can act to make our world more human. Christ will one day transform our habitat into one perfectly suited for human beings, but until then we must do what little we can do humanize our environment. Again, as Eliot reminds us, "For us, there is only the trying. / The rest is not our business."

A benefit of putting hope for redemption in Christ rather than a political movement is that you are less tempted to compromise with evil for short-term political gains. When you believe that you can save your country, it's not difficult to justify lying or the use of propaganda or corruption for the greater good. You may tell yourself, "Technically this isn't true, but the spirit of it is true and we have to save our nation!" Unfortunately, this kind of pragmatic evil has become a chronic illness in American evangelical politics. God, however, does not need or desire our unjust means to accomplish His just ends.

● ● ●

One significant political implication of a Christian anthropology is that identity politics can be replaced by a vision of the common good. If we are all only ever our own, then there cannot be a common good. There may be negotiated tolerance or groups with some overlapping goals, but no good we share in common, no vision of life together that involves desiring and pursuing the good of every member. Most Americans have adopted the belief that human flourishing (which is one of the chief ends of the common good) can only be defined individually.[32] But if we belong to Christ, then the common good exists and we have an obligation to advocate for it. Part of belonging to Christ is living according to His norms, the rightly designed limits He has placed on us as individuals and as communities.

This doesn't mean it's easy to discern what the common good is in any particular instance, but it does mean that politics ought to be aimed at the good of all people. It means, for example, that I have an obligation to care about the quality of the public school system even when my children don't attend a public school. The injustice my neighbor suffers, whether poor or a minority or disabled or unborn, makes a claim upon me because we all belong to Christ and to this particular community. At times, working toward the common good in a community will require me to advocate for causes that cost me or those who look like me. I may be called upon to accept a loss of freedom that I would never accept if I only thought in terms of identity politics. Our conception of the good ought to arise from our understanding of God's revelation in His Word and nature. But we are not starting from scratch. We have thousands of years of Christian tradition wrestling with what the common good looks like, and we may have a few thousand more to go.[33] We must begin with our resources, which include everything from *The City of God* by Saint Augustine to recent work on personalism and incarceration by Anthony Bradley, or O. Carter Stead's *What It Means to Be Human*, a work that explicitly ties the problems with American's bioethics to the belief that we are our own.[34]

The knowledge of what defines the common good is worthy of considerable study and debate, but in some ways, it is less important than the initial choice to envision a common good. You cannot desire and pursue the political good of your neighbor if you cannot imagine the common good as a possibility. For too many modern people, the only imaginable political vision is a private one. That private vision may be extended and combined with others in a larger group, which gives us identity politics, but the vision remains rooted in the private life of the individual. For instance, I may support a Christian legal fund devoted to protecting religious liberty, but if that concern for religious liberty is rooted firmly in my individual good, then I may not care if the religious liberty of Muslims is infringed upon.

Part of the beauty of the common good is that it does not exclude or diminish the importance of social justice in the least. Whenever our neighbors are treated inhumanly, it is in the common good to fight for their justice, even when their oppression personally benefits us or our friends. Because it isn't really their justice—it's God's justice, and because we belong to Him—we must pursue it.

● ● ●

When I study the history of the human race and consider the pace of technological change and our inability to stop it or even contain its unintended consequences, I honestly cannot envision how the world could get better. A world that has cured most forms of cancer is far easier for me to imagine than a world that treats humans as humans. But God is not confined by my imagination. My duty is to remain here, represent God, and wait. That is what it means to "stand with empty hands and palms turned upwards," to "wait without hope." He will redeem His creation. He, not you, will make all things new.

7

OUR ONLY COMFORT

L IFE IS HARD AND DEATH IS TERRIFYING. The only people who don't recognize the need for comfort as we go through life and face death are those who have so effectively numbed themselves that they no longer recognize their numbness as a form of comfort. But how can belonging to someone else, even if it is Christ, be a source of comfort?

For modern people in particular, the idea of not being our own is inherently *un*comfortable. We feel *dis*comfort and vulnerability at the thought of belonging to someone else. Yet, according to the Heidelberg Catechism, it is precisely because we belong to Christ that we may have comfort in life and death—our *only* comfort, in fact. How can something so counterintuitive be true?

• • •

To begin with, belonging to yourself is no real comfort. If the choices are between a Christian anthropology and the contemporary anthropology, then at the very least we are no worse off by believing that we are not our own. Autonomy sounds comforting and freedom is valorized by society as one of the highest goods, but in practice freedom without limits is a kind of hell, as John Milton knew. It's a hell that we carry within us.

This hell may take the form of infinite disappointment in the face of unquenchable desire for wealth or experiences or sex. This is Durkheim's "malady of the infinite." Or it may take the form of choice paralysis—Esther Greenwood starving to death at the base of the fig tree because each fig is too lovely to neglect. Or it may feel like the endless project of inventing and optimizing and expressing yourself. Quite often it appears as the need for approval and affirmation, which is always just a bit too uncertain to be satisfying. If belonging to Christ makes you uncomfortable, consider whether you are actually comfortable belonging to yourself, or whether the Responsibilities of Self-Belonging demand more and more of you, leading you to rely on ever more coping mechanisms to make life tolerable.

•   •   •

Still, it is not altogether irrational for us to cringe at the words "I am not my own." As we considered in chapter five, belonging to someone else opens us up to the worst kinds of abuse. It makes us vulnerable to intimate harm, the abuse of our personhood. If "belonging" to Christ merely referred to the way we owe our existence to God, as a Deist might believe—if that were the entire nature of our belonging—then our discomfort would be warranted. But the Heidelberg Divines did not have a merely creational belonging in mind.

What brings us comfort in life and death is our belonging to a loving, personal God, one who dwells with us, one with whom we have union, one who is able to desire and bring about our good without neglecting His own will. If we belong to anyone or anything else—our passions, a political movement, an ideal, a man or woman—inevitably they will abuse their relation to us by sacrificing our good for their own gain. It may take a while. For a time belonging entirely to a lover might feel right, but eventually they will take advantage of you.

Only in Christ can we find a belonging without violence or abuse, a belonging that grounds and fulfills our personhood rather than effacing it. Through belonging to Christ, we can belong to others in a subsidiary and conditional way. Those conditions, however, are not personal whims, but divine norms. I belong to Christ, who I can trust to desire and bring about my good, and He defines how I belong to my wife, my family, my church, and my neighbor. We find comfort in belonging to Christ because Christ is the only one we can belong to without harm or loss of our humanity.

•   •   •

On the other hand, it's clear that belonging to Christ is difficult. It offers us existential comfort, but it also involves considerable obligations, as we've seen. The faithful Christian life looks like thousands of little deaths to self every day. Thousands of denials of our desires. Some of the desires that God will demand we say no to will feel closer and truer than our own skin. In that respect, some have wrongly described Christianity as another kind of religion of resignation.[1] Christianity requires you to deny yourself, deny your body, and deny the desires that may mean the world to you. Could it be that Christianity only provides comfort through resignation? Someone might say that by belonging to Christ we resign ourselves to a life of denial, and this grants us only the "comfort" of low expectations. If we extinguish our desires, then we cannot be disappointed when we fail to fulfill them. But this is deeply mistaken.

If it were the case that the only comfort offered in belonging to Christ was hopelessness, it would be a false comfort and Christ would not be a good God. No—the denial of self at the heart of Christianity is not a denial of our humanity, beauty, goodness, or joy. It is an affirmation of that humanity.

In our union with Christ, we take on His righteousness, which He works in us. Because we are still fallen humans, we will desire the wrong things, or desire good things in the wrong way or to the wrong extent. But Christ is sanctifying us day by day, and obedience to Him is no real burden.

Christ tells us that His yoke is easy and His burden is light (Matthew 11:28-30), which does not mean that denying sinful desires is easy or without a kind of suffering. The Spirit will call you to deny desires that your flesh holds precious. At the time it may *feel* like the hardest thing in the world. But because we are united with Christ, our obedience is actually His obedience. In that sense, Christ's yoke is a burden He carried for us. We see this principle at work in Paul's letter to the Philippians, where he tells them to "work out your own salvation with fear and trembling"—a command that would be utterly unbearable were it not for the following words: "for it is God who works in you, both to will and to work for his good pleasure" (Philippians 2:12-13). There is no contradiction between the comfort of belonging to God and our obligation to deny ourselves and obey Him because it is Christ who works in us, and that work is always for our good, even when it doesn't feel like it.

COMFORT IN LIFE

Each one of us desires to know that we are okay. As children we look to our parents and teachers to tell us "Good job!" when we try something difficult, or "You're okay" when we are hurt or sick. Most of all we want them to look at us in the face and tell us, by name, that they love us and always will.

Age does nothing to diminish this desire for existential affirmation. If anything, the troubles of the world, memories of our sins and failures, the seriousness of our obligations, the bitterness of competition, and the burden of our choices raise the stakes exponentially. Once a loving word spoken by your mother in the middle of the night could soothe you to sleep, perfectly assured of the rightness of the world and your safety. But as adults our need for comfort seems to be insatiable. It drives some to destructive addiction and others to frantic self-improvement.

We all live before the gaze of someone or something. Our heart's desire is to be affirmed by that gaze so that our lives are justified, our place in the world is certain, and the trajectory of our moral and social life is clear. As Kierkegaard argues in *The Sickness Unto Death*, we can only be our true selves when we live transparently before God. In the language of this book, we must live aware of our belonging to God. At the center of living before God is *living*—the acceptance that life is fundamentally good and worth experiencing, even when it is painful. Life is a gift that we steward rightly when we understand it as a gift from God. This means that when we get out of bed each day, a choice to live in this world, it is a testament to our belonging to God. Choosing to live in an inhuman world bears witness to the essential goodness of life, which can only be essentially good if it is grounded in God. No matter our circumstances, our life is good because we live it before God who intentionally created us and sustains us. We respond to His gaze of love by striving to live faithfully to His norms, His laws. This too would be unbearable, except that His gaze of love is dependent upon the sacrifice of His Son, not upon our faithfulness. When we live before God in grace rather than in shame or despair, we communicate to our children and our neighbors something of the character of God.

Living before God, Kierkegaard's way of describing our belonging to God, is no trivial duty. But it is beautiful if understood in grace.

The experience of modern life reveals just how incredibly fragile we all are. The desire to know that we are okay grows into a much more complex cluster of needs. Yes, we need to know that our lives matter. But we also need to know that our ethical choices are good enough, that we have an identity that can be addressed and known and loved, that the meaningful experiences we have are not merely accidents of evolution and biology and emotion, that justice is real and worth fighting for, and that we have a place in the world.

Much of this book has been devoted to the varying ways modern people feel these needs and try to meet them. In a technologically sophisticated society like our own, we have a growing number of techniques that simulate the feelings of importance and identity and meaning and belonging. My guess is that our methods will only become more effective at producing these experiences through medications, social engineering, and the market. But comfort runs deeper than feeling. It requires confidence in the reality of things, not just our perception.

The great comfort found in belonging to Christ is that we are accepted and loved without reservation. It is the comfort of living before God. That love is not the ignorant love of a human who can never really know us. That acceptance is not the cheap acceptance of modern social psychology, which is only really concerned with producing productive and well-adjusted consumers. Christ truly knows us and His acceptance unites us to Him, sanctifying us by teaching us moment by moment to love what is true and good and beautiful—to love His will.[2]

Modern life is weary, and we are all heavy laden. When we accept and embrace our belonging to Christ, that inhuman burden is no longer ours to bear. Our sins are forgiven and the inhuman demands of our society are exposed in all their hollowness.

Because we still live in a habitat made by humans but not for humans, we will sin. We will forget or deny that we are forgiven and slip back into shouldering the Responsibilities of Self-Belonging again and again. In those times, our task is to remind ourselves of what we know to be objectively true: we are not our own but belong to Christ.

For myself, the greatest comfort in belonging to Christ is that the things most central to my experience of life find their home. Love, beauty, justice, joy, guilt, pleasure, longing, sorrow, delight—it is these things, not in the abstract but in particular moments and with particular people, that give life most of its grandeur. I know I can find alternate frameworks to explain the love I feel toward my wife or the pleasure I experience reading a great novel or the righteous indignation that fills me when I witness injustice. But none of those accounts can avoid impoverishing the very things I find most true about life. In Christ I take comfort that the truest things in life are real things.

A COMFORT IN DEATH

The prodigal God who teaches us to live by grace also teaches us to die by grace. In the shadow of death, where we all live whether we acknowledge it or not, we feel the tremendous pressure to accomplish enough, experience enough, take care of our family enough, or improve the world enough to die content. And if we are our own, we should feel that pressure because this is the only story we get to tell and an incoherent or meaningless ending would be intolerable. We have to believe that it meant something, that it was worth all the pain. No wonder we run ourselves ragged.

Even in the moments when we feel that our life has been enough, we're left with the haunting prospect of nonexistence. For most of us, dreamless sleep sounds like a welcome relief from modern life, but non-being is something else entirely. We don't seem to have the capacity to imagine our consciousness ceasing. It is utterly foreign to us because our only experience of the world has included us right at the center. But usually, we don't worry about this. We are experts at self-medicating and diverting our attention from such unpleasant realities. Life feels as if it were made for eternity. And so it was.

While writing this book, I lost a good friend, Larry Prater, to cancer. It had been a long time coming, but the Covid-19 pandemic prevented me from seeing him before he passed away. Prior to the pandemic, he had surgery to remove the cancer in his spine, and we were hopeful that he would recover, but it returned two months later, and as it did his pain increased. In March of 2020 he was admitted to the hospital for another back surgery to relieve his pain and something went wrong. He fell into a coma and we nearly lost him. As he slowly recovered, outside his room Covid-19 was spreading, and eventually his doctor told his wife that it was not safe for him to remain in the hospital any longer. So his daughter drove him and his wife, Judy, six hours from Houston to their home in McAllen, Texas, but he never recovered.

At the time he hadn't been told that he was facing imminent death, but he was a wise man and I'm sure he knew. I expect that six-hour drive was the longest of his life. I can't imagine how it must have felt to be told by your doctor that you are no longer safe in the hospital and that you need to flee to your home and hide in isolation from a deadly virus. Is nowhere safe? Death stalking, chasing you from the hospital bed to the hospice bed.

I had hoped that Larry would be able to hold on until the pandemic passed, but that was unrealistic. After a few months at home, the cancer and pain spread, and it paralyzed him from the waist down. Larry had been an avid runner right up until the cancer made him stop. It gave him joy to run and kept him healthy. It felt too cruel that he should lose control over his legs in the end. Not long after the cancer paralyzed Larry, his doctor placed him on hospice care, and I realized that I would never see him again.

What bothered me most was the thought of him facing death in isolation with only a few family members able to visit. From conversations I had with him prior to his hospitalization, I knew he was anxious about death. He worried about his wife and his grandchildren, whom he had devoted his last few decades of life to raise. He worried about the pain and whether or not he'd be able to bear it. He worried that he would be a burden to his wife, that he would forget to be grateful and would grow bitter and cranky as his body failed him.

So I wrote him. And I think if I had been honest to myself at the time, I would have recognized that I was writing to my future self, imagining how deeply I love my family and how terrifying it would be to give up the responsibility of caring for them and to accept death—how terrifying it *will* be. I knew Christ was a comfort in death, but how can you feel that comfort in the end? How can you know it deeply enough not to grow hopeless or desperate?

I include the following paragraphs from the last letter I wrote to Larry Prater, both as a tribute to a good man to whom this book is dedicated and as my own earnest attempt to communicate the comfort in death we have in belonging to Christ:

There is nothing you need to do right now. Nothing you need to fix or provide for your family. You can rest. Your time right now is good. It's good for you to see Judy's face, to talk with your son, to breathe God's air. It may hurt a great deal, but it is good. Try to rest and delight in these moments, but don't fear or sorrow because there is nothing good or beautiful or true that you can lose that you will not gain back in unspeakable fullness. God has turned His face on you, and He sees His Son's righteousness and He loves you.

The same God who gave you breath each moment of your life will continue to preserve and love you. As real and tangible as your being in this world feels right now, whether it be pain or agony or fear or even a kind of dullness, His love for you is more real. And your peace in Him is more real, even if you don't feel that peace right now. Although I hope to God you do. Christ's resurrection was as bodily and visceral as the bread and the wine, and yours will be too. And mine. That is all the hope we can ever have.

Larry Prater passed away on October 19, 2020.

There is comfort in death through belonging to Christ, but it is a hard comfort. Because it asks us to stand before God every moment, never denouncing or rejecting the gift of life, but taking each opportunity to delight in God, enjoy His creation, and extend His grace to others so long as we physically can. This is true even when we suffer physically and mentally, even as we lose control over our body and must depend more on others. We can be comforted that before God there is no burden to use our life efficiently, to accomplish enough or achieve enough, to do enough with our limited time to justify our life. We are comforted that the unimaginable prospect of annihilation is unimaginable precisely because it is unreal.

And when we stand before God, we have the comfort of knowing that He will see His Son, and He will say, "Well done, good and faithful servant." Which is all we ever really wanted to hear anyway.

ACKNOWLEDGMENTS

ALMOST EVERY PAGE OF THIS BOOK owes its existence to someone other than me—to some conversation, some act of kindness or grace, some piece of wisdom or criticism. I wish you could hear all the voices I hear when I read this book—voices of friends and loved ones. Here are a few I am grateful for.

My wife, Brittany, helped me understand how dehumanizing our society can be. She gave me examples and sharpened my thinking. She also believed that this project was worth the sacrifices our entire family made. I am blessed. Brittany, along with my children—Eleanor, Quentin, and Frances—gave me the space to write and the unconditional love I needed to persevere. The students in my 2017, '18, '19, and '21 Contemporary Literature classes at Oklahoma Baptist University inspired me to write this book. Their honesty and trust and their love for literature taught me so much about living in this society and the burdens we all carry. Melody Berry (Pierce, at the time) spent tens of hours watching my children in the summer of 2019 when I was supposed to be writing but couldn't get out of bed because of fear. Jonathan Callis talked with me through nearly every section of this book, contributing ideas, recommending books, sharpening my thinking. More importantly, he came to my house and sat with me when I broke down. Find a friend like that. He and my pastor, Matt Wiley, and my friend Bobby Griffith selflessly bore my burdens when I couldn't bear them myself, which is far too often. Richard Clark and Derek Rishmawy prayed for me and for this book and encouraged me. They are good friends. Spence Spencer and Chandler Warren helped me think through early drafts of this book, sharing wisdom and advice and encouragement. Jake Meador and the Mere Orthodoxy Slack gave me guidance. Josh Spears and the Academy of Classic Christian Studies; Michael Stewart, the Verge Network, and my Verge coaching cohort; and Mark Ryan, Covenant Seminary, and the 2021 DMin cohort (who listened to me lecture for three days in a Covid-19 delirium) each allowed me to try out these ideas on a live audience. Your feedback was immensely helpful. Thanks to Judy Prater who allowed me to share the story of her husband. Thanks to everyone who sent me an encouraging note. Thanks to my CaPC family. Thanks also to my agent, Don; my editor, Ethan; and my parents.

NOTES

INTRODUCTION: AN INHUMAN CULTURE

[1]Alain Ehrenberg, *The Weariness of the Self: Diagnosing the History of Depression in the Contemporary Age* (Montreal & Kingston: McGill-Queen's University Press, 2010), 7.

[2]Isaiah Berlin famously called this "negative freedom" in his 1958 essay, "Two Concepts of Liberty."

[3]As with many other items in this list, there is nothing inherently wrong with antidepressants or other psychiatric medication. They can be used responsibly and in healthy ways. They can also be overprescribed.

[4]"Heidelberg Catechism," Westminster Theological Seminary, accessed January 22, 2021, https://students.wts.edu/resources/creeds/heidelberg.html.

[5]Søren Kierkegaard, *The Sickness unto Death*, trans. Alastair Hannay (New York: Penguin Books, 2004), 44.

[6]T. S. Eliot, "Four Quartets," in *Collected Poems 1909-1962* (London: Harcourt, Inc., 1991), 189.

1. I AM MY OWN AND I BELONG TO MYSELF

[1]Georgia J. Mason, "Stereotypies: A Critical Review," *Animal Behaviour* 41, no. 6 (1991): 1015-1037.

[2]The term was coined by animal welfare activist Bill Travers in 1992 according to his foundation's website: www.bornfree.org.uk/zoochosis.

[3]For more on Zoochosis, see Laura Smith, "Zoos Are Fun for People but Awful for Animals," *Slate Magazine*, June 20, 2014, https://slate.com/technology/2014/06/animal-madness-zoochosis-stereotypic-behavior-and-problems-with-zoos.html.

[4]Carolyn Crist, "Mental Health Diagnoses Rising Among U.S. College Students," *Reuters*, November 1, 2018, https://www.reuters.com/article/us-health-mental-college/mental-health-diagnoses-rising-among-u-s-college-students-idUSKCN1N65U8.

[5]American College Health Association, "National College Health Assessment II:

Undergraduate Student Reference Group Executive Summary Spring 2018," Silver Spring, MD: American College Health Association, 2018, https://www .acha.org/documents/ncha/NCHA-II_Spring_2018_Undergraduate_Reference _Group_Executive_Summary.pdf.

[6]L. A. Pratt, D. J. Brody, and Q. Gu, "Antidepressant Use Among Persons Aged 12 and Over: United States, 2011–2014," NCHS data brief, no 283, Hyattsville, MD: National Center for Health Statistics, 2017, https://www.cdc.gov/nchs/products /databriefs/db283.htm.

[7]Benedict Carey and Robert Gebeloff, "Many People Taking Antidepressants Discover They Cannot Quit," *New York Times,* April 7, 2018, https://www.nytimes .com/2018/04/07/health/antidepressants-withdrawal-prozac-cymbalta.html.

[8]"CDC Director's Media Statement on U.S. Life Expectancy," Centers for Disease Control and Prevention, November 29, 2018, https://www.cdc.gov/media /releases/2018/s1129-US-life-expectancy.html.

[9]Anne Case and Angus Deaton, *Deaths of Despair and the Future of Capitalism* (Princeton, NJ: Princeton University Press, 2020), 212.

[10]Anne Helen Petersen, "How Millennials Became the Burnout Generation," BuzzFeed News, August 2, 2020, https://www.buzzfeednews.com/article /annehelenpetersen/millennials-burnout-generation-debt-work.

[11]This is part of a much larger theme: mediation. Terrorism is mediated through news reporting. Death is mediated through hospitals. Memories are mediated through photos and videos. As a direct result, our lives have a sense of unreality.

[12]Laura Sullivan, "How Big Oil Misled the Public into Believing Plastic Would Be Recycled," NPR, September 11, 2020, https://www.npr.org/2020/09/11/897692090 /how-big-oil-misled-the-public-into-believing-plastic-would-be-recycled.

[13]Liz Faunce et al., "Why the World's Recycling System Stopped Working," *Financial Times,* October 25, 2018, https://www.ft.com/content/360e2524-d71a-11e8-a854 -33d6f82e62f8.

[14]In *The Denial of Death,* Ernest Becker calls this the "primary miraculousness of creation" (New York: Free Press, 1973), 50.

[15]This is oddly similar to the "fetch-quests" you find in video games. Many games tell you the percentage of the "main story" and the "side-quests" you have completed. It seems to me that in video games we sometimes rehearse the ways we imagine our lives.

[16]A few hours after writing this sentence I learned of another friend who had just ended their marriage after a midlife crisis and an affair. It really is depressing.

[17]Dante Alighieri, *The Divine Comedy,* trans. John Ciardi (New York: New American Library, 2003), 1.1-2.

[18]Emily Esfahani Smith, *The Power of Meaning* (New York: Crown, 2017), 5.

[19]Johann Hari, *Lost Connections: Uncovering the Real Causes of Depression—and the Unexpected Solutions* (New York: Bloomsbury, 2018).

[20]Steven Pinker, *Enlightenment Now: The Case for Reason, Science, Humanism, and Progress* (New York: Penguin Books, 2018), 267.

[21]See *The Myth of Sisyphus* by Camus and *Existentialism Is a Humanism* by Sartre.

[22]Alasdair MacIntyre, *After Virtue*, 3rd ed. (Notre Dame: University of Notre Dame Press, 2007), 31.

[23]Fyodor Dostoevsky, *The Brothers Karamazov*, trans. Richard Pevear and Larissa Volokhonsky (New York: Farrar, Straus and Giroux, 2002), 589.

[24]Dostoevsky, *The Brothers Karamazov*, 592.

[25]See *Thus Spoke Zarathustra*.

[26]Charles Taylor, *A Secular Age* (Cambridge, MA: Belknap Press, 2007), 571-572.

[27]Taylor, *A Secular Age*, 572.

[28]Pinker, *Enlightenment Now*, 168-176.

[29]Pinker, *Enlightenment Now*, 402.

[30]In his chapter titled "Humanism" in *Enlightenment Now*, Pinker acknowledges the strong relationship between humanism and utilitarianism and argues for the superiority of the latter over theistic morality. Throughout the book he is enamored with the self-correcting power of reason in all areas of life.

[31]Brené Brown, *Braving the Wilderness: The Quest for True Belonging and the Courage to Stand Alone* (New York: Random House, 2019), 40.

2. HOW SOCIETY HELPS YOU BE YOUR OWN

[1]I place "authentic" in scare quotes to stress the contemporary secular understanding of authenticity. In this definition, authenticity is entirely keyed to the individual. But there are other ways of thinking about authenticity. Søren Kierkegaard (in *The Sickness unto Death*) and Charles Taylor (in *The Ethics of Authenticity* and *The Malaise of Modernity*) show us that authenticity can instead describe an effort to live transparently before God, accepting the self that God has made in us. At the end of this book, I will advocate an anthropology that is very much in line with Kierkegaard's and Taylor's view of authenticity, but since the prevailing cultural understanding of "authenticity" is the contemporary secular one, that's the way I will use the term.

[2]Michael J. Sandel, *The Tyranny of Merit: What's Become of the Common Good?* (New York: Farrar, Straus and Giroux, 2020), 146-147.

[3]David Foster Wallace, *This Is Water: Some Thoughts Delivered on a Significant Occasion, About Living a Compassionate Life* (New York: Little, Brown and Company, 2009).

[4]For an example of this, see Neil Postman's *Technopoly*, particularly his chapter "The Great Symbol Drain" (New York: Vintage Books, 1993).

[5]See especially *Desiring the Kingdom: Worship, Worldview, and Cultural Formation* (Grand Rapids, MI: Baker Academic, 2009).

[6]Kursat Ozenc, "Rolling Chairs, Wagging Cars, & Designing Ritual Interactions for Autonomous Cars," *Medium*, April 11, 2018, https://medium.com/ritual -design/rolling-chairs-wagging-cars-designing-ritual-interactions-for-auton omous-cars-e5815382b488.

[7]Zygmunt Bauman, *Liquid Modernity* (Malden: Polity Press, 2012), 14.

[8]Jacques Ellul, *The Technological Society*, trans. John Wilkinson (New York: Vintage Books, 1964), xxv.

[9]Ellul, *The Technological Society*, 369.

[10]Lindsey Tramuta, "To Avoid Burnout, Work Less and Ignore 'Productivity Propaganda,'" Bloomberg.com, May 11, 2020, https://www.bloomberg.com/news /articles/2020-05-11/exercising-eating-right-won-t-prevent-burnout.

[11]Investigating, prosecuting, and dealing with the physical and mental fallout of sexual abuse, for example, is highly costly.

[12]Jane Coaston, "There's a Conservative Civil War Raging—over Porn," *Vox*, December 12, 2019, https://www.vox.com/policy-and-politics/2019/12/12/21003109 /pornography-obscenity-barr-doj-conservatives-libertarians.

[13]Madeleine Kearns, "Pornography Is a Public-Health Problem," *National Review*, February 6, 2020, https://www.nationalreview.com/magazine/2020/02/24 /pornography-is-a-public-health-problem.

[14]Sandel, *The Tyranny of Merit*, 133.

[15]Charles Taylor, *The Malaise of Modernity* (Ontario: Anansi, 1991), 117.

[16]Jordan B. Peterson, "Intro to Self Authoring," August 25, 2015, YouTube video, 8:47, https://youtu.be/qa9u5t3C0AI.

3. HOW SOCIETY FAILS US

[1]This question gets to the heart of a common barrier we have to accurately criticizing technology. It is difficult to observe technological or cultural change when there is some continuity with the past. Texting is merely a faster version of writing letters, so texting isn't really new. The GPS and maps features on your smartphone are just a more convenient and reliable version of a Rand McNally map, therefore it isn't really new. The internet is just a much bigger version of a library, therefore public access to massive amounts of information isn't really new. And so on. But at some point, a technology or practice changes so much that it's more appropriate to understand it as a new thing than as a continuation.

It may resemble or be related to the old version, but something fundamental has changed. And with this change come new meanings and consequences and risks. It may be that where the old iteration was tolerable or even helpful for society, the new one is quite harmful. But if we can't identify it as something new, we can't seriously assess it. We'll just assume that all the old rules apply.

[2]Gillian Friedman, "Jobless, Selling Nudes Online and Still Struggling," *New York Times*, January 13, 2021, https://www.nytimes.com/2021/01/13/business/only fans-pandemic-users.html.

[3]This point and my wider discussion of pornography was influenced by Matthew Lee Anderson's article "How Pornography Makes Us Less Human and Less Humane," The Gospel Coalition, August 26, 2019, https://www.thegospelcoalition .org/article/pornography-human-humane.

[4]J. D. Salinger, *Franny and Zooey* (Boston: Little, Brown and Company, 1961), 26.

[5]Alain Ehrenberg, *The Weariness of the Self: Diagnosing the History of Depression in the Contemporary Age* (Montreal & Kingston: McGill-Queen's University Press, 2010), 9.

[6]Arthur Allen, "Antidepressant Side Effects: Sexual Side Effects, Weight Gain and More," WebMD, March 9, 2011, https://www.webmd.com/depression/features /coping-with-side-effects-of-depression-treatment#1.

[7]See Robert Bellah and his coauthors' *Habits of the Heart* and Taylor's *A Secular Age*.

[8]Albert Camus, *The Myth of Sisyphus and Other Essays*, trans. Justin O'Brien (New York: Vintage Books, 1955), 91.

[9]Anne Helen Petersen, "How Millennials Became the Burnout Generation," BuzzFeed News, August 2, 2020, https://www.buzzfeednews.com/article /annehelenpetersen/millennials-burnout-generation-debt-work.

[10]Derek Thompson, "Workism Is Making Americans Miserable," *The Atlantic*, August 13, 2019, https://www.theatlantic.com/ideas/archive/2019/02/religion -workism-making-americans-miserable/583441.

[11]Salinger, *Franny and Zooey*, 30.

[12]Malcolm Harris, *Kids These Days: Human Capital and the Making of Millennials* (New York: Little, Brown and Company, 2017), 20-23.

[13]Harris, *Kids These Days*, 26.

[14]Michael J. Sandel, *The Tyranny of Merit: What's Become of the Common Good?* (New York: Farrar, Straus and Giroux, 2020), 181.

[15]Sandel, *Tyranny of Merit*, 25.

[16]Sandel, *Tyranny of Merit*, 59.

[17]Josef Pieper, *Leisure: The Basis of Culture*, trans. Alexander Dru (San Francisco: Ignatius Press, 1963). See especially chapter four.

[18]Petersen, "Burnout Generation."

[19]I owe some of the inspiration for these categories to Bruce Rogers-Vaughn's book, *Caring for Souls in a Neoliberal Age* (New York: Palgrave Macmillan, 2016). Rogers-Vaughn identifies many of the same symptoms and causes for our modern crisis as I do in this book, but he frames it from distinctly Marxist terms. While unpersuasive at times, *Caring for Souls in a Neoliberal Age* is insightful.

[20]Note that I say it is an endorsement of contemporary society as it is, not an endorsement of creation as it is. In fact, Affirmation is premised upon the belief that we are responsible for fixing creation.

[21]Sandel, *The Tyranny of Merit*, 123.

[22]Alain Ehrenberg, *The Weariness of the Self: Diagnosing the History of Depression in the Contemporary Age* (Montreal & Kingston: McGill-Queen's University Press, 2010), 44.

[23]Sylvia Plath, *The Bell Jar* (New York: Harper Perennial, 2005), 2.

[24]Plath, *The Bell Jar*, 2.

[25]Plath, *The Bell Jar*, 2.

[26]Plath, *The Bell Jar*, 2.

[27]Plath, *The Bell Jar*, 32.

[28]Ehrenberg, *The Weariness of the Self*, 9-12.

[29]Plath, *The Bell Jar*, 30.

[30]Plath, *The Bell Jar*, 77.

[31]Emile Durkheim, *Suicide: A Study in Sociology*, ed. George Simpson, trans. John A. Spaulding and George Simpson (New York: Free Press, 1979), 252.

[32]See Zygmunt Bauman, *Liquid Modernity* (Malden: Polity Press, 2012).

[33]Plath, *The Bell Jar*, 247.

[34]Plath, *The Bell Jar*, 223.

[35]Plath, *The Bell Jar*, 223.

[36]Plath, *The Bell Jar*, 242.

4. WE ALL SELF-MEDICATE

[1]Victoria Cano, "CBD Plus USA," Victoria Cano, accessed January 22, 2021, https://www.victoriacano.com/cbd-plus-usa.

[2]Paul Monies, "How Recreational Is Oklahoma's Medical Marijuana Market?," Oklahoma Watch, June 12, 2020, https://oklahomawatch.org/2020/01/19/how-recreational-is-oklahomas-medical-marijuana-market.

[3]Alain Ehrenberg, *The Weariness of the Self: Diagnosing the History of Depression in the Contemporary Age* (Montreal & Kingston: McGill-Queen's University Press, 2010), 232.

[4]The following is entirely hypothetical and not at all based on my own experience with my lovely children during the summer of 2019.

[5]This is the premise of his book *Enlightenment Now*.

[6]Steven Pinker, *Enlightenment Now: The Case for Reason, Science, Humanism, and Progress* (New York: Penguin Books, 2018), 40-43.

[7]Zygmunt Bauman, *Liquid Modernity* (Malden: Polity Press, 2012), 14.

[8]Johann Hari, *Lost Connections: Uncovering the Real Causes of Depression—and the Unexpected Solutions* (New York: Bloomsbury, 2018), 10-11.

[9]In 2017 the United States had reached a level of sustained stagnation or decline of life expectancy that we had not seen since WWI and the Spanish Flu pandemic: Lenny Bernstein, "U.S. Life Expectancy Declines Again, a Dismal Trend Not Seen since World War I," *Washington Post*, November 29, 2018, https://www .washingtonpost.com/national/health-science/us-life-expectancy-declines -again-a-dismal-trend-not-seen-since-world-war-i/2018/11/28/ae58bc8c-f28c -11e8-bc79-68604ed88993_story.html. In 2018 the US saw a very modest uptick in life expectancy. But the Covid-19 pandemic at the time of this writing and corresponding economic crash have almost certainly reversed this trend: Sabrina Tavernise and Abby Goodnough, "American Life Expectancy Rises for First Time in Four Years," *New York Times*, January 30, 2020, https://www.nytimes .com/2020/01/30/us/us-life-expectancy.html.

[10]Ehrenberg, *The Weariness of the Self*, 38-39.

[11]Ehrenberg, *The Weariness of the Self*, 9.

[12]Ehrenberg, *The Weariness of the Self*, 221.

[13]Ehrenberg, *The Weariness of the Self*, 218-219.

[14]Ehrenberg, *The Weariness of the Self*, 226.

[15]Ehrenberg, *The Weariness of the Self*, 4.

[16]Ehrenberg, *The Weariness of the Self*, 209.

[17]For a related study of the way anxiety and anxiety medications are a natural response to an inhuman society, see Heather Zeiger, "Our Uneasy Tranquility," *The New Atlantis: A Journal of Technology & Society*, no. 58 (Spring 2019): 15-27.

[18]Jacques Ellul, *The Technological Society*, trans. John Wilkinson (New York: Vintage Books, 1964), 401.

[19]Ellul, *The Technological Society*, 332.

[20]Think about the use of GPS maps. You may decide that you won't use a smart phone or any other GPS device. You'll only rely on maps and written directions and your own sense of direction. But it turns out that using maps is not just less efficient than using a GPS device, it is less efficient than using maps *used to be* before GPS was widely available. You quickly find that people no longer give out

written directions on the party invitations and physical maps are harder to find. Technique is difficult to resist.

[21]According to a manager quoted in a Verge investigation, most of the moderated content is "very mild." Because of privacy concerns, user content is carefully guarded so there is no independent verification of the manager's claim that I am aware of. However, there are two well sourced investigations of social media moderation contracts that extensively quote employees about the graphic content they see. Casey Newton, "The Trauma Floor," The Verge, February 25, 2019, https://www.theverge.com/2019/2/25/18229714/cognizant-facebook -content-moderator-interviews-trauma-working-conditions-arizona.

[22]Newton, "The Trauma Floor."

5. YOU ARE NOT YOUR OWN BUT BELONG TO CHRIST

[1]Paul Moser points out the "who am I?"/"whose am I?" distinction in *The Elusive God* (Cambridge: Cambridge University Press, 2008), 148. Special thanks to Josué Rodríguez for pointing this out via Twitter. See, Twitter is good for something.

[2]Jacques Ellul, *The Meaning of the City*, trans. Dennis Pardee (Eugene: Wipf and Stock Publishers, 2003), 5.

[3]Ellul, *The Meaning of the City*, 6.

[4]Ellul, *The Meaning of the City*, 5.

[5]"Heidelberg Catechism," Westminster Theological Seminary, accessed January 22, 2021, https://students.wts.edu/resources/creeds/heidelberg.html.

[6]Alain Ehrenberg, *The Weariness of the Self: Diagnosing the History of Depression in the Contemporary Age* (Montreal & Kingston: McGill-Queen's University Press, 2010), 7.

[7]See Anthony C. Thiselton, *The First Epistle to the Corinthians* (Grand Rapids, MI: Eerdmans, 2000), 478. Also, Murray J. Harris, *Slave of Christ* (Downers Grove, IL: InterVarsity Press, 1999), 107.

[8]Harris notes in *Slave of Christ* that under Roman law, slaves were considered the only human "thing" (107).

[9]The following discussion of union with Christ is inspired by Grant Macaskill's *Living in Union with Christ: Paul's Gospel and Christian Moral Identity* (Grand Rapids, MI: Baker Academic, 2019).

[10]Ernest Becker, *The Denial of Death* (New York: Free Press Paperbacks, 1973), 55.

[11]Søren Kierkegaard, *The Sickness unto Death*, trans. Alastair Hannay (New York: Penguin Books, 2004).

[12]"On atheistic assumptions, as Sartre holds, a fundamental responsibility for oneself has no meaning, for there is no one to whom such a responsibility may

be owed, no one to impose obligations and relieve us of them." Robert Spaemann, *Persons: The Difference between 'Someone' and 'Something'* (Oxford: Oxford University Press, 1996), 168.

[13]"Moral responsibility must be relieved of the weight of universal responsibility, and the relief is called 'religion.'" Spaemann, *Persons*, 100.

[14] Thanks to Matthew Anderson for drawing my attention to the loose way evangelicals use the phrase "identity in Christ." https://mereorthodoxy.com/trouble-with-talking-about-our-identity-in-christ/.

[15]Zygmunt Bauman, *Liquid Modernity* (Malden: Polity Press, 2012), 8.

[16]Kierkegaard, *The Sickness unto Death*, 59.

[17]Rowan Williams, *Being Disciples: Essentials of the Christian Life* (Grand Rapids, MI: Eerdmans, 2016), 29.

[18]"Persons have faces, by which they are known to one another. Persons exist *for* each other, and therefore exist only in the plural." Spaemann, *Persons*, 134.

[19]In different ways, Johann Hari (in *Lost Connections*), Anne Case and Angus Deaton (in *Deaths of Despair*), and Emily Esfahani Smith (in *The Power of Meaning*) all make this claim.

[20]Jacques Ellul, *The Technological Society*, trans. John Wilkinson (New York: Vintage Books, 1964), 351.

[21]This is along the lines of the argument David Graeber makes in his essay, "On the Phenomenon of Bullshit Jobs: A Work Rant," *STRIKE!* magazine, August 2013, https://www.strike.coop/bullshit-jobs. This was later expanded into a book titled *Bullshit Jobs*.

[22]Charles Taylor, *A Secular Age* (Cambridge, MA: Belknap Press, 2007), 489.

[23]Josef Pieper, *Leisure: The Basis of Culture*, trans. Alexander Dru (San Francisco: Ignatius Press, 1963), 48.

[24]Jacques Ellul, "The Ethics of Nonpower," in *Ethics in an Age of Pervasive Technology*, ed. Melvin Kranzberg (London: Routledge, 1980), 193. Kindle.

[25]Pieper, *Leisure*, 72.

[26]Ellul, *The Technological Society*, 321.

[27]Friedrich Nietzsche, *The Gay Science*, trans. Walter Kaufmann (New York: Vintage Books, 1974), 181.

[28]Brené Brown, *Braving the Wilderness: The Quest for True Belonging and the Courage to Stand Alone* (New York: Random House, 2019), 40.

6. WHAT CAN WE DO?

[1]T. S. Eliot, "Four Quartets," in *Collected Poems 1909-1962* (London: Harcourt, Inc., 1991), 186.

[2]A simple way to see that Eliot does not mean us to abandon *all* hope is the fact that waiting always necessarily implies hope. No one waits unless they have hope that someone will come. Even in *Waiting for Godot,* Samuel Beckett's famous play about waiting for a God who never arrives, what makes Vladimir and Estragon's condition tragic is that they have hope.

[3]Josef Pieper, *Leisure: The Basis of Culture,* trans. Alexander Dru (San Francisco: Ignatius Press, 1963), 65.

[4]Eliot, "Four Quartets," 186.

[5]Eliot, "Four Quartets," 189.

[6]For a wonderful study of *acedia,* see R. J. Snell's *Acedia and Its Discontents: Metaphysical Boredom in an Empire of Desire* (Kettering: Angelico Press, 2015).

[7]T. S. Eliot, "Choruses from 'The Rock,'" in *Collected Poems 1909-1962* (London: Harcourt, Inc., 1991), 164.

[8]Eliot, "Choruses from 'The Rock,'" 149.

[9]Jacques Ellul, *The Meaning of the City,* trans. Dennis Pardee (Eugene: Wipf and Stock, 2003), 5.

[10]Ellul, *The Meaning of the City,* 16.

[11]Ellul, *The Meaning of the City,* 36.

[12]Ellul, *The Meaning of the City,* 42.

[13]Ellul, *The Meaning of the City,* 22.

[14]Ellul, *The Meaning of the City,* 169.

[15]Ellul, *The Meaning of the City,* 41.

[16]Ellul, *The Meaning of the City,* 182.

[17]Ellul, *The Meaning of the City,* 75.

[18]Ellul, *The Meaning of the City,* 76.

[19]Ellul, *The Meaning of the City,* 76.

[20]Ellul, *The Meaning of the City,* 181.

[21]Ellul, *The Meaning of the City,* 170.

[22]Ellul, *The Meaning of the City,* 182.

[23]Wendell Berry, "Sex, Economy, Freedom, and Community," in *Sex, Economy, Freedom, and Community* (Berkeley, CA: Counterpoint, 2018), 137.

[24]Pieper, *Leisure,* 48.

[25]Thanks to Heath Hardesty for helping me understand this experience.

[26]Michael J. Sandel, *The Tyranny of Merit: What's Become of the Common Good?* (New York: Farrar, Straus and Giroux, 2020), 193.

[27]Jacques Ellul, "The Ethics of Nonpower," in *Ethics in an Age of Pervasive Technology,* ed. Melvin Kranzberg (London: Routledge, 1980), 193. Kindle.

[28]Jacques Ellul, *The Technological Society,* trans. John Wilkinson (New York: Vintage Books, 1964), 37.

[29]Bob Goudzwaard, *Capitalism and Progress: A Diagnosis of Western Society*, trans. Josina Van Nuis Zylstra (Toronto: Paternoster Press, 1997), 187-188.

[30]Goudzwaard, *Capitalism and Progress*, 244.

[31]Charles Taylor makes a case for Subsidiarity in *The Malaise of Modernity* (Ontario: Anansi, 1991), 119.

[32]Sandel, *The Tyranny of Merit*, 133.

[33]For a recent discussion of this, see Jake Meador's book, *In Search of the Common Good* (Downers Grove, IL: InterVarsity Press, 2019).

[34]O. Carter Snead, *What It Means to Be Human: The Case for the Body in Public Ethics* (Cambridge, MA: Harvard University Press, 2020); Anthony B. Bradley, *Ending Overcriminalization and Mass Incarceration: Hope from a Civil Society* (Cambridge: Cambridge University Press, 2018). Bradley's book is a good example of applying *human* criteria to matters of justice. As he shows, a personalist approach to justice centers on caring for the good of people rather than seeing them as statistics.

7. OUR ONLY COMFORT

[1]See Nietzsche's comments about Christianity as a slave to morality in *Beyond Good and Evil*.

[2]While I was revising this paragraph, my son interrupted me to announce that he learned to blow up *and* tie a balloon. As he yelled "Daddy, Daddy!" and I pulled off my noise-canceling headphones to hear him, I was tired and bitter. Doesn't he understand that this interruption will set me back? I guess Salinger's Zooey Glass was right when he said, "There are nice things in the world—and I mean *nice* things. We're all such morons to get so sidetracked." J. D. Salinger, *Franny and Zooey* (Boston: Little, Brown and Company, 1961), 152.

ALSO BY ALAN NOBLE